WAYFARER

a memoir

D1563856

JAMES S. ROCKEFELLER JR.

Other Titles from Islandport Press

A Life Lived Outdoors by George Smith
Closer All the Time by Jim Nichols
Ghost Buck by Dean Bennett
How to Cook a Moose by Kate Christensen
Settling Twice by Deborah Joy Corey
Sea Change by Maxwell Taylor Kennedy

WAYFARER

a memoir

JAMES S. ROCKEFELLER JR.

ISLANDPORT PRESS

ISLANDPORT PRESS

Islandport Press
PO Box 10
Yarmouth, Maine 04096
www.islandportpress.com
books@islandportpress.com

ISBN: 978-1-944762-57-5
ISBN: 978-1-944762-58-2 (ebook)
Library of Congress Control Number: 2018942579
Printed in the USA

Dean Lunt, Publisher
Cover and book design by Teresa Lagrange, Islandport Press
Photographs courtesy of the author unless otherwise noted.

To Marilyn, who made this memoir possible.

In gratitude to all those between these covers who were building blocks of this book, and those who helped bring it to light: Marilyn Moss, Jane English, Scott Wolven of The Writer's Hotel, and Genevieve Morgan of Islandport Press.

Tom Neale, Suvorov Island

TABLE OF CONTENTS

James S. Rockefeller Jr. (Pebble) and his grandparents, Bertha and Andrew Carnegie

PREFACE

Memories are framed by time, place, and circumstance. They are like portholes on a ship, offering glimpses of the ocean of experiences as we rise on the crests, or sink into the valleys. A memoir is a collection of these portholes from which the view keeps changing with the rising and the falling and the course of time. What follows are a few chosen views— sometimes connected, sometimes with little relation to one another. Some are more recent, some peer into another time when social morés and cultural expectations were far different than they are today. When one has lived almost a century, and in particular this past century, the world one is poised to leave is almost unrecognizable as the world one came into. Some of these retellings may sound a bit dated in places and biased, perhaps. Some chapters were taken, almost verbatim, from letters and journals I kept, writing down everything I thought important at the time. Many of these adventures took place in the mid 1950s, shortly after World War II. I was younger, by sixty-one years to be exact, so perusing these journals recently was like reading about someone else's life. Much has fled from memory with the passing of the years, and my thoughts now are often not the same as back then. The following, taken as a whole, is intended to render more an ambience of the journey than a definitive accounting of one man's trudge from birth toward death, traveling on an ocean so infinite that ships and passengers may come and go with only a passing wink.

—James S. Rockefeller Jr.
Camden, Maine 2018

The author as a young man

CHAPTER ONE

Childhood

Stirring the bouillabaisse of childhood remembrances, I see Jack Frost pop to the surface. There he is, or was, crouched on the windowsill silhouetted by the moon, humpbacked, hairy. Oh, so sinister. It was 1930 and I was four.

"I won't let him hurt you," Mother said, putting her hand on my burning forehead, pressing me back against the pillows. "There! Look! He's gone."

My mother had ordered him to go, so of course he went, along with the bout of pneumonia shortly afterward. She was born to command, Jack Frost included. From her Scotch/Irish ancestry came a no-nonsense approach to life, reinforced with the will and courage to traverse the most rugged path to its logical or illogical end. The Irish side gave her whimsy, an artistic sense, and a great outpouring of caring for those around her and the community at large. She strode through my childhood like a benevolent commander of troops, bulldozing obstacles aside, pulling her children along behind her with a combination of love and single-mindedness that made one feel secure behind the impregnable defense, if at times removing mastery of one's fate. It was good to have Mother on our side.

Father, or, as his friends called him, "Rocky," beholden to his German and Dutch genes, and admitting to my mother in the dark of night that he never felt loved by his own mother, was painfully shy, introverted, and communicative as a polar bear and as frightening when aroused. Weekdays and Saturdays he disappeared early and returned late from a distant place called Wall Street, driven to and from the Greenwich Station with such repetition of commuter timing that one morning my mother was halfway down the driveway before realizing my father was not occupying the other seat.

This unlikely pair had met on a boat voyaging to Paris in 1924. My father was the captain of the Yale crew. He was on his way to the 1924 Olympic Games, his event to be rowed on the River Seine. Mama recounted, when in a sentimental mood, how she had watched the race from atop one of the many bridges and spat on his bald head as he passed underneath, tugging mightily at his blue sweep, mere minutes away from winning the gold medal at the world championship. The significance of this gesture we never fully understood as she married him shortly afterward, on April 15, 1925, much to the trepidation of her family who found him far removed from their easygoing ways. Dr. Benjamin Spock was also one of that illustrious rowing group. Unfortunately, by the time I should have been ready for his medical jurisprudence, my father considered him "pinkish," which was then an expression for someone who didn't conform to a certain way of thinking. Other rowers on that Olympic boat became captains of industry or pillars of the financial scene and were present at our dining table from time to time. The four oars from my father's four years of tugging at the sweeps hung in the library of our house—long, blue, wooden badges of valor above the wildfowl etchings.

Dad was always in marvelous physical shape. In the early years he strained away at his rowing machine every night. His doctor said the four years at Yale had enlarged his heart and if he gave up strenuous exercise too abruptly he might drop dead. Later, the rowing machine gave way to a yoga mat, which in turn was replaced by a sledgehammer and crowbar. Over the years the two latter instruments transformed the family grounds in Greenwich, Connecticut, into a Maginot Line of stone walls and shooting butts—a staging area for the forty-year war against crows, blue jays, certain species of squirrels, and other feathered, furred, and creeping beings. The double-barreled Purdy or its American counterpart, the Parker, enforced his concept of faunal law and order. It was our first introduction to racial discrimination and we children thought it somewhat unfair that if you were a bird colored black, or blue and white, or were a small mammal with a red coat instead of gray, you were tagged for extinction. Dad was a crack shot despite being nearly blind without his glasses. On the other hand, if genes dictated that your feathers be red or brown or yellow there was an elaborate array of feeders on which you were enticed to peck at seeds of varied shapes and sizes and when replete retire to a city of peaked or slanted houses with entrance holes tailored to your stature.

While my father was breaking or piling rocks, shooting or catching things, or off to that far distant mysterious place of Wall Street, Mother rigorously held the social services of the community together, stamping them with her personality. The energy expended was phenomenal: her own caring Maginot Line. Each organization required a different uniform. A look into her closet suggested a great general was in residence. The phone was continually ringing with reports from one front or another and our "chief of command" would issue daily directives to shore up a defense, chop heads, or initiate a charitable charge.

An organization for which there was no uniform was the one dealing with birth control. The phone calls revolving around this cause made for lively dinner conversation, ranging as they did from dire threats issuing from the religious hierarchy and their following, to women who sang paeans of praise for having been saved from physical, mental, and monetary tragedy. Mother was a pioneer in the state, helping to establish the Greenwich Maternal Health Center in 1935, and commanded immense respect from both sides of the issue. There is a letter from Margaret Sanger, who founded Planned Parenthood, in praise of some project of Mother's. Some of her best friends were priests who overlooked this aberration in thinking because of her great caring and concern for people's welfare.

The house that sheltered us had an inner life of its own, with a pecking order structured like a beehive. Mother and Father were at the top of the heap—the supreme command. Then there were four children: me, differentiated from father by my nickname, "Pebble," my sister Nancy, my brother Andrew, and the baby, Georgia. We populated our limited operating area between supreme command and the general staff, whose jobs were to take care of us and manage the house and grounds. The width of "wiggle room" between these powerful factions depended on one's ingenuity for compromise, strongmindedness, intrigue, and friendship, proving an excellent training ground for later life.

Looking back to this time, when the twentieth century was in its younger years, I see that my early childhood was more a panoply of faces than places. Katy was the Irish cook. Under her served a succession of pot scrubbers and potato peelers, not to mention her husband,

Mother Nancy

Pat, the houseman, whom mother would occasionally have to bail
out of jail for imbibing too much from a quarrelsome bottle. Poor
Katy; she coughed out her life with tuberculosis in the bedroom next
to mine and for once my mother was not master of someone else's
fate—despite her unflagging administrations. Pat used to shoot pool
with me in the cellar. Here new words entered my vocabulary, centered around genitalia and other enticing subjects for a young boy.

The pantry quarters housed a potpourri of nationalities, depending on the year. Joe Beruti of Lebanon was one of the more memorable. He was known as the "green lizard" for his striking uniform worn at formal functions. His inscrutable yet lugubrious expression bespoke of dungeons past, deaths, and other troubles compounded. The parlor maids came in various sizes, shapes, and degrees of vivacity and sex appeal. There was Marie of gay "Paree," who when dressed in black with white trim, coupled with a little French accent that Somerset Maugham could have used to good advantage, made me think that there was more to women than I yet knew. The attentions I could not render her were aptly fulfilled by Art, our chauffeur and handyman, who followed her about (more about dear Art in a moment). Marie left one day after a tiff with the "green lizard." The lizard came to my mother more lugubrious than usual, with the complaint that Marie had whacked him with a banana, blackening one eye.

"She has impugned my country," he said, sighing with utter sadness. "Either she or I must go!"

Moving down into the back basement one entered the laundry with its gas stove, copper cauldron, electric mangle, double soapstone tub, and scrubbing board. Here the Irish employees were firmly entrenched, but the conversation did not have the zest of the others, so I would bolt outside to the vegetable garden to visit with Tommie, the Polish gardener who could bring green from a stone, working at a pace that was as ordered and serene as the nature he tended.

Andy Anderson, the handyman, arrived from Maine one day, introducing me to skunk oil, which he had boiled from various luckless donors. Rubbed on the chest, amber and musky, it was supposedly good for croup and far more preferable to the mustard plasters favored by my mother. I love the smell of skunk to this very day.

Another original was Thigh Sherwood, our neighborhood farmer, who came occasionally to prune trees and perform other grounds-keeping duties. Thigh, pronounced as "Thee," was slightly over five feet tall, gnarled as a hemlock root, with a face that was so red and pointed it could have been dreamed up by the Brothers Grimm. Thigh was an old bachelor, the archetypal Yankee, who every autumn laid down several barrels of apple cider, which time soon converted to a headier brew. Thus it was that come November his concentration developed lapses. One sparkling fall day, the elfin creature sawed himself out of an apple tree with a crash that brought us all running. Two days later we looked up to see him sawing away at his arm, mistaking it for a branch. Blood dripped alarmingly from his sleeve. My mother sent him to the doctor to get stitched up and then home to regain his concentration. But when he didn't show for more than a week, my mother, not one to let things take their natural course, went down to his house to see what was going on. The grapevine had reported that Thigh was cellar-bound. Mother took me along, I suppose, as some sort of moral lesson.

"Thigh!" she called in her best general's voice on sweeping into his kitchen. "I know you're here."

No answer came back, just a slight scuffling noise emanating from under the floor. She threw open the cellar door and peered downward. "Thigh, I know you're down there. Come up this very minute!"

More scuffling ensued, then a "thonk" as if a bung were being driven home.

"Thigh! I'm going to go call your brother!"

More scuffling, then a squeaky little voice filtered up to us from the blackness. "Not comin'. Ain't fit to talk to a red squirrel."

On the way home, piqued by the failings of men folk, Mother firmly led me to understand that her side of the family could not tolerate alcohol and the same was true in certain instances on my father's side. She was a teetotaler, her father was a teetotaler, and my own father was abstemious except for an occasional beer. However, during prohibition there was a gray tank that gave off bubbling noises in the cellar. No alcohol was ever served unless guests came to supper.

My first encounter with the heady grape occurred a few years later when Thigh had broached his last cask. The episode is still vivid. There comes a time in a young man's life when he must break new ground for whatever reason. My breaking arrived one weekend when our parents were away. Being the oldest of the four, I required less supervision from the general staff than my brother and two sisters did, leaving me to my own more creative devices. The forbidden is seldom boring and the young are sometimes bored. This, coupled with a certain peer pressure from school and topped with the delicious complication of outwitting a combination lock, set the process going.

Next to the laundry room was a room used for storage, or in later years to start plants under artificial light. However, at one end there was a padlocked door. Behind it my father kept his bottled goods, safe from the staff, children, and other would-be marauders. It took one whole morning for me to crack the combination. Then I waited for dark. The bottle I selected after a thoughtful process was labeled Monongahela Whiskey, 1898, 100 proof. The label smacked of the mysteries within, and the dust and cobwebs heightened its allure. Even at that tender age I was a romantic. A marvelous burning sensation accompanied each sip, while the taste and smell were somewhere between mellow woodchips and well-tanned English leather—exotic, different, forbidden. I wasn't prepared for the whirling sensation that soon overtook my balance. Up to now I had grown accustomed to traveling in a linear manner but suddenly, circles seemed to be in vogue. I tacked up the corridor, making slow progress to windward, until at last reaching what I thought was safe harbor in my double-decker upper bunk. However, laying head to pillow brought on a connection with my stomach that soon catapulted the contents of the bottle over the bunk boards down past my poor sleeping brother in the bunk below. It made me understand perfectly old Thigh's remark about red squirrels.

However, it is Art who brings back the most memories. His domain was the garage and all things mechanical or in need of repair. He could plumb. He could wire and lay up bricks. He could carpenter. He could tear an engine apart and put it back together. Above all he had the precious ability to make a project fun, whether it was replacing a broken pipe, shingling a roof, or changing spark plugs. Of Welsh background, he was short, powerfully built, with hands callused and scarred from myriad encounters with putting things to right. His nose was long and pointed, somewhat elfin like Thigh's. Below it invariably resided a pipe or cigar. His heart was as big as the skill in his hands and looking into his mischievous hazel eyes made one think that life was a marvelous adventure not to let slip.

As both my mother and father were busy in their respective worlds, it was Art who was my mentor, guardian, companion, conspirator, best friend, and teacher. He guided my childhood development until I left the parental nest. Art would often drive us to and from the Greenwich Country Day School, one of those institutions where students wore uniforms and were taught to conform in thought as much as in dress. Feeling sorry for my plight, Art would take me homeward by way of a little dairy. Here he introduced me to hot milk squeezed straight from the cow's udder, swearing me to secrecy as my mother had a fetish about the dangers of ungulate fever stemming from unpasteurized udders. Art was also a farmer, and although we

My Indian motorcycle, which I owned while I was in the service

didn't have livestock, he raised chickens behind the garage and had a little Boston bull terrier who was a fearsome ratter. Half the fun of raising chickens was making war on the rats. On special nights we would marshal a cunning scheme, rush into the little chicken house from two sides, release the dog, and, to the consternation of the roosting hens, flail about with our respective cudgels. No big game hunter could have felt as proud as I did, holding aloft a small brown pelt.

My father was an inveterate tinkerer and workshop enthusiast. To encourage my mechanical education under Art, he financed a ravaged Model A Ford with enough defects to assure that I could sit for a master's in automotive engineering if we got it running. Out behind the garage were thirty acres of woodland, complete with a small pond and trails that voyaged uphill and down. This was inducement enough to a potential Barney Oldfield. The stream of oil-streaked garments brought increasing complaints from the washing facility in the basement, augmented by the mischievous Art who enjoyed encouraging his protégé's greasy badge of learning. To this day I don't feel comfortable in clothes that I can't get down on my hands and knees with, and I don't mind getting dirty.

Anyhow, there came a day when the four-cylinder engine spoke for the first time with an authority out of all proportion to its fifty-four tired horses. With Art at the controls, as I could not yet drive, we roared down the straightaways in second gear, crossed swales, veered around corners, up the very steep hill, down into hidden valleys with the branches clutching at what was left of the stripped-down body. Two days later Art had to go off on an extended errand. By the time he returned I knew how to drive. I think I was ten.

From the Model A Ford I graduated to a 1920 Indian motorcycle discarded by my older cousin who lived next door. The transition from four tires and cylinders to two fomented double the excitement in as perverse a way as the earlier arrival of the "A." What is there in man, and I presume in women, that demands "change, travel, excitement," as was so succinctly stated by Toad in that delicious volume, *The Wind in the Willows*. Perhaps it is the quest for our individual holy grail, an evolutionary process that—God forbid—never ends. Anyhow, that ancient oil-dripping, push-rod clattering, fire-spewing, limb-endangering piece of machinery reeked of romance. A large car battery, kept alive by constant charges, resided atop the rear fender giving a higher center of gravity than the designer had intended. The boy—I would be twelve soon—had thighs and legs that looked as if they had been worked over by a waffle iron, branded as they were by the hot cylinder fins. The skills learned on that machine probably saved my life some years down the pike, but then again if I hadn't developed those skills I wouldn't have gotten myself in that later predicament in the first place. That old motorcycle was living at its best.

The damn thing was indestructible. Once it got away from me climbing a rutted track that was steeper than both its capability and mine. Dumped over on its side, engine racing, gas squirting out the gas cap vent, my darling caught fire, burning with an intensity that handfuls of dirt failed to extinguish. I sprinted home, gasped out my tale of woe to Art, and we rushed back to the scene where the old girl was still spouting flame like a dragon.

All the wiring was burnt out, the grease encrustations were gone, and other bits and pieces had been reduced to carbon. However, Art recognized heartbreak when he saw it, and by evening I was again thundering down the straightaways and over hill and dale.

Aside from the mechanical and do-it-yourself training with machinery, I had a little vegetable garden that was my pride and joy.

Eggplants were my greatest achievement. There was something about the shape of an eggplant, the color and texture of the skin, that toot-led my inner trombone. Cut into slices and fried in deep fat by Katy, the eggplant's growing, harvesting, and eating process produced a rounded satisfaction that I strongly felt but couldn't articulate. Some-time later on one of my first serious communications with the other sex, I was asked what I liked to do. Still painfully shy outside my own little private world, I blurted out that I liked to grow eggplants. The girl looked at me puzzled, shook her head, and walked away.

I also developed an interest in hunting, fostered by my father, graduating from slingshots to BB guns, to a .22 and more lethal cali-bers. Hand-loading one's cartridges was a further fascinating pursuit. Hunting trips with my father were his one way of communicating with his son. He was such a silent man. My mother said it was the family Stillman in him. Decades later when he was expecting his twelfth grandchild, a wag of a cousin remarked, "Who do you think will talk first, Stillman or the grandchild?"

He taught me a great love for the outdoors, along with an appre-ciation of quietude. Indeed, I don't know whether it was my father, the Stillman genes, or the way we were raised far from the madding crowd that resulted in my becoming a very private person, self-suffi-cient, happiest when left to my own devices or to help Art with one of his projects. On the flipside, I dutifully went to school, did my home-work, played on the athletic field with some distinction, got respectable grades, and even went to dancing school in a blue suit, white shirt, and tie. I did what was expected but my heart was back there with the egg-plants, the acres around our house, the monkey wrenches, my books, or the corner cabinet in my room that I had made into a museum. In it were polished petrified wood, an oriole's nest, old Chinese coins with holes in the middle, a rock streaked with gold, and myriad items I can't remember now. They created a comfortable ambience like a shaman with his bones and rattles. When I came back from World War II the corner cabinet had disappeared and with it my childhood.

—⁓—

My early childhood was ordered, "ran on rails," so it was no surprise that I awoke one morning in a small room of a 1700s house in the Connecticut Valley, which supposedly had genuine arrow marks in the front door. The house was now my Deerfield Academy dorm. Delivered to boarding school, as I had been, I felt neither glad nor sad. It was the way it was. I was gently feeling my way, biding my time until adulthood, and boarding school was a part of the progression to be endured. Three-and-a-half years slid past with hardly a ripple while I did what was required in the classroom and gave myself, albeit reluctantly, to the rigors of the playing field. Being blessed, or cursed, with a well-muscled frame, propelled me along to varsity play in football and lacrosse, even though my heart wasn't really in it. Whenever my opponent would get in a good blow while I was crouched in line as a tackle, the prongs of my braces would be driven into my gums, creating a sensation not compatible with my sporting instincts. Equally bad was being elected captain of the lacrosse team. Still extremely shy, I was as frightened of being in the spotlight as a mouse confronted with a cat. Having to say something before a crowd was far scarier than losing control of my old motorcycle on that steep hill. In addition, running up and down the field with a big stick and occasionally knocking someone off their feet took no great brains or emotional maturity. In fact, it was in this period that I found myself often looking afar at my physical frame's doings, letting my mind go off exploring larger arenas. A certain cunning came to surround my time and space, and I decided to finesse authority by volunteering for another—the Army Air Corps, an organization that I believed might not be so confining.

Looking back at my time at Deerfield Academy, I have a few worthwhile memories but mostly blanks in the graph of days, which is a failure on my part, not the school's. The arrow marks in that historic front door of my dorm were worthwhile. On dull days I would run my hand over the weathered wood panels, across the arrow grooves, and put myself in a different time. That door did for me what the school didn't. Riding ice flows down the river and being hauled before the headmaster on several occasions for unacceptable behavior were also worth remembering. "The Head," as he was called, one of the great headmasters of his time, was a diminutive figure who exuded authority and wisdom. I was a respectful adversary. Even while being dressed down for riding ice flows or slipping out of my room at night and camping up on the mountain with certain supplies, my detached eye felt sorry for him having to waste his time on a little fish like me for affairs of no importance to either of our destinies. His last words to me came in the form of a bleat: "Pebble, when are you going to grow up?"

I did not have the articulateness, *savoir-faire*, or insight to reply that my rebelliousness might be tacitly applauded as a harbinger of better things to come. I blithely went off to military service with a song in my heart, thinking that tucked between new surroundings and exotic machinery, I could be my own man.

My childhood was very privileged. There were no material wants. The food was plain but wholesome. Tapioca and junket still remain my favorites. Some years had to roll by before I came to see the greatest gifts given to me in those years: growing up with loving parents, caring friends, who ingrained rules of ethical behavior, self-reliance, and caring for others. Wealth, as I grew to be aware of it, was not to be flaunted, but I didn't know back then that my family had it. My contemporaries all walked in the same park. The people who cared for our family in that large house were my coin of the realm and as much like family to me as those related by blood. The first segment of my life ended with me going off to the Air Corps in April 1944. It was my last year at Deerfield and, upon graduation, most students went into the service. I was more excited than frightened at the time, looking forward to many adventures. In sculptural terms I was still a rough block of stone that had yet to be chiseled into some kind of finished state. The process of molding is partly a do-it-yourself kit, part fate, part genes, and part mystery. Within the given walls of possibility there is always room to chase a thousand avenues down a never-ending maze. When the final nail is driven home, looking back, I would probably give myself a C for childhood.

CHAPTER TWO

The Road to *Mandalay*

When I signed up to be a pilot in the Army Air Corps during my senior year at Deerfield, World War II was approaching its atomic end. Enlisting, as most lads did, offered immediate release from a constricting school environment while assuring a desirable branch of the service. I was exhilarated at the prospect.

After Fort Devens boot camp in Massachusetts, our class took a battery of tests to determine if our thoughts concerning individual prowess matched actual capabilities. They proved irrelevant as we were soon told that pilots, navigators, and bombardiers were no longer needed. However, the attrition of gunners had been favorable to our cause, so we still stood a chance of seeing action in the blister of a Flying Fortress or B29.

Waiting for openings to gunnery school, I found life good for a young trainee away from family and school, and with a background of limited breadth in many matters pertaining to the young. We were dispatched to an advanced training base in Aloe, Texas, where it was our duty early of a morn to warm up the T-6 advanced trainers with their 600 horsepower Pratt and Whitney round engines for the student pilots. We young Walter Mitty types would mount the wing, slide back the hatch, and adjust our hard, little athletic buns to the leather cushion beneath the panel full of gorgeous dials. It was a setting about as close to heaven as an eighteen-year-old could get when he pumped the primer plunger, flipped the master switch, pressed up the inertia starter toggle, listened to the flywheel gaining momentum with an increasing scream, and then hit the engaging toggle that linked it all together.

The great silver prop would slowly rotate and if things were right, out would erupt a puff of smoke, a mighty harrumph, repeated in increasingly fast cadence until a great streamer of white smoke billowed out the right side and was swept aft by the raging torrent of wind. Of course, we wore our caps backward.

However, if things didn't go right and one gave her too many pumps of prime, or the finicky god of aircraft engines was having a bad day, things could become truly exciting. The inertia flywheel would eventually run down, the engine would come to rest, and a small pool of gas would dribble from the large exhaust pipe like snot from the nose on a frosty morning. It took but a few retries, a few too many pumps on the primer, and one backfire, to set the 100-octane dribbles to flaming. Young lovers are fickle, and affection quickly turned to hate. If one couldn't get the SOB going very quickly and blow out the fire, it was on to the radio for reinforcements if the fire truck wasn't already on its way, accompanied by the curses and fist pounding of the crew chief. He was a fearsome figure with enough hash marks on his sleeve to fabricate the rungs of a Jack-in-the-Beanstalk ladder.

The comings and goings of aircraft were another ongoing treat. The P47 Thunderbolts, Twin-tailed P38s, P40s with their shark

James S. Rockefeller Jr.

In the Army Air Corps

mouths, and sleek P51 Mustangs all salivated our imaginations. Landing gears collapsed; poor technique was good for laughs. When several times a month some luckless soul augered in, marked by a black plume, we still didn't grasp the concept of mortality.

Extracurricular activities were equally entertaining. I discovered motorcycles for the second time. My buddy bought an Army surplus forty-five horsepower Harley Scout. Not wanting to be left behind, I was soon astride an Indian that had been born to wed a sidecar. The low gearing made it not a desirable steed for the speed devotee, so the price was right. For highway use away from flashing blue lights, the maroon beauty had an exhaust cutout. A kick of the heel brought forth an ego enhancing bellow. Our mentor was a master sergeant astride a black 61 Overhead Harley, now known as a Knucklehead. Weekends he would take us on hills. We grew adept at careening up impossible looking slopes until the machine died and both cycle and rider rolled sideways. The heady physical involvement, the smell of oil, hot grease, gasoline, and disturbed dirt made powerful perfume for our redneck souls. The master rule was "never release the clutch when climbing." I did just once, catapulted backward, and learned my lesson. Never again.

He also taught us to lean the machine far to one side, kicking out a foot while twisting the throttle. The machine would spin on a dime, rubber burning. These skills saved me from serious injury one day while I was tooling down the road behind a large truck. It stopped suddenly. Without thinking I laid my beloved on the crash bars and used her as a sled to slide under the truck. Things happened so fast no thought was involved until the driver jumped down after hearing the rasping underneath. The look on his face started me shaking.

One evening in August my relationship with the motorcycle reached its zenith or nadir, depending on the viewpoint. We two "wild riders" rolled into our little Texas town of Aloe. Main Street was defined by store, bar, store, bar, store, bar, movie theater, barbershop. We cruised up and down its length on enough circuits to check every pane of glass and female leg, ending up next to a jukebox belting out its lonesome bummers, and joining the usual collection of civilians and military who sipped, talked, sometimes fought, struggling to get through another nameless Saturday night.

After a round or two of 3.2 beer, word came that a traveling circus was nearby. Included was one of those motorcycle bowls where mad creatures started at the bottom and wound their way to the top pinned to the round wooden wall by centrifugal force. Youth, motorcycles, and Saturday nights being what they were, it was inevitable that we found ourselves peering down into that lighted, roaring silo through the iron guard rail that separated spectators from the gladiator below. The tattooed denizen of the silo floor reeked a heady mixture of fear and romance. His bike was a frame, supporting two wheels and an engine. The sound ricocheted upward with rider and machine, mixing with the greasy smoke and gasps of the spectators peering down into this fishbowl of action. By our side were two ensigns with their new lieutenant wings pinned to starched blouses. Pressed against them were two girls of exceeding beauty. Words were exchanged. Our only trade goods were two motorcycles and possible acts of daring to lure those two sirens away from their escorts onto the backs of our leather seats.

"I could do that," I said in a voice that probably sounded like a gobbling male turkey. "Hell you could!" replied one of the lieutenants.

His smirk to the girls was a red cape to my baser instincts and, like a young Ulysses (or so I thought), I departed for the door at the bottom of the silo, my stomach singing a song that was more of a wail. Words ensued down there, and a month's military pay passed into the grip of a shaking claw with the admonition, "Don't chop the throttle going up the wall, kid, or your commanding officer ain't going to be happy."

I looked into those two eyes and saw all the misfortunes of the world reflected there, blurred by greed and pity. Thoughts of girls riding on the back of my motorcycle were banished to another universe. This had suddenly become a titanic struggle with myself and myself alone. It was a crazy caper. But I knew about backing off on throttles at the wrong time. I also knew my head was in a noose and I had to be man enough not to turn tail and flee.

After that it was like a sporting event at school once initial contact has been made. The bike was light and maneuverable despite its looks. The engine beat strong and true. Giving a little throttle, I moved onto the transition slope that blended from horizontal to vertical. After a few times around to get the feel, I opened the throttle and it was up onto the wall, around and around, pressed into the seat by one of nature's major maxims. Ever so gently I nudged the machine upward until the metal guardrail was in my sights, then angled down, throttle oh-so-gently retarded. Shutting off the engine I stood up, head spinning, and ignominiously fell over. A hasty retreat was followed with our hero consummating his act by throwing up in the bushes outside.

My last fling with motorcycles came soon after when we were assigned to a field in Florida. My father, also now wearing khaki, was stationed at Fort Bragg, North Carolina, in the 101st Airborne. My plan was to ride there, surprise the family, and head on down to

my new "digs." I said goodbye to my Texas buddy, strapped my duffel bag with travel papers to the rear fender, and shoved off eastward.
The only cloud on the near horizon was the rear tire. Rationing was
on and had dried up the supply of motorcycle inner tubes. The old
Indian was running on a car tire tube, which did not take kindly to
being crammed into a small, narrow motorcycle tire. Resenting being
pinched, it rewarded me with a blowout every hundred miles. I had
eleven in all and it took a week to reach North Carolina. There was
nothing to eat for the last two days so that I could save money for
another car tube and gas. My hands were black, cracked, and sore. My
whole body ached. To increase the challenge, the duffel with travel
papers disappeared off the rear fender.

As fate decreed, my mother called the base the day I left. When
I didn't appear after a suitable period, she alerted all the police in the
Southeast. Luckily, they had better things to do than search for an
errant cyclist. When I reached Fort Bragg the home fires of discontent
were burning fiercely. Father had some travel orders cut so I wouldn't
be considered AWOL and Mother sold the bike to an acquaintance
on the base. I didn't try too hard to protest. Two-wheel transport had
lost its charm.

Time and circumstance conspired to move me on to other pastures. Pressing the trigger of a fifty-millimeter machine gun turned
out to be a suitable replacement for riding like a bat out of hell on a
motorcycle. Firing from the blister of a B17 and then later a B29 was
the next best thing to being a pilot. However, it all came to an end
with the conclusion of the war, long before I was ready to reenter that
workaday world from which I had gratefully departed. I finessed my
return by signing up for another year of service. The duty consisted of
deactivating our airfield. Where there had been thousands of airmen,

The *Mandalay* at anchor

now there were just a handful of us closer-downers. The sizable town next door became a newly opened oyster. I came out of the service as a staff sergeant, versed in arcane military paperwork, with a gunner's rating, and a three-year chunk out of my life considered well spent. I was one of the very lucky ones—so many of my friends did not come back or were scarred for life.

Reflecting today on how wars start is not too far removed from where I found myself that Saturday night stuck on the side of the wooden bowl, determined to prove something to myself and a pair of lovely girls, something that in the end has little worth. Pride goeth before the fall, and though I consider my time in the service transformative, the loss of life and prospects of so many makes me wary of hostile exchanges and puffed-up challenges.

Yale University, that venerable learning institution in New Haven, Connecticut, with its blue banner, was my next four-year stop. We veterans were, by and large, a serious bunch compared to our younger counterparts. We went to class, kept our noses clean, but were still in that gray launching area of being half prepared yet feeling fully capable of taking on real life roles of doctor, lawyer, banker, butcher, baker, and candlestick maker. Of the four years of higher learning I remember two courses. One dealt with cultural artifacts. We called it "Pots and Pans." The professor spoke of furniture, silver, and other artful works of man. The appreciation of the beauty and creativity of our species was a delightful lesson. The other was "Daily Themes." Every day we wrote several hundred words on any subject, despite rain, shine, or runny nose. Ever since "Daily Themes" I have never been far from pen and paper. Writing is a marvelous therapeutic exercise that helps straighten the kinks in the thinking process by placing things in a logical context, rather like viewing a sporting event from a blimp. Writing also teaches the art of how to stare out the window for long periods thinking about very little.

Other interests were two: The first was a delectable creature, friend of my sister, whose chemistry bonded to mine. She broadened my horizon in things feminine to such an extent that I barely escaped being issued that all too innocent paper that automatically materializes when one says "I do." My parents were mostly approving of our late-night trysts, seeing her as suitable flypaper to stick me to an ordered life once college had run its course. Her family was on a like wicket, gracefully accepting my failings. These came to a head one night when cuddled in her wonderful double bed, we heard the front door open. "Jumped-up-mossified-Christ" is the expression that comes to mind.

Her family had arrived back home two days before scheduled. The expression "tail tucked between one's legs" took on special meaning. There was naught to do but play out the scene, hoping they would take a long-range view of things and overlook the immediate. Escape was cut off. My car was in the front yard. Footsteps came quietly up the stairs, down the hall. The door opened oh-so-softly. We lay there, pretending to be sound asleep, trying desperately to emanate youthful innocence. The door closed as quietly as it had opened, and I was gone by dawn's early light. Later I was told that we looked so sweet and innocent that it was impossible to make a scene.

Alas, for the best laid plans of mice and parents. Their forbearance came to naught for my other attachment took over to eventually carry me away from the girl and to the Southern Seas. My other love was boats. It started with a month and a half spent bumming around the

Caribbean on trading schooners with their colorful humanity scattered among coconuts, pigs, chickens, or the occasional horse and donkey. It took us a week to sail from St. Lucia to Barbados. The old Gloucester fisherman did its thing, but the diminutive captain wasn't good at his thing. He couldn't find his island. Yet time meant little. The ample woman berthed above me, raining vomit past my head, was a small inconvenience, far outweighed by the coral sea and tropical sky with its waterspouts, squalls, or glassy calms. The smell of rum, coconuts, and tropical fruits mated with the creak of the rigging and the singsong intonations of the native people, placing me on a track from which there was no escape.

The experience precipitated the purchase of an old Casey cutter called *Mandalay* with my brother Andrew, who taught me the rudiments of sailing. Now that New Haven institution at last became useful for I had taken a course in celestial navigation. We made a cruise to Bermuda and back, encountering a good little blow the other side of the Gulf Stream that ripped the mainsail in two. Luckily, we had a salty type aboard who was adept with needle and palm. With the cutter hove-to under storm trysail, he repaired the break and we made Bermuda with no further delay and were quite pleased with ourselves. On our return we pointed the bowsprit toward the Maine Coast. I was hooked. Here was adventure in a very pure form.

Father saw the starry look in my eyes and the professional storm clouds building. We had a chat (read: intervention) about my future career. The next summer I found myself apprenticed to a delightful Pole who ran a napping machine in a Rhode Island textile mill in which my father's family had a longtime interest. This marvelous contraption ran cotton cloth by a line of gas jets that burnt off the little fuzzies. We stood by adjusting the flames, careful not to let the speeding fabric catch fire. My boss was a burly chap whose two passions were the symphony and the nudist camp. He attended the latter with his family every weekend when the weather was warm enough. I kicked myself years afterward for not having the nerve to break away from my Puritan heritage to accept his kind invitation to be their guest. But then, in all fairness, I was playing a somewhat similar game in a small coastal town some miles to the south with that lady friend, aforementioned.

The mill was a fascinating world of whirring machines, new smells, and people of every variety, all housed in a rambling cavern with long corridors and alleys. In the engraving room several old Scotsmen imprinted cloth designs on copper rollers with little prick punches—a skill not quickly learned. Before the war a gigantic twenty-ton Corliss steam engine drove the generators that in turn drove the machines. Little did I know that thirty years hence the same engine would enter my life in a manner that I could not have believed possible.

The manager of the mill was due for retirement shortly after my scheduled release from higher education. No other family member had stepped forward to take his place. My father's eyes rose expectantly to mine. I failed him by slipping away the following year, selling my interest in the Casey cutter to buy an old forty-foot Friendship sloop of dubious virtue in Annapolis, which I also christened *Mandalay*. The plan was as directional as the North Star—namely, to sail around the world. Napping machines and print rollers, preparing cloth for pajamas and shirts, could not compete with the incense of the Tropics.

I knew little about boat construction back then. The Friendship floated, had a gaff rig, and was dirt-cheap and that was enough. She even had a figurehead—a torso of a sailor whose face looked as if he had been brutally smashed in a barroom brawl. The boat wore two masts of equal length, most odd for a Friendship that nearly always sprouted one. The story goes that the Lash Brothers of Friendship, Maine, who built her, stuck the two tree trunks into their conventional Friendship hull, stood back, and discussed how tall the masts should be in relation to each other. That they both came out the same length said something about family relationships. Somewhere along in her career an owner had added a raised deck. She was a hideosity of design that only an escape artist could love. In addition, she barely kept out water.

The idea to sail around the world arose out of that time spent in the Caribbean. I was in a period when one sequence of events led to another and yet a third. In Puerto Rico I had met a man who was sailing around the world on a small Bahaman sloop. Bob Kingett had recently put his dream on a coral reef beating through the Mona Passage on a calm black night. I joined him on his remote beach where he was living in an abandoned Coast Guard hut on the western coast while trying to salvage his boat *Jack Tar*. Bob had fallen asleep and awoke when the boat struck, pushed there by the treacherous currents. It quickly sank. He found himself on that lonely, gorgeous beach with only a handful of worldly possessions. Working as a graphic artist over the past ten years he had saved enough to purchase the sturdy little native boat and outfit it simply and was headed for Panama and beyond.

I spent a week with him trying to raise the boat—to no avail. But meeting Bob Kingett, eating rice and beans, talking the long nights away between salvage attempts, changed the course of my life. Not another light was visible from our spot on the beach but for the occasional passing boat. The dying trade wind rustled the palms behind the hut. In this Robinson Crusoe setting the stars begged touching as the little driftwood fire outlined our sunburned faces, muscled torsos, and unkempt beards. It was a golden time for me, yearning for happenings swirling beyond the horizon and the context of parental expectations. The cruel blow that had cut Bob's voyage short dealt me the key to escape from a life I did not wish to lead once formal schooling had run its course and blown my cover. Bob was knowledgeable about boats, a skilled woodworker, a good companion. We forged a pact and I purchased the old Friendship. We moved her from Annapolis to Milford Harbor, Connecticut. Bob took up residence aboard while I commuted from academia whenever my forthcoming diploma did not appear in too great jeopardy.

Captain Bradley, the harbormaster, and his wonderful wife, Eleanor, mistress of the ducks, oversaw Milford Harbor. There were white ones and black ones and speckled ones, interspersed with geese and itinerant fowl. The focal point of this delightful ménage was Brad's tiny waterfront shack that served as office, house, meeting place, and boatshed. The yard was littered with moorings, chains, buoys, old anchors, derelict boats of assorted sizes and shapes, old engines, and other marine salvage sufficient to squeeze film out of any visiting camera. Cap Bradley had the proportions of a square-rigger's windlass and possessed as much pulling power. He could walk off with a 200-pound mushroom anchor as if it were a tea tray.

When Eleanor came out of the house in the morning, pandemonium reigned as the feathered horde rose on beating wings to swoop down on the Milford Saint of Duckdom for their morning handout. Tall and thin with a beautiful, serene face, Eleanor was perfect to wear that halo of ducks.

Come spring, cockpit repairs were slowed when one of her flock took up residence in a box next to the bilge pump to hatch her young'uns, just to port of the companionway. She would cluck away irritably when we had to pull on the pump's wooden handle, but bread and other delicacies eased her maternal concerns to the point one would be called in the morning to do what she considered necessary. If the call was not answered, one faced waking up looking into two beady eyes with a clacking beak several inches from one's nose. When she finally went over the side with her dozen yellow balls of fuzz we felt bereft.

Captain Brad and Eleanor were kindly guardians of a peaceful kingdom. It was with unspeakable lumps in the throat that I shook that gnarled hand and hugged Eleanor's sparse frame when it was time to leave. I looked on them as beloved grandparents, perhaps never to be seen again. Chugging out the harbor we looked back to see Brad giving a last wave before picking up a huge chain and making for the mooring barge. Eleanor was starting on her morning rounds trailed by the usual train of ducks.

Cumberland Island, Georgia

CHAPTER THREE

Connecticut to Cumberland Island

The next watering hole for us not-so-ancient mariners was Muzzio's Yacht Yard at Stamford, Connecticut, on Long Island Sound. The Brothers Muzzio, Bill and Emil, treated us like kin when they learned of our dream. They saw our earnestness to make it happen and understood within a few days we were no threat to machinery or yard operations. Bob was given run of the power machinery in the woodshop. My friend and boatmate, Roger, kept them amused with his humor and I always tried to break away from what I was doing to give a hand when needed. Bill Muzzio was wise in the way of boats, the sea, and youth, with all its innocence and failings. He would drop by most every day to check on our progress. His suggestions became our command, which was high praise from young lads who thought they knew everything. I will always recall with a warm feeling, his small compact figure, with the deep lines around the eyes and strong artisans' hands, appearing from among that collection of boats and boatyard gear.

Yards were different then, the boats and the people. There was a family atmosphere. Boaters weren't golfers, and seldom did we spot a boat owner with clubs or other sporting gear. Back in those days one didn't have a long list of different activities to fill leisure time.

Those who loved boats were found in boatyards or on the water. The rest were somewhere inland doing things, to our minds, of smaller consequence.

I remember one of Bill's tenants. She was in her forties, perhaps, and would show up several times a week. Her joy was a Matthews cruiser, the kind we would call an old classic today. Back then they were all classics but newer. She never came with family or a husband to help take her boat for a little run on the sound of an afternoon. Bill introduced us, and we sensed he was protective of her; either because she was a woman skippering a good-sized boat by herself or he knew about her past, which perhaps had not played out kindly. He asked if one or two of us would care to go along with her from time to time to help if needed. Roger and I were like Labradors. We loved anyone who would come play with us or pay us attention. Bob was a more serious breed, focused on what he was doing. It was hard for him to drop saw and hammer and give up an hour or two while the afternoon was slithering by. So sometimes I would go and sometimes Roger and sometimes both of us. She seemed genuinely happy to have us along and would thank us warmly on our return. But nothing personal was ever said, no intimacies, nothing of the past, the future, or what her life was all about. We were too shy to pry, so she remained a mystery woman. We made up fantasies about her that ended when we sailed away.

That woman has stuck in my mind this half century. Why, when bigger things are soon buried under the detritus of passing days? The unanswered is so often more powerful than the answered. Encounters in life, these little incidents, nothing in themselves, have subtle significance in the larger frame; rather like a stroll through one's personal garden, smelling the smells, touching and being touched.

Coming out the other side there is nothing tangible to show but a sense of wonderment.

Another image from that yard was the rigger, a diminutive and ancient Dane. He was the color and texture of leather, but it was his hands that riveted the eye. They were hands of a much larger man, dexterous hands built of horn. The callous on one index finger had been shaved so the end was pointed. He used it as a marlinspike when splicing rope or wire. He had worked on square-riggers in his youth and with his muscled arms, one could picture him on the end of a yard in a howling gale, those piercing blue eyes peering through the snow and sleet for a lee shore off a surf-lashed one. He was the most authentic deep-water man I have ever encountered. Here again, his kindness to us was so in keeping with that yard. Watching him splice was like watching a cat chase a mouse, so fast did his fingers move— through, around, up and down. Not a piece of rigging broke on our voyage, which was a testament to his knowledge and the wisdom he so generously shared. "Tings happen," he would say to us. "Sometimes you fault. Sometimes no fault. Make strong."

When not at the yard, our headquarters was my family's house. Father and Mother were more tolerant of our presence than they had need to be, seeing how to them the proposed voyage was a waste of time, a needless hazard to life and limb, a potential destroyer of an ordered future for me—and possibly worse. In their estimation, the commuter train was the proper lifeline to a career of worth. We did enliven the dining table, however, which otherwise was a one–sided conversation with my effervescent mother at one end and my taciturn father at the other. I remember one meal when my mother, exasperated with his uncommunicativeness, threw a plate down the length of a table at his head. He bent his head to one side to let the missile sail past and went on eating.

One evening, in an unexpected burst of talkativeness, Father mentioned that his bank was running a contest for a catchy phrase to promote deposits. The following evening Roger stood up.

"Mr. Rockefeller, I have a little ditty that might do the trick."

My father nodded for him to go on.

"Don't be left sucking hind titty,
Bank your money with National City."

My father's mouth twitched ever so gently. "Very good, Roger. I will pass it on to the advertising department."

They also put up with two of my other friends. Henry was sequestered on the top floor, attempting to write his first novel. I can't remember quite how he arrived or when he departed, but he brought a cultural gloss to our more hedonist group. He was not part of our band of three, except at mealtimes, but his dedication to his task impressed us all. Searching for our own path made us tolerant of others attempting the same. I don't think the novel ever came to light, but he did become the head of the English department at a prestigious southern university.

My closest friend was not of the *Mandalay* crew. He was D.P., a small creature, thin, with expressive hands that painted images with their motion. A photographer by trade, he worked with the Rapho Guillumette agency that sent him hither and yon. Davis did not like entering by the front door. His favorite access was through a small kitchen window over the sink. It was this that led to my mother's greeting, "Don't let anybody see you, and stay under cover." He came to stay for a few days and remained on and off for years with arrivals and departures at odd hours like the local tomcat. He would be

gone for days, months at a time, suddenly appearing at the breakfast table one morning as if he had never been gone. And like a tomcat his love affairs were legend. Women found him irresistible, and
indeed, it was through my sister that he first entered our lives. But he
was more a guru figure, a mentor, than the passionate lover. His focus
never remained long on the same place or person. He would simply
wave those hands and disappear through the kitchen window, knapsack clamped to his back. D.P. demonstrated to us a freedom that
was envied but never could be copied. Often, I imagined climbing a
mountain to find him at the top, seated before the mouth of a cave
with his legs crossed and face pointed at the sky. I imagined saying,
"What in hell are you doing up here, George?" (We called each other
George.) He would reply, "Just getting a bit of peace and quiet. I've
been watching an eagle for the last three days. He has a feather missing on his left wing tip."

Some days, I could come into a room and find him in the corner standing on his head, or just as likely see him running down the
beach stark naked with his arms spread wide as if hugging the summer breeze. My mother adored him, my father didn't understand
him, and his room was always waiting. He was also a treasured corre-
spondent. We poured out on paper to one another the current things
weighing on our minds. We filled a vacuum in each other during that
period of our youth. As the years passed and those voids were filled
with wives, children, and other commitments, our paths no longer
crossed with such frequency. Then one day he up and died, becoming
another folder in my "life file cabinet"—like that woman at Muzzio's.
A part of advancing age is the enjoyment of a cabinet of memories
such as this, pulling a folder here and there at random, rewriting the
events in the current mind's eye, often with a different perspective.

That fall, more than half a century ago came with its usual chill imported from the north, tearing leaves from their birthing place, sending migrating flocks south, and turning our thoughts in their wake. Severing ties with the shore is never easy. There is always that last little job making ready for sea, that last box of provisions, that last commitment. Eventually the urge to leave overcame the inertia to stay and we glided away from the dock on a warm day in November, carried the tide past Hell Gate, and found ourselves in open water off the Jersey Coast.

The wheel of *Mandalay* nested nicely in our palms, and the jib, loose-footed main, and mizzen pulled us along at a sedate four knots. I had chosen loose-footed sails as being easier on the nerves when running before the wind and sea, without worry about jibing. Having booms charge across the deck with a sudden roll of the ship on a black night, scud flying, was a bad story about to get worse. The old girl would go to windward like a ladder, but that was all right. We had plenty of time and the route was mostly all downhill once below the fortieth parallel. For the trades we had rigged two jibs, winged out on booms. The booms were heavy, unwieldy, and a misery to get up and down. *Mandalay* was primitive. There were no winches, only block and tackle. Running lights were kerosene lamps on boards and gimbaled kerosene lamps below. Canned goods resided in the bilge and the leaky old hull soon dissolved the labels, causing meals to be a continual surprise. We were strong on Argentine bully beef, corned beef hash, Brunswick stew, and other delicacies of the coarser palate. Beans in all shapes and sizes were staple fare, blended with rice and canned tomatoes. Black-eyed peas, sliced onion, olive oil, and vinegar made a splendid salad. The Shipmate coal stove served for cold climes. Gimbaled above it was a two-burner Primus stove, fine for lower latitudes.

At the bottom of the companion to starboard lay the chart table with a rack for navigation books. Then there was the sextant, a Zenith transoceanic radio for time signals from the Bureau of Standards to correct the chronometer, and of course, charts. Their team effort did the job. We were able to arrive at our chosen ports at the calculated times with a regularity that made navigation a nonissue. Mating the sun's lower limb to the true horizon was a fun challenge. Capturing the Man in the Moon was child's play. Navigation in those days turned one's eyes to the wonders of the sky rather than a dial with numbers. If moon or sun or stars were too coy to show their faces, the taffrail log and dead reckoning were pathfinders for the heaving highway. The chronometer was another valued hook into history. Time was important for accurate navigation. The gain or loss of a few seconds a day of the clock resulted in miles off course, thus the reason for the correcting time ticks. Those ticks from Station WWV, Washington, giving the precise second were a nice anomaly to the irrelevance of time in our slow plodding across the lines of latitude and longitude.

But there was more to the interior of our little ship than a place for navigation—lockers, a dinette that made into another bunk, two bunks, one over the other, and a head, and forward was the lazarette, holding those bits and pieces so necessary to a nautical sojourn far removed from the local hardware and grocery stores. Much of the cabinetwork remained to be completed in the warmer climes so things like the paper coal bags rested in the open against the sheathing of the hull on the trip south.

We were pleased with our progress as the Jersey Shore slowly passed to starboard. We congratulated ourselves, thinking this first leg of our voyage was going to be a cakewalk. Those ancient mariners ashore with their words of doom about traveling around Cape Hatteras in November did not know what we knew. We became less sure a few hours later.

Off the Virginia Shore the sky clouded over, the wind rose, and the next ten days became an adventure we had not counted on quite so soon. By the time we had shortened sail twice, the clamp of *mal de mer* had loosened, and our attention focused on the tendency of our little ship to leak. She was an old boat, a tired boat, and her frames were not as resilient as they used to be. But we had not realized she was quite so weary. There was a large bronze bilge pump bolted to the side of the chart table that soon became the most essential piece of equipment aboard if the voyage was going to reach a successful conclusion and we were to remain animate entities on this most glorious of planets. A dinghy hung from davits out over the stern, representing transportation to and from shore when it was a few hundred yards away in calm harbor. There was a rubber raft that took half a day to inflate, but no ship-to-shore radio, emergency transmitter, or other modern items that today we include when venturing beyond the harbor's mouth.

The seas became rougher, the wind kept increasing, and soon we were hove-to under reefed staysail and a sliver of jib. The old girl rode the waves like a duck, albeit a leaky duck. Heaving-to with the bow forty to fifty degrees off the advancing seas is a gracious way to weather a storm if pumping isn't required. Roger was the first to notice that water was lapping the bottom of the coal bags. Twenty minutes devoted to the pump handle caused the bilge to suck dry. The coal bags dissolved. Coal and black slurry sloshed on the cabin sole.

During the next two days the wind would die then come on again just as soon as we would get up a little sail. By the third day we were hove-to twenty-one hours out of twenty-four. Thirty minutes of each hour were spent at the pump.

Adventure, here we come.

The seas really increased, to the point where the valleys were so deep that the sails flapped at the bottom of the watery canyons. Every once in a while, a large fish shape would flash down those slopes. It was like being in an aquarium. The sea took on the color of green whey. The tops of waves were decapitated by the wind and blasted to leeward. Our easterly drift had pushed us into the Gulf Stream. Wind and the stream are rough playmates. They rile each other up, making it uncomfortable for those caught in the middle. The wind would blow forty to fifty knots from the north and six hours later would be honking just as hard from the south.

The crew remained resilient. Roger bunked in the fo'c'sle. The deck above him developed leaks. One drip would hit him on the forehead and another on his privates. But his humor never flagged. One breakfast he came up with a new ditty:

If I ever go down to the sea again
It will be on the Cunard Line
With girls and showers and cocktail hours
And a crew of eighty-nine.

One especially dark night with the wind a full gale, the cabin was suddenly flooded with light. We stumbled from our bunks and looked out. Three hundred yards away a freighter lay motionless, a spotlight directed on us from the bridge. The Aldis lamp began to blink. Our Morse code expert, Bob, translated:

"Are you OK?"

Bob blinked back with a flashlight, "OK."

The freighter departed into the night leaving us in the swirling blackness, somewhat shaken, but with a warm feeling of being connected to the world. Our little vessel was a poor radar target at best and in those seas even worse. We carried no running lights. The kerosene wicks blew out as soon as we tried to light them. After that encounter we always had a man on watch ready to shine a light on the sail. It gave one something to think about aside from pumping.

Time stood still as the days passed with the vessel hove-to. We pumped, stepped around the lumps of coal, cooked beans and porridge, listened to the keening of the wind, and kept repeating to ourselves that this was adventure at it best. On the tenth day, time stirred again. The sun came out, the wind went down, the sails went up, and two sights showed us 125 miles east of where we had first hove-to at about the same latitude. We trundled along at our usual four knots under the gentle northerly, headed for the jetty off Fernandina, Florida, gateway to Cumberland Island, which my mother's family had owned since the late 1800s. Best of all, the pumping decreased to ten minutes out of every hour. We draped the deck with sodden clothing and bedding, feeling like tried and true salts ready for the next go around with the war gods of the sea. That evening we toasted the setting sun with a glass of rum laced with lime juice to ward off scurvy. Our thoughts turned to warm climes where the trade winds would push us down the long South Pacific swells, leading to dark-skinned maidens, blue lagoons, and adventures under the palms.

CHAPTER FOUR

Cumberland Island

The door to Cumberland Island was the entrance to Beach Creek. Here, one entered a ribbon of water twisting like a lazy dragon between mud banks topped with marsh grass, fanning out for several square miles to form a plain of various shades of brown and green. This was home to many that swam, flew, or slithered among the swaying stalks, with evidence of human population well back into the second millennium BC. It was a paradise for man and beast and a suitable entrance for the wonders that lay ashore. Porpoises rolled ahead of our bow in search of schools of mullet, flinging them up the banks with a whack of their tails and catching them in their mouths as they slid back down into the water. Marsh hens clattered deep within their grassy kingdom, and birds, large and small, brightly colored or modestly brown, flew about their tasks under flocks of wood storks bound for their roost in a swamp farther up island.

Cumberland Island off the coast of Georgia was bought by my great-great-grandfather, Thomas Carnegie, in 1881 as home for his wife, Lucy, as Mama Carnegie was called, and their children. She had fallen in love with the place on a prior visit. In a storybook plot deserving of a wide readership, she resolved to live and bring up their children. Grandfather died five years later of pneumonia, leaving Lucy and their nine children on this eighteen-mile barrier island, connected to the mainland only by boat. Here my grandfather had grown up and my mother, Mama Carnegie, the matriarch, built the house my grandparents inherited, called Stafford, where I had spent spring vacations since 1926, at the age of three months. The original house, called Dungeness, now a relic of a different era, was an imposing stone-and-brick Queen Anne-style structure at the southern end of the island overlooking the marsh and creek, a few steps from where we tied up at the Little Dock to begin a six-month outfitting sojourn that would alter my life in subtle ways of which I had no inkling.

Outbuildings, like chicks around a mother hen, stretched out for several acres around the great house, interspersed with fields and live oaks and a white water tower on metal legs rising above the tree tops across the road from the pool house with its bachelor's quarters. The large white stucco stable with workshops had stalls for twenty horses. Out behind were the manager's house, refrigeration building, and power plant, the latter two now leveled. The separate white and black sleeping quarters (segregation was in effect then), commissary, and mess hall guarded the rear. In the far northeast corner, next to the woods, was the carpentry shop, but that is another story.

More than thirty years prior, in the 1920s, the place had been a little kingdom, complete with barbershop, squash and tennis court, a huge vegetable and flower garden, and a flowing fountain and folly with a turning waterwheel. In addition, there had been a bakery and Mrs. Rickard's compound where chickens and other livestock started their journey to the dinner table. At the time of our arrival, the place was more like a great ship, sinking slowly. In the big house there were but echoes of the past with only the olive-wood paneling to stand as a poignant reminder of those days when the great dining table seldom seated less than twenty family and friends. By the time we arrived with the boat, I was twenty-six years old and the estate of my great-great-grandmother was breaking up, as all estates eventually do with the succession of generations. The family was in the throes of formulating a plan for the division of the island, with the intention of preserving its integrity. Who was to get what, and where, was a conundrum my parents' generation wrestled with, and they did so with an eye more focused on conservation and accessibility than on large houses. It was a time of change between the old and what was to come, and into this slender crack of time the crew of the *Mandalay* fit well. Family machinations were peripheral to our primary focus of outfitting an old boat and sailing around the world.

Transportation on the island back then was a black Model A Ford Phaeton, lovingly called "Lady Cumberland." My father had bought it new in the twenties and it meant "Cumberland" to us kids as much as the island itself. The main road connecting the various family houses was coated with white oyster shells. It ran up the middle of the island under a canopy of live oaks that obscured the sky. One traveled this arboreal tunnel in the company of deer, birds, snakes, coons, and wild horses, bathed in a mosaic of light worthy of a cathedral's stained-glass windows. Off this main artery was a network of more primitive roads so even the most remote areas were accessible with a little walking.

Passing the front steps of Dungeness, where my mother and father had been married in 1924 (the last time the great house was fully opened), a right turn took one out through the wrought iron gate with masonry pillars. Then on past Coleman Avenue branching to the left, leading to the main dock and Captain's House, where in normal weather the island boat of the time was tied and in the old

Me, Liv, and our children, Liv and Ola, in "Lady Cumberland"

days, supply schooners and large yachts discharged cargo or took on passengers. Continuing on, the next marker was One-Mile Pine, a long-leaf giant marking one mile to or from Dungeness. Then came a narrow road between the palmettos that passed a deep pit where, legend has it, Blackbeard had buried a treasure. In truth there was no better explanation for the mysterious excavation. And anything was possible on Cumberland.

Greyfield, home of my Aunt Lucy, was the location of many grand adventures, a house out of *Gone with the Wind*. The front steps swept upward some fifteen feet to a long porch, offering an appropriate viewing stage for arrivals and departures. From the porch one commanded a view of the front yard comprising several acres of grass interspersed with ancient live oaks and cedars. Like all the family houses, it had an ample stable and a clutch of outbuildings. But unlike the others, here animals outnumbered people. Many were not the usual run of the island creatures.

Master of the two-legged and four-legged was Aunt Lucy, my mother's cousin. (Lucy was a favorite family name.) She had long raven hair, a diminutive build, and the eyes and temperament of a magpie. Wearing a red bandana wrapped around her head, and with blue jeans and blouse, sharp features, and a deeply tanned face, she could be mistaken for a gypsy or Seminole Indian. Her acquisitive nature, coupled with deafness caused by a childhood bout of scarlet fever, caused her to harbor a deep suspicion of what was going on around her. As a son remarked, "Say something behind her back and she can hear very well." Lucy related better to animals than people and was well connected with the circus crowd and their world of exotic animals. At various times she had Ticker Tape, the tapir, who was indestructible until one day he was fed an arsenic sandwich to purge him of worms. There was a black Labrador and his constant companion, a large buzzard. "Buzzie" had a thing about black. A black raincoat to Buzzie was the reverse of red to a bull.

An ostrich in his time created a legend. A vicious beast who was uncompromising of his territorial rights, he one day extracted a goodly portion of wool from the head of a young hand, who had stuck it between the slats to give the bird his daily ration. It was decided the ostrich had to go but the going was complicated. How could one get a vicious ostrich down the main road and onto a boat back to the mainland? He was too valuable to render into meat. I was never told how he got there in the first place. Anyhow, for delicate matters such as this, Aunt Lucy had a contact on the mainland called Alligator Joe. Joe, a not so gentle man, arrived one evening with a pint of whisky and a big black sock. When his audience had reached an appropriate number, Alligator Joe rushed up to the bird. The bird went for his head but not fast enough before the sock went over the bird's feathered one. This marvel of exotic animal control jumped on his back, road him down the road and onto the boat, or so the story goes.

Then there was the black bear cub at a time when Lucy's kids were still babies. The bear was friendly—too friendly. One night he climbed up the iron fire escape, clawed in the screen, and was found in the morning fast asleep with one of the children. Like the ostrich, he was banished, but he was in good company. Some of my own two-legged kin fell into this category for reasons not to be related here. I almost forgot about the kangaroo that came to an unhappy end, when peering over a palmetto bush, he was mistaken for a large deer by a poacher.

Lucy's easygoing husband, Uncle Bob, was the opposite of his wife and a great favorite of us children. It was Uncle Bob who came up with the much repeated phrase, "the great vulvocracy," pertaining to the dominant nature of the Carnegie women. Originally from Maine and a member of the Georgia Legislature, he epitomized a genial innkeeper with malice to none. In truth, a few years ahead, Greyfield would become a family inn. Uncle Bob had the art of laughing at himself and regaled us with how a tapir peed backward and once got him square in the eye. Ticker Tape had incredible aim; information hard for a child to forget. Uncle Bob tolerated and enjoyed his wife's eccentricities, like the time they were in the Jacksonville Airport. Lucy was in her buckskin dress and wearing a western hat and a big feather in the rim. I forget what kind of exotica Aunt Lucy had in a basket at her feet. An acquaintance sidled up to Bob and quietly inquired who that person was sitting next to him.

"Her? Just an old Arapaho friend," he replied.

Lucy would often sleep in the bathtub when her back hurt. With her would be a rabbit that was always chewing through the wire of her hearing aid, a pine lizard she fed ant eggs on the end of a pencil, and a gosling. Bob's only remark was, "When I go in there, there is always something in everything." A family trip to Europe was a typical epic, as related by one of Lucy's two daughters. On the way to the Wilhelmsen Freighter with four children, husband Bob and the family parrot, she spotted a box turtle crossing the road. Bob didn't want to stop, but Lucy pulled a hissy fit, so the turtle joined the entourage. On the Atlantic crossing, the turtle and the parrot were given the bathroom. A clothes hanger in the shower suited the parrot just fine. Just one dark cloud lay ahead: parrots weren't allowed in Europe. Parrot fever, a severe type of influenza contracted from the species, was a dreaded disease before the advent of penicillin. On arrival, parrot, turtle, and the tin potty for the youngest child were stuffed into a suitcase. In the middle of the train station, the suitcase sprang open and the tin pot hit the concrete. The parrot escaped, screeching at the top of his lungs. Eventually all the contents found their way back into the suitcase and the family checked into their hotel. The turtle and parrot had a room to themselves. During the night the turtle laid an egg under the radiator. Up to this time the sex of the turtle had been unknown. The chambermaid found the egg with the turtle and became alarmed, never having seen one before. She was hushed up with appropriate gifts before the news could reach the ears of management.

The trip home was uneventful. Lucy had large eiderdown pillows made for all the children, with springs in them, designed for the storage of brandy, parrot, and other sundries. When the family went through customs, an inspector felt on one side of a pillow and remarked it felt lumpy. The parrot was seen on Cumberland in the wild for years after. The turtle probably joined Lucy in the bathroom.

Going north to New England one summer, Lucy brought a fawn, called Diana, into the Pullman compartment. She was nested in a large wicker basket and was used to make acquaintance with interesting people on the train. On this particular trip it proved to be a prominent writer. Another time the deer was shipped up to Washington, D.C. in a crate. Lucy and Bob tried to get the crate in the taxi but it wouldn't fit. So one end was opened and the deer shot into the taxi, jumping from the back to the front seat, intriguing the cab driver. He wanted to drive around town showing off, but Bob pointed out the meter was still ticking. In later life Lucy's son Ricky said, "Until I was twelve, my best friend was a chicken." Cousin Rick finally went to school at the age of twelve.

But the real legend was J.B., Lucy's right-hand man, whose storied past was known far beyond the kingdom of Cumberland. He was short, compact, and strong as a windlass, with a face of tanned leather, deeply creased from a life spent outside catering to sundry, demanding activities. One afternoon in his rum-running days, he was approaching the Georgia–Florida line with a load of bottled goods. A cruiser, flashing its blue lights, hove-up alongside him, motioning him to pull over. J.B. was a man who focused on the job at hand. He calmly picked up his double-barreled shotgun, cradled it in the arm deformed by an encounter with some man or machine, and pointed it so the trooper's eyes were looking into two twelve-gauge orbs. The sheriff's car pulled sharply to the left, landing in a ditch, and J.B. crossed the line with his cargo intact. He told us that the revenuers' greatest friends were the intoxicated hogs. When the fermented mash was dumped on the ground the hogs were soon upon it and staggered around in the bushes making a god-awful noise. J.B.'s long experience with the law earned him a deputy's badge to keep the peace on Cumberland, protecting it from evildoers. One night in 1959 he bloodied a poacher with a number six shot and shortly after, Dungeness was burnt down in retaliation. This was after we had left on *Mandalay*.

J.B. had another side in that he was at one with nature, making him a favorite of Lucy. He could call a hawk down out of a tree or summon a flock of crows. He could also call deer, coons, or most any other living thing, including earthworms. For earthworms he would get down on all fours and drum on the ground with his fingers to simulate a heavy rain. Sure enough, after a minute or two, up would pop big night crawlers. It was J.B. who taught us how to wrestle gators. This sport seemed to link itself to a certain consumption of beer or Sweet Lucy, generic for a jug wine that was cheap and came in gallon jugs.

My sailing companion Roger vividly remembers our first episode with J.B. and alligators:

"The first time you and I met him, we discussed the fact that he could call gators. A touch of skepticism crept into our conversation, so J.B. bundled us into that station wagon with no doors, one night, and headed up the road to a slue, home of a big gator. We shined a light around. It was pitch black but we didn't see anything. Then J.B. began making strange grunting sounds, saying he was calling a baby alligator, explaining how the female comes to protect the baby and the male comes to eat it. It soon turned out something was coming, because the light shone on two of the biggest red eyes I've ever seen—like the reflectors on a motorcycle. J.B. whispered they could move really fast on land. That's all we needed. We were out of there and never doubted his word again!

The main thing with gator wrestling was to keep the beast coming, once one activated it by grabbing it around the waist. Propelled by its tail, the gator, once out of the water, was flung to one side while the participant moved rapidly to the other. A favorite place for this was at the Plum Orchard Beach House, which had a freshwater drain from the swampy land behind, running into the ocean between the sand dunes. Often at a noon picnic with J.B. in attendance, after a few belts of the gentle grape, egged on by us youngsters, the entertainment committee chairman would cast his practiced eye upon the waters. Wading in would soon create a thrashing scene, egged on by yells of appreciation from the bank. If the victim was small, he would bring it to shore and turn it belly up so we would rub the white tummy until it was hypnotized into sleep. When it awoke he would demonstrate how a gator has no strength to open his jaws and one could hold them closed with one hand. But better not get in the way when they were slamming shut."

On one occasion, J.B. went north to attend a wedding of one of Aunt Lucy's children. In the midst of the party, J.B.'s absence was suddenly noticed. Then grunting noises were heard coming from the bathroom. Fearing the worst, a rescue party burst open the door. There was J.B. down on his knees trying to call his shoes out of the toilet bowl. Afterward, when the spirits had worn off, he said somewhat sheepishly, "Well they were made of alligator hide."

If Greyfield was one side of the Cumberland coin, Stafford, my grandparents' house, was another. Continuing on the main road past Greyfield, one came to a divide in the road. The reason went back to 1908 when there were two cars on the island. They crashed, head on, at this slight bend in the road and thus inspired this parting of the ways for a hundred yards. Murphy's law was written especially for my mother's family.

Beyond the bend to the right was the skeet field where as a boy I used to shoot with my grandfather and his contemporaries in the afternoon after he had his nap. The family were all crack shots. Grandpa could knock down a deer with one shot with his 30-30, while standing in a car bouncing along a rough road.

A hundred yards farther on behind a clump of palmettos was where Cousin Perkins, in earlier times, was wont to set up shop at the cocktail hour, complete with easy chairs, table, family retainer, and shaker. His mother, Aunt Floss, had forbidden her boys to drink, so this Cumberland evening custom for some family members was moved to the main road to offer evening refreshments to any passing guest. Floss was my grandfather's sister and lived in one of the outbuildings at Dungeness just beyond the pool house. In my time she was quite elderly and confined to her bed from time to time. A visitor knocking on her bedroom door would get the hail, "Friend or enema?"

Once in her old age, traveling with Aunt Lucy, she peed in the lobby of their hotel behind a potted palm. Aunt Lucy was mortified, although I could quite picture her doing the same. Floss asked why her niece was so embarrassed, saying, "I was the one who did it."

The next point of interest on the way to Stafford is the "big field" several miles up the road on the right—a large, level expanse comprising some hundred acres that was a cotton field back in the days of slavery, long before my great-great-grandfather purchased the property. The chimneys of the slave quarters are still standing on the farther side among the live oaks. Nowadays, a grass landing strip runs down its middle, creating grazing for wild horses, deer, feral hogs, and attendant bird life. Cumberland was famous for its long-staple cotton in olden times. Robert Stafford was the major planter and landowner back then. The 1850 U.S. Census showed him owning 348 slaves. He had six children by his mixed-race slave, Elizabeth, and built them a house in Mystic, Connecticut, where the children were brought up and educated. From 1852 on he spent his summers north, having business holdings in both the north and the south.

Stafford's house overlooked the big field. He died in 1877 and it was from his heirs that my great-great-grandfather bought Cumberland. The original Stafford house burnt down and it was on that site Grandma Carnegie built the existing Stafford; a three-story, stucco, T-shaped building residing inside Robert Stafford's old tabby walls. The long porch fronted on the lawn with its palm trees, umbrella shaped cedars, and flowing fountain in the center of a circular gold-fish pool. The low wall kept out the cattle, hogs, and horses, but was no barrier for the deer that nibbled the climbing roses and enjoyed the flower and vegetable gardens out behind. Across the main road to the east, the big field created a daily parade of wildlife, while to the north was a small nine-hole golf course, fenced to keep out the livestock. I clearly picture Grandpa ringing the large bell to call his caddy. The young figure would come running up from the stables, a hundred yards farther north at the end of a stately avenue of live oaks before one hit the bamboo thicket.

It was a childhood paradise and it was also a paradise for us three young men during those months in 1952 that we spent outfitting the boat. Toward the marsh behind the house rose a tall windmill and water tower. The windmill was replaced in later years by a water ram that worked on hydraulic pressure generated from the artesian well.

This pumped the water up forty feet to the tower where it ran into the house by gravity. Its muffled beat, between a bonk and a clunk, was a classic Cumberland sound. Next to the house was the laundry building from Stafford's day, made into a tiny schoolhouse where my mother was taught as a child, and attached to it was another tabby structure housing the Kohler plant, which provided electricity, and a small garden shed. The twin two-cylinder, magneto sparked engines powering the generators were tired by the time we appeared on the scene. They served to sharpen our mechanical skills. When we failed to bring them to life there were always the foolproof kerosene lights and candles, harking back to plantation days.

But the beach was, is, and will always be the crown jewel of Cumberland. That is why it is a national seashore today. The road to it runs between the big field and the now forgotten golf course, under magnolias, cedars, and live oaks of monarch proportions. It goes past the site of Stafford's slave cabins, with only a few chimneys still standing, on through the forest, finally tipping over a wooded sand dune and several smaller ones, out onto the hard sand, a good hundred yards wide at low tide, running the entire thirteen miles of the island. In the days I spent there as a young man there was often not another soul in sight. One could drive its length at a goodly speed, dodging conks that might puncture a tire and avoiding other treasures washed up from the deep. In places along the gently sloping beach were slues, depressions in the sand, where on a rising tide one could catch red bass, drum, whiting, catfish, and sharks. Behind the beach rose the sand dunes. The valleys between them were a catchall for those things brought by past spring tides and violent storms.

Standing there with rod and reel, bathed in the beat of the surf, with wheeling birds overhead, warm sun on the bronzed back, nothing in sight but a small herd of wild horses enjoying the southwest breeze away from the insects of the forest, we felt at one with Mother Earth. The essence of the island was part nature, part history, part family. For an hour or more, time could stand still. Only the sun moved, the flocks of birds, the horses, the black buzzards soaring over the white dunes beneath the blue sky.

But there was also work for the three of us: food to gather, a boat to outfit, social engagements—a whole circle of encapsulated life never to be repeated in such perfection. Most mornings we arose with the dawn, breakfasted, and rode down to the little dock in Lady Cumberland, where *Mandalay* lay waiting for our eager hands. Bob, the skilled woodworker, was in charge of rebuilding the interior. I was master of the engine room and Roger lent a hand where needed when he could tear himself away from scraper, sandpaper, and brush.

My challenge—the engine room—was the size of a shoebox. One entered from the after deck. Light entered through three portholes in the sides of the little raised house. The engine was an ancient Gray Marine, weary with age and years of saltwater coursing through its cooling sections. The manifold and block resembled a cross between a porcupine and a wart hog, bristling with half-inch pipe plugs to excavate the rust and sludge that created hot spots as the salt ate away the metal. I would bore another hole, clean out the debris with a wire, and tap in a plug.

Surrounding the tired, old mechanical lady was a layered accumulation of bosun's gear, engine parts, tools, and most anything faintly associated with a sailing vessel undertaking a lengthy voyage. In behind were tucked the soldered copper gas tanks and galvanized water tanks. The former would put us in mortal danger on the other side of the Galapagos. I spent hours, days, down in that gloomy hole, both at the dock and at sea, working on the hot spots, cleaning the carburetor when it became choked with debris from the tanks, and keeping a spark to the plugs. We had a love-hate relationship that changed daily, and it was a great mentor for patience and innovation.

In the meantime, Bob was doing his wonder work below. *Mandalay* was one of the few vessels that could sport a dinette table made from olive wood. The exotica came from the paneling in Dungeness. It had been sawed on the island from a grove of trees that had expired in a great freeze before the turn of the century. Other materials came from the carpenter shop. This was a long, low structure tucked under arching live oaks, housing a collection of machinery that looked as if it had come from back in the industrial revolution, which some of it had. The centerpiece of this long shed was a large dragon of an engine with flywheels as tall as a man. Built in 1895, it represented a significant landmark in the evolution of the internal combustion engine, being the creation of Nikolaus Otto of Germany, who invented the four-stroke engine in 1876. The historical significance was lost on us at the time but would reappear in my life some decades later when I moved to Maine. It was a one-cylinder giant with make and break ignition, generating twenty-one horsepower at 240 rpm. But what horsepower! It weighed more than a ton.

The carpenter shop was the ultimate do-it-yourself facility. It came equipped with an elderly family retainer who handled Old Otto as one would a Stradivarius. On a cold winter morning Mr. Fred would cock his head at his monster, much as Mr. Robin would while listening for the succulent rustle of an unsuspecting worm. Then he would turn on the fuel valve below the fifty-five-gallon drum of gas outside the shed, amble with haste back inside, twist this and tweak that, spit on his palms, and grab the great flywheel and heft it slowly back and forth as if telling his old friend that it was time to wake up. Next he would leap nimbly on one of the spokes, let the flywheel revolve from his own weight, jump off, and throw the wheel the other way, helped by the compression.

If Fred's stars were in alignment, Otto would give a mighty "har-rumph," followed by great sighs and hisses like a genuine dragon, until exploding again, gradually building up momentum with smoke rings billowing out the straight cast-iron pipe beside the drum of gas. The sound ricocheted off the live oaks arching overhead and could be heard all the way to the Big House. Mr. Fred would throw a long wooden handle hanging down from above and the whole place would go bananas. Overhead belting and pulleys whirred, chirped, and snapped, and as successive handles were pulled more noise and motion erupted when the planer, shaper, buzz saw, bandsaw, and huge wooden lathe came on stream. One knew when Otto was coming up to speed, as a large blacksnake would shoot out from underneath the building. That shop, with companion Bob Kingett, rebuilt *Mandalay*, making possible our storybook voyage to the South Seas.

Meanwhile Roger, remembering his experience with the leaky deck on our way to the island, laid rolled roofing on the forward deck. It wasn't yacht-y, but the flint stone surface was no-skid and kept out the leaks. The smell of tar in which it was bedded, on a sunny day, made us think we were on a sailing ship of yore. Roger was also good with the cast net. At low water he would catch us a mess of mullet to use for bait or to give to James. James was the yardman and gar-dener at Stafford from my grandfather's day and was now retained by my mother and her sister to look after the place. Months would go by with no one staying in the house and it must have been lonely for him. For company he kept an alligator in the pump house. On a quiet evening we could often hear him having an animated talk with his scaly friend. I'm sure some of Roger's mullet found their way into his large jaws.

As Roger remembers:

"The variety of wildlife on Cumberland was prodigious. It ranged from the alligators and diamond-backed rattlesnakes to deer, raccoon, otter, armadillos, birds of every description, and even giant sea turtles that came ashore in the spring to lay their eggs. There were also domestic animals, horses, donkeys, razorback hogs that had reverted to the wild, not to exclude the free-roaming cattle raised by the family for revenue. So in the words of Bob Ferguson, 'A prowl around the gum pond was always rewarding.' I remember I was on just such a prowl, creeping through the woods entirely convinced I was the second coming of Natty Bumppo. The only problem being that after thirty minutes Natty wasn't seeing anything. Then I got the uneasy feeling I was being followed. Like the old Westerns, 'It was quiet— too quiet.' So I wheeled around and there, right behind me—I mean two feet away—was the gentle face of a Sicilian donkey. There were, in fact, two and they had been following me for God knows how long and I hadn't heard a sound. So the question is, why would those amiable creatures be following the blood brother of the Mohegans? Turns out, Sicilian donkeys, at least these ones, were nicotine fiends. They loved cigarettes. So we sat around and had a cigarette. I smoked mine and they ate theirs."

Living at Stafford was a joy for me, evoking as it did so many childhood memories. As a boy, I came with my family every spring vacation for three weeks. Three weeks was the time off given to executives, as it was possible to "cook the books" when gone two weeks but not three.

In those days, we entered Stafford by way of a central room and were greeted by an elaborately carved table from the Far East on which reposed a Tiffany lamp. The table was called Old Black and had come from Dungeness, representing the excesses of the Victorian era with its dragon feet, every square inch of the five-foot length carved in bewildering grotesque complexity like a completely tattooed body. My mother called it a hideosity but it was an old friend and the lamp was gorgeous. To the left in an alcove was the gun rack with a rifle, several shotguns, a Civil War musket, and fishing tackle. Farther left was a room with bookcases, a card table, a fireplace, and a couch where Grandpa took his nap after lunch. To the right was a cozy corner with a fireplace where people sat before the fire on cold evenings in leather mission chairs. The library was beyond, arrayed with those volumes of the classics one bought back then, more for the bindings than the content. In the center was a partner desk where my grandparents sat to pay the bills, make out menus, and handle island affairs. At the farther end was another fireplace.

Grandmother, Bertha Sherlock Carnegie, was tall and lean. One could spot the Irish and Scotch ancestry in her patrician features. She spoke in a voice soft and gravelly from a bout with typhoid in her younger years. She was an authoritarian figure to us as children and we never disobeyed her. Even though she appeared frail there was a ramrod quality about her one could call "presence." Grandpa, her husband, Andrew Carnegie II, was short and compact with a neatly trimmed, pointed beard. He always wore a tweed suit and tie, often with knickers, in even the warmest weather. His eyes were blue and twinkling like Saint Nick. I loved my grandfather and spent hours playing Whist with him or Dominoes and Parcheesi. He taught me how to shoot skeet. Grandpa was a teetotaler and a responsible trustee of Mama Carnegie's estate and the overseer of island affairs. He did like a cigarette from time to time. I used to feel for him when he would closet himself in the downstairs bathroom to have a puff with his friend the blacksnake who came out from behind the toilet when the bowl was flushed.

"Andrew! Andrew!" Grandma would call in her most disapproving, scratchy tone. "Is that you in there smoking?"

"I'll be right out, Bertha," would come the reply, and he would sheepishly emerge.

His other vice was cockfighting. The chauffeur, mechanic, and handyman, Frank Lynn, kept fighting chickens down at the stables. Periodically there would be a get-together there with Uncle Bob from Greyfield and the sheriff of the county. It was an accepted southern sport at the time, but here again my grandmother disapproved. When Grandpa went missing for any length of time she would question us as to his whereabouts, never mentioning cockfighting by name but skirting around the bush with phrases like, "Was that a chicken I heard making that noise down toward the stables?"

Our reply would go along the lines of, "I think it was that Rhode Island red laying an egg. Frank says she's awful noisy."

Come 6 p.m. every evening Grandpa would have his ear up to the radio, with its domed case and smoked dial window, listening to Lowell Thomas spout the news. At such times he did not like to be disturbed. But afterward he told of the old days. A favorite tale was what happened on that day down at Dungeness when he was growing up. First, Great-great-grandma broke her arm falling between the boat and the dock. Then Uncle Frank shot Uncle Morris in the head inside the Tabby House office where they were target practicing. Next Annie Meekam, the housekeeper, was thrown out of the carriage while turning left at Dungeness toward the stables. The rest of the passengers saw it coming and jumped. Annie said she decided to stick with it. A wheel ran over her.

Frank Lynn's wife, Katie, did the cooking on a large coal stove, always supporting several kettles and a pan or two. A most delicious cornbread was forever coming from the commodious oven along with enough cookies and cakes to satisfy the most insatiable sweet tooth. The smells of cornbread inside, and those of camellias and honeysuckle outside, still linger in my nose. Food came to the dining table via Clayton or Bird. Clayton had finely chiseled features and had killed a man found in his wife's bed. Grandpa used to whisper to his guests that they were being waited on by a murderer, which was always good for a gasp. Clayton recounted to us as children how he had met the Headless Horseman coming back from Dungeness one night. From then on, we made a habit of looking over our shoulders when outside after dark. Bird was huge with a leonine head. Half Croatan Indian, he was an imposing but gentle figure who padded around quiet as a cat in his uniform. Stafford was a gracious and kindly place. Family frequently dropped by, like Uncle Bill, Grandpa's older brother. He was short, thin, and wiry, and in his younger days could jump in and out of a tall barrel from a standing start, my mother recounted. She could never understand how he did it. Uncle Bill lived in the old Stafford house before it burned in the late 1890s and was rebuilt. When his wife died he had her buried in the front yard so he could look at her grave from his window. The night after she was buried he dug up her remains and cut off the long braid of golden hair she curled around the top of her head. He carried it in a locket around his neck for years. We were told he was the great sport of the family—he drove the fastest cars, starting with the electrics. A great golfer, he had patented a new club and was responsible for the golf course near the house. He brought a Scotsman, Tom Hutchinson, over from the old country to design and build it. The poor man fell off a horse and was killed during the process. He was buried with Mr. Stafford in the cemetery. His brother came over to complete the job and teach the family how to play. When Uncle Bill's new wife, Gertrude, died, he moved away, and Grandpa was given the new Stafford house.

We children were on our best behavior at Stafford. It was the kind of place where any other behavior would have seemed inappropriate. Talk at the table was always interesting—fish caught, a rattlesnake killed on the steps, wildlife seen, livestock goings on like the periodic cattle dipping in a large trough for parasites, a dog eaten by an alligator, or a successful duck hunt.

After Grandmother died, Grandpa rented a summer house near ours in Greenwich to be close to my mother. In that period between military service and returning to college, I spent a lot of time with the old man, then in failing health. I think he talked to me of things he wouldn't to others. He reminisced about growing up at Dungeness in privileged circumstances. How Mama Carnegie was a good and loving mother but kept her children too close, rather than sending them out to the bigger world to create their own lives. While they were away at school she would write about how well the fish were biting, how good the hunting was, or other wonderful goings on that they should come home and enjoy. As a result, their education was desultory. Too much time was spent secluded on Cumberland, where challenges were lacking and hedonism was king. It was no wonder many of Grandpa's brothers drank more than they should and died early, not particularly happy. He recalled how much he envied my father, who had a nine-to-five job that kept him extremely busy with the challenge of running a large bank. Grandpa introduced me to death by dying in our house of cancer, slowly wasting away. I would sit by his side talking and reading, although near the end I doubt that he heard me. When the pain was severe I would hold his hand that grew colder day by day. At his death I helped the nurse take out his false teeth. That simple act of doing something for one I loved acted as a personal closure of our relationship more poignant than any funeral.

My companions Bob and Roger also grew to love Cumberland and talked about our stay years later. Unlike me, however, they experienced it as a momentary stop on the road to an even bigger adventure. I knew other adventures would come, but I would always eventually return here, which I, now an old fellow of ninety-two, have done, every year of my life.

CHAPTER FIVE

MWB

Days became weeks on Cumberland, with the boat coming closer to completion. Then, without warning, came a mystical evening in the spring of 1952 that changed my life. The magnolias were in bloom and the setting sun painted the grasses of the great western marsh in old gold as our tribe of three emerged from the forest, rattled across the cattle guard in Lady Cumberland, and drove on to the great lawn with its ancient live oaks. Beyond an avenue of cedars, towering like honor guards, rose an iconic building in white: Plum Orchard. The oyster shell drive welcomed us to the marble steps leading up to a wide porch. The massive front door, flanked by bronze sconces, lay centered beneath a canopy supported by four gigantic Corinthian columns. On either side were ten-foot-high windows, topped with a small glass-paned fan. Even when I was a child, mounting the steps was like entering a bygone time. This evening it was to become part-and-parcel of my life ever after.

Plum Orchard was built in 1898 for George, one of Mama Carnegie's sons. It was the gorgeous statement of Peabody and Stearns, a prominent Boston architectural firm, and placed in park surroundings. The creek, bordering the marsh to the west, offered deep-water

Margaret Wise Brown, Cumberland Island, on the bow of *Mandalay*

of acres until arriving at the Inland Waterway. Behind the mansion a small pond, protected by bamboo and live oaks, offered largemouth bass for sport and nearly always a gator for further interest. To the right, at the end of a line of magnolias, was the garage. In older days it housed carriages, riding horses, and the equipage for transportation of another era. Farther away by a few steps were sizable buildings for those who raised the chickens, ducks, and green things, or managed the holding pen at the edge of the creek for terrapin turtles. Adding to the tropical splendor were Canary date palms, sago palms, and other trees rarely seen on the island.

Plum Orchard was a fun place filled with family and friends. It epitomized Cumberland, an island of many wonderful structures, much beauty, and an experience waiting around every corner. Up the broad steps we went that evening in our shorts and beards, lugging a gallon of Sweet Lucy, a wine from unheralded vineyards, with power beyond its monetary value. Entering the foyer, we bore left, toward my favorite room, a place where the family gathered in the evening. I made for a position to the left of the fireplace, which was framed in red tiles and had a leather bench in front. The water lily wallpaper gave me a sense of peace, mixing well with the smell of old leather, gun oil, and bourbon. This branch of the family came from Kentucky, bringing with it a history of graciousness and all the manners of civilized living and enjoyment of people with like interests.

My glance went around the room, checking the familiar faces until they fell into eyes I had never seen before. The instant exchange of energy between us was so intense that it was as if a sudden curtain had descended. It was only the two of us, alone, in that large gathering. My mind cast loose from my body and I found myself moving forward to shake hands with this mysterious woman, not realizing I had crossed the room. Her hair, the color of the glowing marsh, surrounded eyes and a mouth that drew me in with every last strand of my being. What we said after the touching of hands was of small significance. I'm sure it was the niceties. She introduced herself as Margaret. Our proximity did the real talking. To this day that moment remains a milestone in my life. It was only later that I learned her full name was Margaret Wise Brown.

The following dawn found us walking the high dunes overlooking the beach. The air was warm, birds sang, and a surprised deer bolted into a nearby thicket. I used the moment to reach out and casually touch her hand. Instantly she took mine and the rote of the surf was a background drumbeat to my heart.

MWB at Stafford, Cumberland Island

I told Margaret how this was my favorite time on Cumberland, walking with the dawn to catch the sunrise while the white mist floated like feathers above the awakening land. This was the time the island enfolded into itself, banishing the pattern of the day to another slot in time. I didn't say it like that but that was what I tried to convey. She seemed to understand for she gave me a look out of the corner of her eye—an animal look I quickly grew to love. She told in turn how she wrote children's books, seventy-two to date. The latest she had called *The Noon Balloon*. "I hope to write something serious one day soon as I have something to say, but I am stuck in my childhood and that raises the devil when one wants to move on," she told me.

She said that someone had told her the Queen Mother of England kept *The Little Fur Family*, one of her creations, by the side of the bed. Margaret enjoyed the image of such a regal person keeping something so small and fuzzy close to her. The cover was made with real rabbit fur.

In the days to come, I came to see how Margaret walked in her own sunrise and sunset, cloaked in the mists of her art that hid the petty daily doings from sight until she was forced to face them. I remember her saying, "Evening is like morning to me—full of change and renewal and excitement. My low time is from eleven to lunch. Noon, the light is all glaring and blatant and some of the magic seems gone from the day."

From those first moments together, she pulled me gently into her world. Perhaps it was seeing me as such a willing disciple of her fantasies that made her turn those hazel-flaked eyes from her old schoolmate, my cousin, whom she had come to visit at Plum Orchard, and fasten them on me. She walked the dunes with me that fateful morning, as she would on so many mornings to follow, a kindred soul to share in her world. Later I learned how her dear friend Michael Strange, wife of John Barrymore, had died right before Margaret's arrival at Cumberland. I must have helped fill the vacuum even though fifteen years separated us in age.

On our third day together, I asked if she had ever been married.

"I am too busy and too selfish to get married," she said, again giving me that corner of the eye look, half teasing, half serious. She had to return the next day to her New York publishers and business. Jealous, desperate at the idea of having her go, I asked if she liked her literary world and the big city.

"Telephones terrify me. They are so black. And my days are too filled with fidget wheels of time." But leave she did.

It was a new experience for me to have the absence of a person leave such a void. Walking the dunes at dawn, recalling her hand linked in mine, I wrestled with feelings never before encountered. About to embark on a voyage to the South Pacific, I realized my excitement for it had fled. The daily tasks of outfitting *Mandalay* lost their glow as if a setting sun had turned my world black. Evenings found me at the typewriter, pouring out my soul in letters to my new-found lady of the morning mists, while my companions viewed me as if a foul disease had taken its toll, threatening their very existence.

Re-reading my childish prattling these sixty years hence, makes me wince. I was better at splicing rope and wire than conjuring words. But they were heartfelt, which must have conveyed my feelings, for the envelopes soon flowed both ways. I told how the fawns were dropping as they did each spring, tugging at my heart as they scampered after their mothers. Diana, the tame doe that hung around Stafford, had a fawn. It was a delight to see it nursing on the front lawn.

Margaret wrote back, "The first time I ever held a baby lion in my arms it was just like a living toy or a child's dream come true. And that warm clean smell of that little armful of something I couldn't believe was real and the tenderness of that small great beast will always fill me with wonder. Love Tim." At the time she was ghost writing a book for Osa Johnson on her African adventures, Adventures in Paradise.

Margaret had many nicknames—Tim, The Bunny, and The-Bunny-No-Good. I called her "My Bunny" and she called me her "Warlock" because I looked "so fierce" in my dark beard. I asked how things were going in the land of black telephones and fidget wheels.

"I am trying to get to a short story as a longer and sustained piece of writing. But the days are so chopped up and I can't focus on one theme. I am completely amazed and delighted that life is not at all the way it is supposed to be."

I desperately wanted to believe that the last sentence related to me. I guess it must have, for after not too long she returned to Cumberland at my pleading and we spent an idyllic month together at Stafford.

Throughout, I continued to work on the boat. Sometimes The Bunny would come to work alongside us. Otto, the big one-cylinder engine that ran the carpenter shop, delighted her. When it let out its throaty report she would ask what kind of beans it had eaten for breakfast. She and the resident blacksnake got along beautifully.

When not with the *Mandalay* crew, Margaret would write or explore the island for story ideas or pleasure. She was fascinated with animal tracks as windows to peer into the creatures' lives. Raccoons were everywhere, along with deer and wild horses, and the friendly Sicilian donkeys belonging to Aunt Lucy. There were the feral hogs with their piglets, big boars with tusks and red eyes, and great sows with their milking stations hanging down. She liked the shadow crabs on the beach, living in their round holes in the sand, scuttling sideways when one approached. Squirrels jumped from limb to limb. Rabbits timidly hid in the shadows or fed on the grass at dawn or dusk. There were the scaly alligators, and the chameleons that changed color as they ran along ledges and pursued food. She loved the bustling wrens with their cries of *teacher, teacher, teacher*. On to brilliant cardinals, gossiping mockingbirds, hummingbirds, storks, eagles, hawks, and of course the myriad beach dwellers. Sandpipers and terns, gulls, oyster catchers with their yellow leggings, formations of pelicans playing follow the leader, inches above the breaking surf, all were candidates for her fantasies and pen. She soon had stories about them all.

After a few days listening to her I wasn't sure whether people acted like animals or animals like people. Mr. and Mrs. Toad would come out every evening as we sat on the steps of Stafford sipping our Sweet Lucy. She would talk to them as intimates, asking what they did in their spare time and if they didn't get tired of always sleeping on their tummies, especially if they were full of juicy bugs.

When my turn came to hunt the weekly larder deer, I asked if she would like to go along, hesitant that her love of animals would stand in the way. "Don't you know me better than that? Of course I want to see my Warlock kill something. Will your hands run red with blood?" She wasn't an easy one to pigeonhole. She shed skins as easily as a chameleon, living in her fantasy world where change was the only constant, balanced by a sharp mind when it came to dealing with publishers and business affairs. So off we went one evening to my favorite place to hunt or just to walk. Lady Cumberland chuffed us up the beach around the slight bend at Stafford Shoals. Here a sandbar extended far out to sea causing breakers that were a hazard for marine interests but a boon to fishermen surf casting from the beach. I stopped where the band of live oaks ended along the mid-dunes, bent to the north with the prevailing southerly wind. Parking above high water in the white sand, we walked inland toward the forest. The dunes, undulated like the sea that had formed them, blended into a smooth constant rise of pure white sand, decorated here and there with blasted skeletons of live oaks overcome by the white avalanche tossed up by the surf.

The meeting of sand and forest was a magical place. Twenty feet down the steep incline, the forest floor spread out under a canopy of branches, blending into little clearings, marsh, and small shallow ponds. It was the jungle primeval, seemingly as far removed from civilization as the wilds of the African bush. Down the steep slope, plunging into the forest were myriad animal tracks, branching into many game trails before becoming obscured from sight. The breeze was coming from the west so we couldn't be scented. I picked a place beside a clump of bushes atop the dune and we sat down to await our prey with the fast approaching evening. For half an hour we waited, The Bunny silent with her nose twitching as if seeking a scent in her story world. A coon came by, kneading the bottom of a little pond with its feet and searching for food. A doe passed below us, but I held my fire, not wanting to shoot a mother—although there was no fawn. Then came the buck, stopping every few feet to test the air. When he was within fifty feet I ever so slowly raised Grandpa's 30-30 rifle and carefully squeezed the trigger, wanting the kill to be clean. The deer fell, twitched and lay still. I propped the rifle against a bush and started down, half walking, half sliding with the precipitous slope. I sensed Timmie right behind.

It was a struggle hauling us and the deer back up the dune. We were panting before reaching the top. A button of my mate's blouse was torn off with her exertion and the look in her eyes was that of a terrier with a bone. We paused for breath, then with one of us at either side of the head grasping a horn, we made for the beach. Dusk was coming fast. At the water's edge I shed my shoes, took out my hunting knife, and opened up the buck's belly, momentarily forgetting she was there. Carefully laying aside the liver and heart I removed the other organs until the cavity was bare. Only then did I glance sideways to see The Bunny on her knees holding the heart in her palm. I questioned her with my eyes.

She looked out over the darkening sea and said, the heart still in her palm, "How strange it would be for you as a man, being you, to live a life and never have this experience." It was like so many of her remarks that appeared from midair, plucked from her special tree hanging the fruits of her creations.

We drove home in silence, her hand in my lap, and the deer riding in the valley between fender and engine. The only sound was the chuffing of Lady Cumberland and the rote of the surf.

The following week we were driving down the beach and saw a knot of people at the water's edge looking out toward the breakers where an old shrimp boat was being rolled in the surf like a child's toy. The owner was a wizened black, shrunk by age and adversity. His son was with him and their clothes clung to their thin bodies, wet from wading ashore. The family's manager arrived, an English major, a product of India whose viewpoint ran along the lines of "us" and "them." The old man stared at his life savings, shoulders hunched, asking the major if he could arrange for help in getting the boat towed off. Back in those days old engines, worse from wear, caused many boats to come ashore. Only a few got off from the Cumberland shore at great expense.

The Major was not helpful. He was on the way up island to meet someone and let it be known that he had more pressing things on his mind than arranging the rescue of a tired shrimp boat with a black crew. Tension built. The manager and I exchanged words. He departed north and I told the two men to climb in the back of the Model A. We took them to Dungeness at the south end and arranged to get them to the mainland where they could organize a rescue. Margaret was quiet on the way down the beach and all the way home. That evening sitting on the front porch she said suddenly, "The wind-up toy boat danced on the sea, not knowing it was the last dance. Thank you for saying what you did."

"That does not sound like the start of a children's story," I said.

"I feel comfortable with animals," she replied. "Animals are friends. When I have something to say about grownup people I enter a wilderness where I lose my way. Do you think they will get the boat off?"

"No," I said. "It is old and tired, nail-sick and wracked. If they did manage to tow it off it would probably sink."

"A tragedy for those two."

"Yes," I said. "The sea serves up many tragedies." Then to lighten her mood: "The bones will whiten on the beach. Children will play in and around them. They will make up fun stories if that is any solace. I have many remembrances of wrecks from my childhood here."

"I like that," she said. "We will dedicate the place to that man and his son."

Secretly, I wondered if that man's family had worked for my forbearers, or before that as a slave for Planter Stafford of Stafford. From whom and where one entered the world was a roll of the dice. By all odds, it could as well have been us looking out to sea where our "toy, wind-up boat" was foundering.

One afternoon we climbed to the cupola of Dungeness, the old family mansion. Sitting on the circular seat we overlooked the marsh. I thought of the old days when a boy would be sent here to keep an eye on Mama Carnegie while she went rowing on the creek. She had been known to fall asleep and be taken downstream by the tide. But now, even more, I thought about the two of us, Margaret and me. During the month together, we had drawn ever closer until it was impossible for me to foresee a future without her. Nonetheless, she had to leave in a few days. The plan was to meet in St. Thomas where we would set sail together for the South Pacific, getting married at the first place whose name took our fancy. There was much for her to do before casting loose from a past life of black telephones, commitments, and publishers. She looked far out from within her different world to where the marsh bordered the main channel, and said more to herself than me, "You can never in this world love anyone you love enough."

Then she said something else that was powerful medicine to sip in the coming days when we were apart. "Pebble, it is as if I was only half alive and you have given me a transfusion of your own blood."

After she left for New York, I reviewed the days together and they seemed too good to be anything but a beautiful dream. One of our favorite places had been the Plum Orchard Beach house. It was one small room with a fireplace and a large sliding door opening to the dunes. A small stream, draining the wetlands behind, ran between the house and beach. With darkness, a cozy fire burning on the raised hearth, we listened to the sound of the surf and night noises and felt a million miles removed. The Bunny would take two great cockle shells, place a dab of butter in the bottom, push them near the coals and when the butter was melted, pour an egg in each one and add assorted herbs she had rounded up from goodness knows where. Making a glove of Spanish moss we pulled them away from the fire when done, decanted red wine into two glasses, and commenced the evening feast. After the eggs would come, perhaps, a fish we had caught several hours before, baked on a plank that stood up at one side of the fireplace. Then we would talk into the night about those things that wafted from the depths of the coals. Or sometimes we sat silently, bodies touching, minds and stomachs in nirvana. Such moments one banks in memory for those times when the path grows thorny and hope becomes a stranger. Looking back more than half a century, picturing us there, I see the scene take on dimensions molded by the intervening years. Today, I am still transfused with a sense of well-being that approaches the mystical.

After The Bunny left, long days were filled with purpose. The sooner the boat was done and sailing, the sooner we would be together again. The evenings were a time to touch each other through letters or thoughts brought on by the night. Reading through the correspondence with the insight of all these years, I marvel at the difference between our writings. Hers were poetic masterpieces alongside my childish scribblings. It certainly wasn't my literary skill that had her write sentences like, "Pebble, you are wonderful in the subtle ways you answer my own thoughts and strengthen me to really step right out of those fidget wheels of time." Or, "No one has so disarmed all the me's to reach that first one, who you have touched."

She had the skill to describe a happening in few words. What wasn't told, one instinctively knew. She had gone for the weekend to a friend who ran a cow farm in Litchfield, Connecticut. "I went to sleep last night with an old piece of bacon tied on the bottom of my foot, to draw out the splinter I got from dancing in my stocking feet—very late."

So the days spun on toward that one when the sun rose and my companions and I determined to depart. The readying of a boat for a long voyage is an incremental exercise never completely done. There has to be a cutoff or otherwise the weeks continue to multiply with no movement and no course. The Bunny was the rainbow at the end of my tunnel. Her letters kept tugging me forward. She was now at her summer cottage on the island of Vinalhaven in Maine, a magical habitat, I sensed, that she drew around her like a cape.

It was easy to imagine when she wrote, "The song sparrow is singing and a clowning gull is down on the shore trying to crow like a rooster and cluck like a hen and laugh like a gentle maniac, all at the same time. The house is a boat, only the weathers and fogs and times of day and night sail by the house instead of the house sailing away."

One evening while sitting on the back porch of her cottage she called "The Only House," she wrote, "I must tell Pebble how easy and comfortable it is to bake things—just pop them in the oven and eat them with butter and coarse ground pepper and very red meat and redder wine."

I could see myself there. From the descriptions in her letters I recognized every rock, wavelet, and birdsong. A new plan was forming in my mind—one that would bring me to Margaret—even as our crew finally pulled up anchor and departed from Cumberland. We sailed *Mandalay* to Miami and up the river to a little private dock belonging to a friend. Through Margaret's introduction, we met Jean Watts who drew mischievous little reindeer, along with a whole world of creatures who parodied their human relatives. It so transpired that Jean introduced us to Monica Flaherty, daughter of Robert Flaherty who created the documentary "Nanook of the North" about Eskimos. Monica was a trim, attractive woman. Roger took more than a liking to her and soon she had Roger running in and out of her igloo, while Bob looked on with growing dismay. I saw my plan approaching fruition. The Bunny was never far from my mind.

The fates surveyed the scene from on high and their fickle fingers soon jibed with my heart's desire. We would temporarily interrupt the voyage so Bob could go down to the Gulf and work on a shrimp boat to earn some money. Roger would also go shrimping, while continuing his studies in Monica's igloo. I, in turn, would venture north to see The Bunny on Vinalhaven. Our lives began to spin in different orbits and we innocents sensed it, even if we did not speak our thoughts aloud.

CHAPTER SIX

A Writer of Songs and Nonsense

Islands can be personal castles or prisons depending on how one views their moats of water. That summer of 1952 when I traveled north from Cumberland Island to be with Margaret on Vinalhaven was a sweet sojourn. I saw immediately that this place at the head of Hurricane Sound was her castle of fairy story proportions. Margaret called it The Only House, because looking out at night, more often than not, no other light was visible.

No road existed. The surrounding forest was yet another barrier against the outside world. Our entry started at the little fisherman's cottage of Mildred Brewster and Maynard Swett on the edge of a small tidal drain behind Strauson's Point. Mildred had done the cooking in the boarding house at Wharf's Quarry back when granite was king. Maynard, well past seventy, lobstered out of his white peapod with the green gunwales. They were devoted to Margaret and here she kept her gray flat-bottomed skiff built by a local shipwright called Skoog. It comfortably held the two of us, her Kerry blue terrier called Crispin, groceries, a case of wine, and other household necessities. The twenty-minute pull up the sound was a pleasant interval on that warm and sparkling day of my arrival as we were gently pushed along by the southwest breeze.

Dog and Margaret occupied the stern sheets. Crispin glared at me while I eyed his mistress. Crispin was disagreeable by nature, but then in all fairness, it was not easy for him being in the proximity of another male who also loved his person. The Bunny wore her usual working costume of white slacks, espadrilles, and a blue blouse open at the neck. Her straw-colored hair, tumbled by the wind, was a perfect frame for those crinkly blue-gray eyes that looked at me, through me, while absorbing everything within sight. She trailed one hand in the water, lifting it eventually to extend a dripping finger to a passing dragonfly. To my amazement the insect landed on this perch as if it had no other choice.

"Warlock," she said. "What must it be thinking, flying over all this bright blue water? Must be all these lobster buoys look like flower beds."

With Margaret one lived an ongoing series of mini-adventures. Deeply involved with the smallest event, she pulled her companion along through a magical world she composed on the spot.

Too soon we arrived at a tiny beach hidden behind a long boulder of rounded granite. Entrusted with the case of wine, I walked up to the tiny house through the tall grass of the miniature meadow dappled with hawkweed. The high-pitched roof, black attic window, black framed windows of the lower two floors, and gray, weathered clapboards made it intensely appealing yet mysterious. It was as diminutive as a child's playhouse but one sensed immediately the inhabitant was neither child nor casual rusticator.

Saluting an ancient pear tree, one mounted steep steps, almost a ladder, that teetered upward to a circular porch fifteen feet above the ground. This platform in turn was guarded by a granite ledge to the west that resembled a beached but happy whale, and an apple tree that intruded over the railing to the north. Ice-cream-parlor chairs and table formed an eyrie for eating, talking, or just surveying the warblers, woodpeckers, ospreys, gulls, and terns that considered the place their own, which delighted Margaret. The long, narrow, steep steps were yet another psychological barrier against things and beings beyond the forest and water. "Here I am in my snug little ship safe from storms of that other ridiculous world," she would say, talking about her frenetic winters spent in New York with agents, publishers, and a host of social commitments.

From this roofless treehouse one entered a tiny kitchen, off of which opened an eight-by-ten-foot room holding a love seat, a reclining couch, a potbelly stove, and a long table in front of the window where Margaret did her writing. To the left of her writing station was a door that swung out to a ten-foot drop to the ground below. It bore a brass plaque saying "Bell McCann." Bell had owned the house before it was jacked up and a floor was added underneath to house animals for milking and to create the larder. In winter, heat from the warm bodies leant a helping hand to the old potbelly. Off the sitting room was an even smaller bedroom with just enough room for a double brass bed and dresser. The whole place was the size of a ship's cabin.

The window behind the writing table commanded the granite wharf from quarrying days, and Hurricane Sound with its myriad little spruce tipped islands arranged with an artist's touch. This was the view that inspired *The Little Island*, one of her most charming books. I am sure some of the original script was written with a quill. A bird's feather, sharpened at one end for a writing instrument, gave her great pleasure. The search for an appropriate quill followed along with all our walks.

Kerosene lamps were the sole illumination. A rose-colored globe hung over the tiny kitchen table on an adjustable chain. Another standing glass lamp, this one ruby-tinted, lit the writing table, while two companion pieces were moved about as needed. A pair of exquisite small, rococo candelabra created a floral display on the vertical paneling between sitting room and bedroom, adding further soft ambience when darkness fell.

Of an evening with perhaps a red spaghetti sauce laced with garlic bubbling on the kerosene stove, and wine in goblets, Margaret would seat herself at the table that had witnessed many things, her eyes shining in the fairy-story light. She was definitely the queen of this special kingdom. I say "queen" for everything in the tiny house appeared to be her personal subject, chosen for shape, color, or adding catalytic power to the overall sense of a cozy den, yet in such an unstudied way as if to be a natural extension of herself. Eggs were stored in a glass bowl for people to enjoy their shape and to facilitate their use. Wildflowers winked from glasses, cups, vases, or copper pots. The sublime imbued the whimsical with a frame typical of their originator's genius.

Margaret loved fur and there was a lot of it around: a fur rug on the floor, fur on one of the couches, a fake leopard skin covering the bed. "Remember we are animals," she was wont to say.

Rabbits were a special totem. Margaret had long eyelashes and would sometimes accent the corners of her eyes to suggest an almond bunny look when she was in her Bunny-No-Good mood, uttering statements like, "I'm going to buy all the bird-brains egg cozies for Christmas," when exasperated at some human stupidity.

In earlier times before her reign, goats, chickens, and a cow had lived downstairs. Now the space was for a workshop and spartan guest room. The latter also served as a gallery for her paintings. She

Margaret looking out from 'The Only House' in Vinalhaven

explained that from early on she knew she could be either a credible painter or a writer. Deciding that writing was her commanding drive she had taken up painting for relaxation and to sharpen her eye as to color, place, and position to aid her storytelling. She worked closely with her illustrators and in so much of their work one could see her perceptive genius. There was an oil painting of a dog with long rabbit-like ears lying on the loveseat. Through the window in the painting peeped the Little Island. Another featured the horse weathervane she had mounted on the end of the stone wharf. Yet another showed a white china water pitcher filled with wildflowers exuding a tour de force of colors. The last conveyed a different mood. The Only House stood somber in its black trim under a lowering sky. A small drab figure huddled against the stoop. This she had done after the death of her dearest friend, Michael Strange.

"When I can no longer write, paint, or read, that is the end," she once said to me.

Even going to the outhouse was an adventure. First met was an apple tree that shaded a washstand with white ewer, pitcher, and soap dish. A classic mirror was nailed above them on the trunk. Next one passed the icebox—a covered well with floating containers housing butter, milk, cheese, and other perishables. The white wine floated alone. Only then did one enter a short section of woods, rush up an incline, throw open the Dutch door, and choose one of two holes. As Billy Brown, her caretaker, put it, "Darn thing is so far away you're pressin' your luck."

Once one was enthroned, the best was yet to be enjoyed. The view took in the rear cove with the large grout pile of Wharf's Quarry rising on the other side. Across to the left was a rock with a fissure that from half-tide down cast the silhouette of an Indian maiden demurely bending forward at the edge of the limpid tidal pool.

I asked Bill what he thought of the maiden. "Haven't told my wife," he said. "Might get jealous."

The rest of Margaret's dominion held other landmarks. Along the path leading eastward was the dug well where one hauled water up with a bucket. At the edge of the spruce forest dwelled the magic mouse in his mouse hole. From there the trail wove between the trees around several corners until bursting forth upon a small clearing with a cabin Margaret had built for Michael Strange. On entering, one met a large, ornate, gilt frame set with glass that revealed the picture out-side—the best picture window I'd ever seen. The front of the cabin perched at the edge of a large, perfectly smooth ledge that sloped down to the sea. The roof, as if to emulate the ledge, also swooped downward forming two points, pagoda-like. These were supported by wood columns from her favorite antique store in Rockland. Convention to Margaret was as red to the bull.

Walking up the granite escarpment behind the cabin, one came to a flat expanse of stone some one hundred feet in diameter. As we approached, she would press fingers to her lips for silence. Here was the fairy ballroom where "the little people" danced at midnight over-looking Hurricane Sound far below. It was always just possible, even in broad daylight, that there might be one peeping from behind a bayberry bush.

I loved to go up there of an evening. We would stand on the edge of the rock cliff and watch dusk enfold the sound. Dawn and dusk were important times for The Bunny, as were the languor of noon, the rising of the moon, storms, and calms. Standing on the promon-tory outlined against the darkening bay, she radiated the elemental dignity of a wild thing in its native habitat. Often those eyes of hers would go far away where no one could ever reach, and one evening she turned suddenly and said, "We are born alone. We go through life alone. And we go out alone." I never have forgotten that moment, painful as the words were, for what she said was true as I came to see in the ensuing years. She saw herself in a frame where human beings were but one component of a larger whole.

As one's eyes are drawn to an animal to gauge its intent, so mine were constantly drawn to hers. There was always more going on in there than the viewer could ever grasp. Her look would vary from youth to venerable age to childlike wonder, mischievousness, gaiety, somberness, or the wisdom of a seer.

In the woods and fields Margaret moved like a deer. She told of going fox hunting, running with the hounds for hours. During berry excursions she wiggled through the most impossible tangles at incredible speed and ate berries off the bush like a bear I once had. A herring fisherman who set his nets out in front of The Only House said to me, "That Margaret! If you saw her in the woods come November and she was wearing horns it would take a steady mind not to shoot." Then he added with a wistful grin, "I'd rather take her home, alive, myself."

For venturing on the bay Margaret had a treacherous North Haven dinghy. One day we had a wonderful sail down to Hurricane Island at the end of the bay, trailing the bottle of white wine behind on a string. Margaret puffed on her pipe—she enjoyed smoking a pipe—reciting one of her many lyrics, *The Fish with the Deep Sea Smile*. The ballad begins:

They fished and they fished
Way down in the sea

Down in the sea a mile.
They fished among all the fish in the sea
For the fish with a deep-sea smile.

On the way home the southwest breeze turned into a small gale. We rushed along faster and faster until at the end of Leadbetter's Island the dinghy sailed her nose right under. There we were with the sail up, going nowhere, paddling around in the swamped cockpit. I was mortified, considering myself somewhat of a sailor. But Margaret puffed away on her still-lit pipe, asked if there was any wine left in the bottle, and giggled with glee despite the chilly water. Just then Goldie McDonald, the guardian of neighboring Dogfish Island, happened by and pulled us dripping into his boat. Goldie was one of Margaret's favorites. She even used him as a pen name. Goldie took one look at The Bunny, wet clothes clinging to her athletic body, and said with feeling, "Gawd Margaret! You look better wet than dry."

She laughed all the way home. In her eyes it couldn't have been a more perfect day.

Aside from sitting in the evening bathed in the ruby light from the kerosene lamps, going up to Wharf's Quarry was among my fondest memories. Here the columns for the Cathedral of St. John the Divine in New York originated. Carrying a hamper, towels, and soap, we would take the path around the back cove and plough through an overgrown meadow and tangle of brambles until coming to a granite ledge lying in the gloom of the forest like a forgotten Stonehenge. Over this we pushed and pulled ourselves, emerging on a gently sloping expanse of stone that we followed upward until standing atop the quarry. From there we could gaze down fifty feet of sheer rock wall to the pool of water. To the left stretched Hurricane Sound and straight

Margaret and me on Cumberland Island

ahead to the west was Leadbetter Narrows with the Camden Hills as a backdrop.

The entry to our destination was at the far end of the rock wall. The granite sloped down to cattails and blue iris with stone and vegetation arranged by a master's brush to form a hidden water garden. Here on a flat rock by the water's edge we would spread our things and have our biweekly ablutions. Afterward drying on the sun-warmed granite we would eat lunch in mystical serenity.

Often, Margaret would talk about her writing, returning to her thought that she had nothing serious to say. I would reply that seventy-two books meant she had a lot to say. At the time I didn't comprehend what a pioneer she had become or how revered she was in the writing of children's books. Facetiously I asked once what she would like to have put on her tombstone if not recognition for children's works. She thought a bit, watching the white clouds pass overhead before turning and saying in all seriousness, "You will put 'A writer of songs and nonsense.'"

"Writing nonsense," I asked, "how does one go about that?"

She took my hand and gave it a squeeze. "Sometimes it is easy, sometimes hard, to bring your feelings, your heart, and your interest together." Then she turned mischievous. "I understand in words almost as well as I did without them. That is what one animal would say to another if they suddenly learned English."

It was impossible to conceive what was coming out of that mouth and brain next. When I asked how she came by the title of her forthcoming book, *The Noon Balloon*, she replied, "I was looking out my window in New York at noon when this blimp came sailing by. It had to be the noon balloon to LaGuardia."

More than sixty years have passed since that particular day in the quarry. As we lay in the sun drying ourselves, I had no reason not to believe that our time together was endless and our future secured. The darkness ahead was obscured. Even now, when I think back, that day is as clear to me as if it had only just passed. Like her books, Margaret is eternal and forever loved.

Today, children and grandchildren on Vinalhaven still stop by the magic mouse hole to whisper "Hi." They know *The Little Island, The Runaway Bunny, Goodnight Moon,* and a dozen others. As to The Fairy Ballroom, I am convinced it is Margaret peeping from behind the bayberry bushes, while the Indian maiden holds Billy's hand across the eternal deep divide. And forever, ever, there will be the fish with the deep-sea smile, down in the sea a mile, just a swish of his tail from the Little Island in a world all its own within the enchanted kingdom that will always be Margaret's.

CHAPTER SEVEN

Miami to Panama

After the idyllic time on Vinalhaven, I said a sorry goodbye to Margaret. I had given her a ring, and heartened by the promise of our marriage, left her with no sense of foreboding. I returned to my boat in Miami and to Bob, Roger, and the voyage so long planned. While there we enjoyed Jean Watts, the artist friend of Margaret's who drew mischievous reindeer doing mischievous things. With Jean came her friend Monica Flaherty, whom Roger had taken such a liking to. It didn't take long before he asked if she could come along. I had doubts, and Bob had bigger doubts, as Monica had as sharp a tongue as Nanook's harpoon. Now we were four, bringing dark clouds to threaten the horizon.

Before we left shore, Monica decided she had to go to New York to do something. So off we went to the airport, where Monica being Monica suddenly decided it would not be prudent to leave her Roger alone with Jean of the wicked reindeer and so she canceled. Clothed only in shorts, T-shirt, and topsiders, I grabbed her ticket and was, suddenly, and with no warning, the one airborne. It had been only a few short weeks since I'd seen Margaret, but the attraction between us had grown only more intense since parting. Here was an opportunity impossible to resist. Excited to surprise her, I landed in New York and made a beeline to her railroad flat apartment at 186 East End Avenue on the Upper East Side, across from Gracie Park and the governor's mansion.

"I knew you were coming," was her greeting. She had the sixth sense of a wild animal. Clinging to her, smelling the fragrance in her hair, I had a moment never to forget, like the all too short days that followed.

The next day she introduced me to her writing retreat, Cobble Court, at 1335 York Avenue. It was hidden behind a tenement building owned by Mrs. Healy, whose family had lived there for generations. Navigating a dark corridor, one opened a rear door and came out into an enchanted little courtyard with a diminutive house behind. The tiny place had started life as a cow and goat shed in the 1800s. It was two stories, after a fashion, on the scale of a large dollhouse. Here masterpieces were born. Cobble Court was Margaret's favorite place in the city, a little hideaway, where she tucked herself in, while East End was more formal. Cobble Court she loved, perhaps because it was so small, a dollhouse that appealed to her sense of make-believe. She felt comfortable there. It provided her kind of surroundings like The Only House in Maine. It defeated "the fidget wheels of time"—the distractions of city living. We spent most of the time there. It went with the fairy tale we were living.

What do I remember about those short weeks? I was introduced to her creative circle of writers, artists, illustrators, and sycophants, who trailed her with adoring eyes. They were tolerant of my presence, considering me perhaps a moment's whim that would soon pass. Some of them saw the presence of happiness and were pleased for us both. A walk in the park with Crispin was an entertainment.

Crispin was immortalized in her Mister Dog, "the dog who belonged to himself." I did not take him for a walk; rather he took me. There were rear ends to be sniffed or snubbed, bushes to lift a leg on, residents to be reunited with, or a nosy pigeon to be reprimanded. When all these duties were satisfactorily performed he would direct me back to his mistress and not before. We had an understanding that neither would bite the other.

Before returning to Miami, I saw Margaret off to Cannes, France, on the liner *Vulcania*, with a heavy heart. She was at the rail with Crispin at her side as the liner pulled away from the dock. I looked up and she looked down and it was probably my imagination that Crispin stuck out his tongue at me. In those last moments, the same intensity of our very first meeting across the room in Cumberland was there.

Back in Miami, Bob, Roger, Monica, and I officially took to the sea. The Miami skyline sank beneath the waves, and the changing color of the water that accompanied our entrance to the Gulf Stream became the gateway to our Pacific voyage. The northward thrust of the vivid blue current was also the harbinger of new dramatic forces about to enter our little moving world. By evening we were waiting for the flooding tide to cross the shallow bar into Bimini Harbor, a place dependent on the American sport of catching large game fish to stuff and mount on sportsmen's walls. Our sport was different.

We arrived in Bimini, a different setting with a different purpose. Bimini was to be our base for a few days while we treasure hunted for a fifty-foot schooner that had gone down six miles off the island in thirty-six feet of water a year ago. The owner had dived on it but didn't have the equipment to bring up the six thousand pounds of easily accessible lead, or so he said. He gave us a release and the location. Lead was selling for around $.25 a pound, so the treasure in its bilges was a tempting nest egg for the future. Bob was a good diver, we had the necessary equipment, and the allure of high adventure was a marvelous sauce. If one could have bottled our anticipation it would have been worth far more than three tons of lead.

"We sailed and we sailed many a mile over a shallow sea," as Margaret might have said, looking for that wreck. We took turns in the ratlines and whenever something appeared that didn't seem native to the bottom, over the side Bob would go. Roger was towed behind in the rubber raft as he stared down through a glass bottom box. Once a pilot fish swooped up from the sea floor and fastened himself to Roger's window. Roger said he asked the fellow where the wreck was, but Mr. Pilot replied it was a subject of no interest and asked where we were going.

Our navigation for pinpointing potential treasure was crude as we only had sextant and eyeball. The gentle breeze would drop at dusk, so we would anchor out on the shallow bank, six miles from land, floating on a film of sensually moving glass, orchestrated by the music of bird night sounds and other creatures or the occasional lights from a passing vessel bound northward in the Gulf Stream. It was an eerie feeling, like being naked on a busy street, lying there with no protection but the hope the wind wouldn't get up. In the morning the native boats would glide by on their way to the crawfish grounds, a man in the stern sculling with a long sweep in a rhythmic motion like a dance to entice the gentle breeze. In the evening they would return, laughing and singing and calling to one another across the water. They were good people, with a joy of being alive that gave us an appreciation of our own existence.

Me and Bob Grant

Just when we began to bore of the routine, hurricane warnings arrived via the radio. We fled the quest for lead and under full sail at a stately three knots pointed the bowsprit toward Nassau with its hurricane anchorage. This proved a narrow indentation about the size of a large Jacuzzi into which crammed myriad Bahamian craft. An eighteen-foot sailing dinghy came cavorting in, its skipper yelling to a captive audience, "I'm coming in on the wings or prov–ee–dence." Later he was heard to remark, "I want to go home to my wife, but I have to remain with the ship."

We threw out two anchors. The rest of the fleet tossed over a collection of rusty iron worthy of the scrap yard. A party atmosphere prevailed, a tribute to the concept of Bahamian providence. What would come would come.

Providence was kind. It pushed the hurricane aside. The captain of the eighteen-foot dinghy went home to his wife and I rushed to the post office to check for mail. Those envelopes with their foreign stamps stirred more emotion in me than any hurricane. The first was dated October 10, 1952. Margaret wrote about Florence through her dog's eyes. "All the rooms were as big as a house with people painted on the ceiling all held together by bunches of roses—little fat naked people with curly hair, smiling and waving their toes. They are disappointing as pictures—they aren't really round and they don't move, you can't chase them and they don't smell.

"But there was a real cat and I chased him and sent him cracking.

" . . . my mistress loves you very much and I accept the inevitable—send me an old sock to sleep with."

In the next: "One eats soufflés and tomato provincial and huge lovely salads—but The Bunny has to watch it, and is going to run up and down the goat path in the mountains to the sea so she won't get too fat to climb the rigging for Pebble with her white catalyst ring (the wedding ring I gave her in Maine) flashing in the lightning."

In yet another she wrote about my upcoming passage to St. Thomas. "I will come when the light changes and give you an extra hug so hard your flippers will beat like a porpoise slapping the waves.

"Your rabbit wife."

The last letter was troubling. She had gone into the hospital with pains diagnosed as a cyst in one of her fallopian tubes. The operation was a success and she was fast recovering in time to meet me in St. Thomas as soon as I wired our arrival. She told of "The Barbar hospital" and of old doctors with beards and of happy nuns, going on to say, "I've never been in a situation like this before—a big helpless creature becoming younger and younger in bed. My eyes change constantly and she [the nurse] must always ask how old I am this instant. Everyone is entitled to a certain margin of mystery."

Disquieted by her operation and wanting to be with her as soon as possible, I pulled up the sails and we headed to sea, eager to reach St. Thomas. The future by now had taken a new twist. I was no longer content to be sailing off on a happy-go-lucky voyage around the world. After I met The Bunny we would carry on for a temporary adventure and then return to the States to get on with our life together, whatever and wherever that might be.

The voyage progressed frustratingly slowly, and I was in no mood for the sea's diversionary tactics. Two days out, as we tried to gain some easting for a good slant to St. Thomas, the wind died, and we lay rocking back and forth, rolling forty-five degrees in either direction so violently in the swells that we doused the sails. Pots and pans crashed about and anything not contained flew across the cabin. It was like being ground up in a giant blender. Not to be intimidated,

Bob baked a lemon meringue pie. As he opened the oven door the boat lurched sideways, and the pie arced to the cabin sole where it regarded him lopsidedly.

Five days out we lay heaved-to in a series of squalls, with the boat leaking. The violent motion in the previous calm had opened up the old girl. To pass the time I read Joseph Conrad's *Victory*, Richard Hughes' *High Wind in Jamaica*, and Russian short stories. Squall after squall followed, arising from some breeding source beyond our sight. We had sailed five hundred miles, mostly in the wrong direction.

Writing in the ship's log, cooking, and reading were our major occupations after sail managing, pumping, and bracing our bodies. One meal I baked a rice dish, cooking it first in olive oil and garlic with consommé and fresh chopped onions, then mixing in two cans of roast beef and lathering a cornbread mix on top. Another concoction was potatoes, corn beef hash, and a vinegar salad with canned spinach, which The Bunny had taught me to do.

On the second night out Bob had to luff up to let a freighter go by at a safe distance. The third night I was on watch when lights appeared at the left edge of my horizon, grew larger and larger, then passed to starboard and grew smaller until disappearing below the right horizon like the passing of a celestial body. The passing of another ship on the open ocean invokes a cathedral of thought. Out there, we resided in a small world resting on a floating one, sandwiched between yet another world with its own stars, planets, black holes, and infinite space, all working on concentric courses. It was humbling and exhilarating to be part of a mystery beyond the knowing. Contemplating the wonder helped us pass many long hours, as it has for many mariners over the millennia.

On yet another day a freighter out of Bergen, Norway, hove alongside and asked if we needed anything. We requested our position be reported to the folks at home and they steamed off headed for the Mona Passage. There were fewer little boats back then messing around this far from shore. The freighters were smaller and slower and had better lookouts. The automatic pilot had yet to take over the wheelhouse to dull watch-keeping eyes. Yet one night I had to shine a flashlight on our sails when a ship kept steaming right for us.

Then came the experience that is as vivid today, as it was then, more than sixty years ago. I awoke from a dream in a drenching sweat, muscles knotted, with the unmistakable certainty that Margaret had died. Her face was as vivid as the full moon. She reached out to me with those hazel eyes that held a distillation of all the hours spent together. With the intensity of a burning brand they held me, then slowly drew away and disappeared behind a screen of black.

My crew reassured me that it was just a bad dream. But I knew better. No dream could fuse to the very nerve endings and become an integral part of me. When I was handed the telegram on our arrival in St. Thomas, I went to a quiet place away from other eyes before opening the yellow envelope. She had died in her hospital bed, kicking up a leg to show the doctor how strong she was getting. The motion, so typical of her, must have broken loose a blood clot, which caused her death. Retracing the time of her death I saw that it corresponded exactly with the arrival of her image on the high seas four days from St. Thomas. There are dimensions of communication that transcend the known limits of the mind.

Now came a black time, that same curtain Margaret's image had disappeared behind. Life was for naught. Every task had no meaning. The eyes saw nothing but an endless wasteland, sterile of emotion, hope, or even fear. Good friend Roger put his hand on my back and said, "You can never be hurt as bad again." He kept me going. Days passed in this nether land until Monica said pointedly, rather heartlessly, "Grow up! Get over it. Get on with your life."

The chemistry between us was not good and this bitterness reinforced her words. But somewhere deep inside, though they did not feel this way at the time, they were useful—especially since we were still on a boat and my hands were needed, even if my heart wasn't in the tasks. I used the outburst to unsnap the shackles holding me in the black hole and got on with living. But truth be told, my real instinct was to flee. I made do by trying to stay moving. Panama was next, then Tahiti.

The passage from St. Thomas to Panama was tumultuous. The trade winds blew at gale strength day after day building huge long rollers that rushed us along. We covered one thousand miles in six days, which meant *Mandalay* was maintaining hull speed most of the way. Descending into the watery valleys down slopes as steep as any ski hill meant keeping the seas directly aft. If the boat were to broach rushing downward we would be rolled over and over. The days were bad enough, but the nights were longer with the hiss and roar of water rushing past the hull and the see-saw platform that never stopped. The last two days the wind increased, and we were pooped four times. The roaring and the hissing followed by a crash, left us sitting knee-deep in water in the black of night, an indelible memory of the voyage.

We arrived at Cristobal at one in the morning. The array of navigation lights, blinking, glowing, flashing, was like a lighted Christmas tree. The staysails were winged out and not all that easy to get down. We very nearly piled into the breakwater. The quiet that followed was like taking a breath after being under water too long. The quiet spaces between adventures were treasures as great as the boisterous blips linking them together.

At the Cristobal Yacht Club lay a collection of yachts making for the Pacific and points west or coming back the other way. Like any harbor with transiting boats there was an interesting mixture of crews and a swapping of berths from a voyage gone sour or myriad other reasons. The first to come our way were Jack Bourke and Bob Grant from the forty-eight-foot Alden schooner *Ventura*. They had restored it in Gloucester and were headed for the South Pacific. One of them was destined to join *Mandalay* several thousand miles down the seaways.

We got to know a canal pilot and one day he came aboard looking for Monica. His wife was threatening to take off to the United States with his children and another man. He wanted Monica to mediate. This wasn't her strong suit and I can't remember the outcome, probably because I was not a big fan. All along, she and I had our own rumbles of thunder that grew louder. Roger came to me one day and said that if we could get along without them they would like to leave and set up housekeeping together. It was a sad moment, for Roger was a very dear friend. But as I knew, women were a force that had few equals. The black clouds I had seen on the horizon in Miami were indeed more than an intuition. Now we were down to two, Bob and me.

Two days later the *Nellie Brush* sailed in. A crew member, Tony Richardson, took to strolling past the stern of *Mandalay* several times a day, eying us and the vessel with increasing interest. The saunter and the mustache drew our interest and it wasn't long before he was spending more time with us than on the *Nellie Brush*. He hailed from the corn and Bible belt of Iowa, but his sauntering through life, sniffing the daisies, was not altogether genetic. During the war he had served in the Pacific on the battleship USS *California* where he received wounds that led to his discharge. On the fateful day, he had been blissfully sleeping beneath a large cowl ventilator that funneled the sea breeze to those below. A deck inspection was in progress above. As the officer drew near, a sailor spied a chipping hammer out of place. He snatched up the tool and tossed it down the ventilator. Tony received a direct blow to the forehead. An hour later he was on a plane headed for the naval hospital in Los Angeles. A large piece of his skull was removed and a metal plate was stitched in to protect the hole. He convalesced in a mental hospital for six months and met the famous Menninger and "other most interesting people." Discharged with full disability, he joined a ballet group after several months of practice, having fallen in love with one of the ballerinas. He was a good dancer.

Tony recounted how after a year he and the dancer, Annabel, drifted apart. "I knew ballet wasn't my line. I became disenchanted with those dancing people. All they could talk about were postures and technical tricks about how to stand on your toes or make the audience think you were flying through the air like a butterfly."

With a little income of his own and his disability pay rolling in every month, Tony was free to wander and do what fancy dictated. He became absorbed in boats and boating and eventually found himself aboard the *Nellie Brush*. He was wont to strike poses when met with the unexpected, teetering along on his toes to express his appreciation of the beautiful. As practical as a monkey in a machine shop, he had an everlasting good humor and appreciation of the passing scene that made him excellent company. It wasn't long before he asked to join our crew and I signed him on for comic relief. People found him endearing, so he also provided a key to doors not easily opened. His relationship with the skipper of the *Nellie Brush* was not discussed.

I also had another reason for inviting him along, sensing more dark clouds rapidly approaching. Bob got to disappearing for longer and longer periods without explanation. One morning he came to me with a face more serious than usual. I was not altogether surprised to learn that he had met a woman and was madly in love. If I could find someone to replace him he would like to leave, marry, and go to California to make a living as a graphic artist. I begged a week or ten days to give him a reply. This gave me a chance to take an excursion with Tony to see if the two of us could handle the voyage to Tahiti.

Renting a car, we bounced over several hundred miles of bumpy dirt roads to a place called Carro Punta in the district of El Vulcan, 5,000 feet above sea level. The dirt track went through Indian villages with thatched roofs. We enjoyed seeing the inhabitants sitting around the local bistro playing dominoes, first tying their gamecocks in the designated place, much like tethering a horse or burro to a hitching post. They would slam down the dominoes on the gaming table with a most impressive clatter, accompanied by looks so fierce as to make a western gunslinger blanche. Our Spanish was minimal, but here again Tony carried the day by joining in the occasional game, playing the role of a passing gringo bonanza.

Cockfights often accompanied the dominoes. The chickens were a mixture of Spanish and Panamanian. The Spanish breed would stand in one place until winning or lying dead. The Panamanians were more street smart. On seeing they were getting the worst of it they would change tactics and run about dashing in for a slash or two when they saw an opening. The Spaniards would get furious and peck themselves in a rage.

El Vulcan could have been a Swiss hamlet. Our bungalow was beside a rushing trout stream with mountains shooting up on all sides so that one had to practically crane the neck to see the horizon. The air made one come alive after the heat of the tropics. A sweater in the morning and a blanket at night felt good. Oranges, lemons the size of grapefruits, tomatoes, lettuce, coffee, and strawberries grew in profusion. Meat was 25-cents a pound, lean and flavorful from the local cattle. The trout stream could have been taken from the North Woods with the water rushing over the boulders and falling into little pools. I took a picture of a chap catching a fourteen-inch rainbow trout, who said that on several occasions a fish had been taken off his line by otters. The surrounding countryside had a good number of deer, wild pigs, sloths, tapirs, and what looked like a tiger but was in reality a cougar. A handful of Swiss farming people had settled there building little chalets. The rest of the population was Indian.

But most interesting were the ancient Indian graves containing many artifacts, even gold. In one place it was possible to dig up one hundred pieces of pottery a day. We met a retired oilman who had just returned from a fourteen-day trip to the interior across the Costa Rican border. He had come across a gravesite with a stone table, six by four feet. One end was held up by a carved figure of a chief, another by the queen, and the two others by warriors. All along the perimeter were little gargoyles. It was too heavy to bring out even if the Costa Ricans would allow it, so it sat there, undisturbed. He estimated it was more than a thousand years old. The man made a good living digging up gold artifacts and selling them to collectors for $7 a gram. As for the antiquity part he held no interest.

I was sorely tempted to have him take me in there with my camera gear, but there still remained a blackness in me from Margaret's death, which hounded me forward as if fleeing to Tahiti were a cure.

It took several more months before the compulsion to keep moving began to fade.

We returned to sea level just in time for the bullfights. Panama City had recently built a new bullring, so it was rumored some very brave bulls would be imported to initiate it, as the Panamanian bull was not very brave. Malnutrition, disease, and parasites might have had something to do with it. The city seethed with anticipation. The matadors were quite good—one Mexican, a Spaniard, and a Panamanian. The bulls were something else. One became so scared he jumped over the wooden fence and disappeared. The Mexican matador was a big ham and swaggered about doing wondrous things with his cape and the bull. Arrogantly he considered that El Toro was tuckered out so the matador turned his back. The bull had some turpentine left and by hooking a horn in the back of the matador's trousers left his adversary with a bare behind. With a ferocious glare our Mexican dispatched the bull with a monstrous thrust and the crowd went wild.

We missed the train back to Cristobal, giving us the chance to check out Panama City at night. We went into a fashionable looking bar to find a bevy of the fabled "blue moon girls" awaiting their prey. The Madame approached Tony, asking if there wasn't something she could do for him as he was so far from home and seemed such a nice boy. He answered in the affirmative, requesting a piece of apple pie. We were promptly thrown out.

Cristobal and Colon at night were a world apart from El Vulcan. The many bars were waterfalls of music. The sidewalks were a mosaic of humanity. Lottery tickets were on sale at the front of the Chase Bank, and on Saturdays crowds would gather to ponder what numbers to buy. The little side streets were snug harbors of enterprise and living. People slept in cubicles. A cobbler put on a shoe's sole by the light of a kerosene lantern. We saw a pet coon running around its owner, who was sitting on a box watching his brethren go by. And always there was a blue moon girl or two with one eye out for customers.

On one such a night I ended up with a tattoo. It was not a spur of the moment thing. I had asked Jean, my artist friend in Miami, to create the design of a standing bunny after Margaret died. It had long ears and a red eye, so she would always be there on my left shoulder. The tattooist asked three times if I really wanted it. He was a kindly man and said he was most reluctant to engrave names on flesh, as people changed. Eagles and roses were timeless. He charged me a dollar when I told him my reason. He made $50 a day on the average. "It's a living," he said. All these decades later the tattoo is still there with the red eye fading a little bit.

The trip convinced me that Tony would make a suitable shipmate for the push to Tahiti. He could stand his watch at the wheel and I could handle the practical matters. Bob was greatly relieved. I said goodbye to another dear friend. He ended up on Catalina Island, off the coast of California, with his mate. He earned a living as a graphic artist and we kept in touch until his death.

The canal pilots were an interesting lot and we became good friends with several. They gave me a pass so I could accompany them on passages. All of them agreed that the Greek liberty ships were the worst—disorganized and in bad repair. Losing a propeller was common with them and many carried as many as six spares. On the other hand, the Japanese vessels were immaculate. The skippers would look a person in the eye and their handshakes were firm. I remember one vessel with the most beautiful inlaid stairway. The ships were like yachts.

We passed through the locks to Gatun Lake while tied to a banana boat after our engine stopped. Not to be outdone by a Greek liberty, our propeller shaft had backed up when the setscrew came loose and our prop fetched up against the deadwood. The boat towed us to an anchorage in the lake where seven freighters were waiting their turn. That night the place was alive with jumping tarpon. There were other noises from howling monkeys, shore denizens, and thrashes in the water that did not bode well for human safety if one were to fall overboard. We stayed several days to let the fresh water kill the marine growth on our boat. On reaching the Pacific side, we lashed alongside a grounded barge and scraped the bottom, added paint to the bare spots, and drove home some more boat nails where several planks were bugging out.

The old girl was definitely tired, but we were fully provisioned for a long voyage and the compulsion was stronger than ever to push on. Next stop the Galapagos. I was still fleeing, but now I had The Bunny on my arm, forever.

Me (center), Bob, and Stella leaving Tahiti

CHAPTER EIGHT

The Canal to the Galapagos Islands

Keeping a diary or writing letters is alien in this age of email and the cell phone. It was somewhat alien even back when I was young. I don't know why, but from an early age I wrote letters and jotted down thoughts. There were several close friends to whom I could pour out my heart in writing, saying things I would not say to family and those surrounding me. Letter writing and diary keeping seemed to arrange events and people in better perspective. When we are young, emotion rises easily to the surface, while with age, observations are often wiser but not so vibrantly colored. We grow more guarded, building up barriers against the abrasions of daily living.

Looking back over my letters and diary of the voyage, I see that the incidents, people, and places were like eyelets in a boot. Laced together they became a structure supporting my footsteps along the path to adulthood, from heartbreak to some measure of healing.

As we departed the canal that first night, the gentle wind dropped to nothing. We were only ten miles off Cape Panama and headed toward the Galapagos Islands. From there we had mapped a route that would take us to the Marquesas, the Tuamotus, and then to Tahiti. The sea was calm. Shortly after dusk we were sitting and thinking those evening thoughts that come with the start of a new voyage. Suddenly a flash from beneath the water off to starboard made us start. Then there was another and another until the sea was a pulsing subterranean light show both mysterious and beautiful. It was pyrotechnics on a flat scale from an energy source that tingled the imagination. Here were thousands of candlepower switching on and off with our boat at the apex. Later we learned the light came from schools of jellies and diatoms, but even that knowledge didn't take away the mystery of how one tiny creature could manufacture light and cause all its fellow creatures to instantaneously follow suit. Learning the answer to one mystery often opens the door to another.

That same night we heard rushing water and thought we were being set down on the island off Cape Male, but it was only a tide rip. A lantern hung over the side brought myriad squid and four-foot sea snakes with nasty copper heads. The squid would leap clean out of the water. Trails of phosphorescence followed little fish being chased by larger fish, ending in a shower of sparks and offering the story that there was a city of life boiling just below the surface.

Between Panama and the Galapagos lies a body of water devoid of wind called "the doldrums," famed for the maddeningly long passage time a sailing vessel often requires to cross it. For days on end there is only an occasional brush of a breeze. One's boat lies wallowing and rolling in the long swells. In the age of the square-rigger, ships would hasten to tighten their rigging before the incessant rolling threw their masts overboard. We didn't have to tighten our wire rigging, but the rolling was the same. Our bodies were in a continual brace with the only half comfortable position being flat on the back with legs braced against the sideboards. We had two fifty-five-gallon drums of gas lashed on deck, for future needs in the Galapagos. This increased the rolling. We rolled at the mercy of the elements, read books, and cooked with the Primus stove swinging in gimbals. Being on a lengthy voyage in a small boat is like giving oneself to the tender care of a personal trainer twenty-four hours a day. The exercise never stops. There are few fat long-distance sailors.

So it was we found ourselves floating on the giant mirror of a placid sea, slowly inching south, taking advantage of every little puff. Two weeks out we were within ninety miles of the equator. Our particular doldrums trainer had rolled and lurched us day following day with the equatorial sun crashing down. This was a vacuum where nothing stirred except the rolling of the ship. We came to feel like lost men on a forsaken ocean with the ship a pendulum marking nonexistent time.

One of those days, we were fitfully dozing in our bunks, drugged by the heat and eternal rolling, when there came a fearful clap as if Neptune had whacked the surface of the sea with his monstrous trident. We raced on deck to find nothing in sight but a churning pool of discolored water thirty feet off the bow. Thirty seconds passed before a huge bat-like shape broke water, hurtling upward like some futuristic flying wing and then pancaking back, sending up a giant saucer of spray accompanied by the noise of an exploding mortar shell. The creature, a manta ray, was fifteen feet from side to side with two bulbous eyes set on top of two nacelles and a hooked horn rising above each. Once more it jumped and then was gone, leaving us speechless. The black immensity of the thing, with its long tapering tail and eyes from another planet, was an unknown image to us East Coasters.

We waited, for what we didn't know, liberated from the routine of endless days. Then, like divine providence, came the sound of rippling water above the creaking of the rigging. They came bouncing toward us, the little porpoises of the Pacific. From north and south and east and west they came in little groups leaping clear of the water and headed straight for where we sat. Then they were all around us, jumping, spinning, turning somersaults. The boat was a new toy. Under the keel and around and around they tore, regarding us with their comical old child's eyes, reproachful it seemed, that we wouldn't join them in their revels. They particularly enjoyed playing around the bobstay, that length of chain from the end of the bowsprit down to the bow where it met the water. They would race toward it and jump so their dorsal fins just cleared the chain, spin about, and repeat the fun.

For more than an hour they cavorted before exploding away in search of new amusement, leaving us clapping our hands and whooping in appreciation. We were "crossing the line" at the time, so to celebrate both the show and zero latitude we poured a tot of rum. When a pod of whales came rolling up like meandering elephants, it all seemed quite natural and expected. They wallowed past, blowing lazily at us intruders, who had disturbed their natural grazing ground. We laughed at their assumed dignity, wondering how they would look if outfitted with trunks, for by this time we were into a second glass of rum and the world was bright and cheerful. When they blew it sounded like the muffled sighs of lost souls. We told them to cheer up for the world wasn't such a bad place even though it was nine-tenths water. Their dignity was apparently hurt by such levity and they huffed off to leeward sending up jets of vapor like little steam trains starting up a long grade.

We returned to the last of our rum ration, wondering if the finale had come and passed, but there was yet one more performer to appear. He broke water three hundred yards astern, and his sword-like bill flowed into the silver greens and blues of his long body before ending in the great vee of his tail. He leapt again, this time closer, chasing a school of bonito that were fleeing toward the yacht to hide beneath the keel. He leapt yet again, savagely flailing a luckless victim, sending it spinning in the air. Falling back, it swam around in aimless circles, blood oozing from its gills. Then a huge shape made the surface hump and the bonito vanished, leaving only a puddle of frothing water.

The marlin swam slowly toward us, apparently undecided if it was worth pursuing another mouthful. He prowled slowly around the boat with the bonito keeping the keel between them and their pursuer. It was a monstrous game with sudden death the probable end result. Slowly at first, then faster and faster the chase went on with the bonito racing by the hull close to the surface. We grabbed the harpoon and plunged it down in their midst and then hauled a nice fish into the cockpit where it flopped and spattered blood before being dispatched. The marlin, startled by the intervention, departed and we dined on delicious fish that night.

A word should be said about the mechanical propulsion in the bowels of *Mandalay*. It was a grumpy companion the entire trip, believing it should have been retired years ago to some pleasant junkyard where it could rust in peace. It was tired, calcified, and out of sorts, barely tolerating my constant prodding. We were mostly under sail, because the engine didn't have enough juice to get us very far. I considered myself a dermatologist in reverse when I bored into its block, cleaned out the corrosion in its arteries, tapped the hole, and screwed in a plug, of which I had a goodly supply. It had as many hot spots as an aging maiden has flashes. By the time we finally parted company it resembled an old warthog.

Its food supply was equally suspect. When one of the aged copper gas tanks leaked its contents into the bilge, it was what is known in a South Pacific expression as an *om-a-lavo-pea-soupo* situation, meaning just what the expression sounds like. One false move and it would have been a wave goodbye from us to this world, hoping for the best in the next. We pussy footed about as pussy footing had never been done before. Bailing out the bilge of the deadly contents was choreographed motion.

Toward midnight of the marlin's visit came a breeze. Three days hence we were in the enchanted kingdom of the Galapagos. The entrance door was Kicker Rock, on the way down the coast of San Cristobal to the harbor of Wreck Bay. The monument to nature was as if a sculptor had spent years conjuring a beautiful design that would have all the strength, wisdom, beauty, poetry, and sadness of the world and then composed it as a study in cubes and cones. The sea surrounding it was the frame. It was perfectly calm, so we decided to anchor for the night before entering officialdom the following day.

Just before letting the anchor go we paused as a school of rays moved lazily along beside us, forming a Japanese print with their wobbling rectangles of amber, the brush strokes of the antennae eyes, all undulating softly through the water in a glittering formation, twenty of them in perfect harmony.

Myriad fish swam just above the sea floor ten feet below, so anchor down, we got out two of our Norwegian jigs. First twitch with the jig and we had a five-pound grouper. First twitch with the other jig and up came a two-pound drum that supplied a delicious supper.

Wreck Bay was an open, uneasy anchorage. We cleared customs and were turned over to a jolly little fellow who took us around to help bargain for supplies. He won. We didn't. Later we learned the going rate was $1 for three stalks of bananas, $1 for two hundred oranges, $1 for seventeen eggs, 6 cents for a pound of pork or a pineapple, $1 for a bottle of beer, and $20 for a fifth of whisky. His margin that day could have bought him one of those elaborate uniforms so beloved of small officials.

We satisfied the grasping hands under the table and quickly departed for Academy Bay on Santa Cruz, home of the Angermeyer brothers, whom I had heard so much about and was anxious to meet.

Me and the Duke of Galapagos

CHAPTER NINE

Duke of Galapagos Islands

I was calculating where we were between Wreck Bay and Academy Bay on Santa Cruz when Tony rushed below. "To hell with your navigation—we're here!"

Taking the binoculars, I saw that sure enough, barely discernible in the distance lay Santa Cruz, a flat-top cone on the gray sea. Drawing closer we saw the shorefront of black volcanic rock, pierced here and there by towering cactus. From the water cliff rose perpendicularly from ten to seventy feet, then leveled on to a volcanic plain that extended inward, covered with cactus and scrub. At the inward side of the bay was a playa, or beach, with a little town behind. As we were to learn, the island pushed abruptly upward beyond the cluster of houses and the vegetation grew lusher until, approaching the top of the cone, it flowered into a rain forest. At the summit, two thousand feet above the sea, the country leveled out once more onto a grassy plain from which scattered volcanic craters thrust their snouts toward the sky. Here lived the Scandinavian farming families.

A haunting loneliness and beauty enveloped the place—intensified by the tortured rock and cactus, the crying of the sea birds, and the soft crashing against the cliffs. We thought it looked like a forbidding land, a land for men with strong arms and courage and no terror in their souls.

Sailing into Academy Bay we skirted a treacherous ledge, anchoring bow and stern off Angermeyer Point. Shoreward to our right, an unpainted house sat on a low knoll. To the left was the skeleton of a house under construction set on the cliff overlooking the sea. Behind it squatted a tiny shack topped by a wind generator on a white scaffold. While directly shoreward of *Mandalay*, a mangrove thicket flowered in a thirty-foot fault forming a tiny harbor. A small sloop and skiff were tied there among the trees.

A man, judged to be in his late thirties, appeared with a bevy of children. He wore only denim shorts. His feet were bare, but on his head perched a curious creation. It was made of red felt and ran fore and aft across his head. The brim, curled up at the sides, made a slight visor in both front and back. A feather was stuck in the brim at a rakish angle. The hat's Robin Hood air complemented the grandiose wave its owner gave us as he untied his dinghy, loaded children, and rowed out to us.

The children swarmed aboard the instant the punt touched our side. With warm smiles they politely shook our hands, and duty done, scampered along the deck with squeals of delight, exploring the ship. The man wrung our hands, sweeping off his hat and giving us a theatrical bow.

"I'm Carl Angermeyer," he said, "and those villains who have boarded you are my rapscallion nieces and nephews. Welcome to Angermeyer Point."

We went down in the cabin. "How about a cup of coffee with a dash of rum in it?" Tony asked, always welcoming the opportunity for a tot.

"Are you good men or bad?" Carl inquired. "Once before I had a drink with strangers and no good came of it."

"We're angels," replied Tony, delighted with this Sherwood Forest character. "My captain is kind of stuffy and a bore, but otherwise we are harmless." He took down a bottle from a locker and tilted it into the three mugs.

Carl's golden-haired nieces whispered into their uncle's ear. He pretended to listen seriously and winked at us.

"These are my guardian angels, Hunky and Margaret. They say that my wife, Marga, wouldn't like it if she knew that I was out here sipping from that brown bottle. You see, I'm supposed to be working on my new house." He raised his mug and touched ours. "To happiness and life, and gay times ahead!"

We immediately asked how he had happened to settle in the Galapagos. He told how he had two brothers, Gus and Fritz. The three of them had left Germany when Hitler came to power, detesting the Nazis and their military regime. A sea-captain friend had told them of the Galapagos. So leaving their mother and father behind in Hamburg, they had scratched their way to Santa Cruz after two years of adventure and privation. They intended to have their parents follow when the brothers had made a home in the new land. However, the war came and they never heard from their parents again.

"Things are quiet out here," Carl said. "The boat from Ecuador comes once every couple of months bringing sugar, rice, flour, and our other few necessities. Living is cheap if you don't count the labor. There are turtles and fish in the sea, wild goats on the barrancas, and fresh fruit and vegetables are brought down from the hill when the trail is passable. No doctor, of course, but so far we have been lucky. Most people think we have a lonely life. I guess it is, if you like the bright lights and plenty of people. But we are happy here. All of us are married—Gus and Fritz have kids. Passing yachts like yours give us a glimpse of the outside world now and then."

The children finished their ship's biscuits after exploring every nook and cranny and then asked if they could look at the magazines spotted in the bookcases. Immediately they were lost to the wonderful photographs from the lands beyond the horizon. I caught Carl also looking wistfully at the rows of books. I asked if he and the children would like to take some ashore.

"I sure would. Reading matter is hard to come by here. Which reminds me, let's go in and I'll give you the tour—introduce you to the rest of the family. If I don't come in pretty quick Marga will be suspecting the worst."

We told the children to take all the magazines. They bundled them up with squeaks of pleasure, jumping up and down in excitement. The two goddesses, Hunky and Margaret, insisted on rowing us ashore, one tugging at each oar. Never did mariners have a fairer crew.

On landing we heard bangs and clanking ahead. We crossed a strip of sand and mounted a rocky path bordered with cactus. Walking around the bushes we came upon a rough shed with a squat, muscular man out in front, bent over a box-shaped metal contraption that was not unlike a stove. Seeing us he threw down his tools and shook our hands in a crushing fist.

"Amigos from across the sea," he boomed. "I'm Gus. Welcome to my humble palace. What beards you have. You look like pirates. Johnny! Run and bring a watermelon. This calls for a celebration. Tell Lou we're coming up."

"What are you building?" I inquired.

"It's going to be a stove big enough to bake six loaves someday," Gus grinned, striking the top of it with a hacksaw.

"It seems to have quite a few parts."

"*Ja.* The base is from an old engine. That there is from a Fordson tractor, while this is a rudder from a boat. That big round thing, that will be the firebox. It's an oil filter case off a Caterpillar tractor. For the top I'm going to use the stand from an air compressor. It's all war surplus you might say. The Americans had an airbase on the next island during the war."

"Time consuming," said the impressed Tony.

"Yes. I don't have many tools. But when it is finished, Lou, my wife, will only have to bake bread once a week."

"You certainly have patience," Tony said. "I can hardly keep my mind on a pan of water to boil an egg."

Gus laughed. "We haven't got much down here except time—a lifetime of it. Keeps us busy using it all—so the months roll on and one day my stove will be finished."

As we followed Gus up to his house I sensed that here was an unusual man. There was an almost poetic air about him, yet his shoulders were shaped to fit an oxen's yoke and strength was in his face, tempered with wisdom and gentleness.

We were introduced to his wife, Lou, whose "nice to know you" was gracious and heavily German accented. She was a frail woman, with lustrous eyes, a little tired it seemed to me. Gus put his arm around her as we went into the house.

With quiet charm she made us comfortable on the homemade chairs and went to prepare refreshments. Gus shouted to his sons: "Johnny! Fetch your mother some water. Teppie! Bring wood for the stove. My little Ben, get that loaf of bread your mother baked yesterday. You, Franklin and Tom, play in the corner there and stay out of your mother's way."

Gus grabbed a knife and with grand flourishes cut slices from the watermelon. He took the wood from Teppie and kindled the stove, reprimanded Ben for being slow, and helped Lou bring out the coffee mugs and cutlery. He seemed everywhere at once, breathing fire into his household, making things easier for his wife.

"Lou," he gently kidded her, "this is some gay life we are leading, entertaining admirals from America. Just like the time I found you in Ecuador teetering around on high heels, wallowing in luxury."

"Big change out here," Lou said, laughing and wiping chapped red hands on her apron.

Gus turned to us. "The Galapagos are paradise with such a sweet wife." He swept her into his arms and kissed her soundly.

"Impossible man! You have no manners." She giggled, pushing him away, and escaped into the kitchen.

"Gus," I said, changing the subject. "This house must've been quite a job to build. Where did you find the lumber?"

"That Air Corps base was a treasure," he replied. "Most everything came from there. Building this house was nothing. When we first came out here, we went up into the hills and built our first shanty there. We had to cut down the trees, then saw each plank by hand. For roofing we took sea charts and covered them with tar. Had to make the nails from copper wire."

"Jesus!" said Tony, who was not the best do-it-your-selfer.

"It was a backbreaker," admitted Carl. "Gus thought it was a lark bucking that two-man saw. I must admit I had more fun playing my accordion at our evenings concerts."

"Tell me," Tony exclaimed. "How did you all get your wives? That must have been quite a trick out here."

Carl roared with laughter. "It was like this," he began. "We built that farm up in the hills. It's fertile up there. We thought we'd be farmers, but then after three years we got a hankering for the sea. So down we came to the playa and built ourselves a fishing boat."

"How'd you do that?" I asked.

"We used copper wire for the rivets, and for the washers we took coins we had saved. We caught sharks, boiled their livers, and used the oil for paint. We tarred the bottom."

"What has all this got to do with finding your wives?" interrupted Tony. "Boiling shark liver doesn't sound like triple romance."

"I'm getting to the romantic part. You see we caught a lot of fish, salted them, and took them into Guayaquil on the mainland to sell. That was at the start of the war, and because we were Germans the Ecuadorians wouldn't let us come back here for a couple of years."

"That was my good fortune," bellowed Gus as he jumped up from his chair, bounded into the kitchen, grabbed Lou by the waist, and whirled her around the floor in a waltz step. Carl broke into The Blue Danube, clapping his hands in rhythm for the dancers. Gus whirled Lou wildly, stopped, and bowed low before her.

"Tony, how's that for the first romance?" Gus said with a sweep of his arm.

"I get the picture," said Tony. "You swept her off her feet and clear back to the Galapagos, before the poor girl could think it over twice."

"I try not very hard to run away from Gus," Lou gasped. "He was big and strong and told me wonderful stories about his island of Santa Cruz. A few of them I found were true," she added with a mischievous look.

"OK," said Tony. "We've got you and Lou married; now how about you, Carl?"

"Well," said Carl, "you do ask the most personal questions, but I will tell you anyhow because I see the subject of women interests you immensely and my tale is rather unusual. When we were building our boat and preparing saltfish to sell in Guayaquil, there lived on the playa nearby a Belgian and his lovely wife, Marga, who had hair the color of the sunset. Now her husband was a strange tyrannical man who had lured her from a debutante's life in Hamburg to the wilds of Santa Cruz. They had a fair daughter called Carmen, soon after they came to the Galapagos.

"As the years rolled on the man became more wild and difficult to live with. Poor Marga grew afraid. What to do? No money! Nowhere to go. Then I—brave, gallant, dashing, handsome, irresistible, wifeless man that I was—stepped forward. To make it short, we married in Guayaquil. I saved her from a horrible fate, and at this very moment she is wondering why I'm not working on our new house on the barranca."

"But what about Fritz?" Tony prodded.

"Why, he married Carmen, of course."

Tony shook his head. "Better than a book. Can you introduce us?"

We trooped from the house. Lou waved us down the path. Gus left us at his work shed to fit another piece to his embryonic stove. Coming out on the sandy strip behind the mangroves, we walked past a shed that Carl said was his bodega workshop, then passed his little shack with the glassed-in front, and followed along the water's edge. Here the barranca fell away until it was a scattered tumble of rocks along the shoreline, while inland to our right the sand soon ended in more rocks, thorny bushes, and cactus. Ahead I saw a shade tree of some foreign species, and underneath it in a cradle was a trim double-ender with an inboard motor, looking very new and splendid. A tall, angular man was bending over it, tinkering with something in its guts.

"There's Fritz," said Carl. "He's been working eight months on that boat off and on. He's too modest to tell you, but he took the motor out of a junk heap, built himself a foot-pedal lathe, and turned out new bearings and bushings for it. He even made the clutch and stern bearing. And you should see him carve wood. His birds seem to be about to fly away unless you hang onto them. Fritz doesn't say much. The Ecuadorians call him 'The Monk,' but give him a few tools and oo-la-la."

Fritz looked up, smiled shyly, and held out his hand. "How do you do," he said quietly. "Your boat looks nice."

"It's not as well made as this one," I replied, examining his little runabout with admiration. "Yours is a work of art. Where did you get the plans?"

Fritz shuffled his feet. "Out here we have to go by the materials we can get. I had some plywood and the boat just came out this way."

"I'll be!" said Tony. "You brothers are something. Is your wife around?"

Carl winked at me. "Carmen, Marga," he shouted. "Come out here and meet the two scoundrels off the *Mandalay*."

A small cinderblock house stood some yards away. Voices answered from inside and a moment later two women emerged. One of them had flaming red hair. A parakeet was perched on her shoulder. When it spotted us, it broke into shrill cries, flew from its perch, and made straight for Tony. It hovered over his head, screeching insanely, then swooped on my luckless mate and grabbed a tuft of his hair, attempting to tug it out by the roots.

"Don't let him get your mustache!" Carl yelled.

"Dammit! Ouch!" hollered Tony, batting at the bird.

The children screamed with delight as Tony pranced to and fro, trying to shake off his tiny attacker. The redheaded woman called to the bird in German and finally it let go, returning to her shoulder, evidently much pleased with itself as it voiced soft tweeting noises.

Marga and Carmen shook our hands. Both mother and daughter had blue eyes, handsome features, and bodies well suited to outdoor life. Marga was in the Indian summer of womanhood. Loveliness clung to her, ripened by age like fine wine, while Carmen was still in the blush of youth, popping with vigor and blessed with the beauty of her mother.

Marga apologized for the parakeet, explaining how he hated everybody. Tony asked how they liked the Galapagos and the isolation.

"I was born and raised here," Carmen said emphatically. "This is home and I know I'd be homesick the moment I ever had to leave."

"Yes, once you get used to this outdoor life and making your own fun it's better than living in any city," agreed Marga.

"Come with us right now," urged Carmen. "Fritz and I are going goat hunting. See for yourself how it is out here."

"Sure," Tony said without hesitation. "I couldn't hit an elephant with a scatter gun, but I'd like to see you in action."

"You can help carry them back," Carmen replied with a merry glint in her eye. "The shooting is nothing. It's the shoulder work afterward."

Carl decided he had to work on his new house. So the four of us walked down to the mangrove harbor at the opening in the barranca, and borrowed Gus's sloop. Powering around the point to a cove called Pelican Bay, we eased into a tiny opening between high cliffs and went along a hidden canal. The cliffs rose thirty feet on either side. The channel itself was only ten feet across.

Tying the boat, we climbed up the rocks hand over hand and looked out over the plateau of bushes, cactus, and volcanic boulders. Nothing was in sight, so we set off, single file, across the plain. It was hard walking, for although the ground looked level at first glance, carpeted with vines and thorny growth, it was anything but even. It was necessary to jump from one rock to the next, dodging the deep cracks and razor edges that made it easy to twist an ankle or gash a leg if one took a false step. Fritz set a hard pace and Carmen stayed with him. We kept up as best we could.

We walked for half a mile before stopping to listen. Carmen was carrying a rifle on her shoulder. When we halted, a yellow finch flew down and perched on the end of her barrel, completely unafraid.

Ahead, slightly to the left, a stone rattled and something scraped on a rock. Fritz put his finger to his lips. Stealthily we moved forward again for two hundred yards. Once more we heard the noise, but it was still at some distance.

"They've heard us," Fritz whispered. "I'll circle around to their rear with Pebble. Tony, you stay here with Carmen. Try to work up a little closer."

Fritz and I doubled back for fifty yards, then angled off to circle. The goats were getting warier every year, Fritz explained. Now they always posted an old Billy as sentinel. The only way to outwit them was to go around and approach from behind. They were never prepared for that. The Billy would be watching in Carmen's direction and wouldn't notice us.

When we were well to the rear we sneaked behind a high rock, inched up on it, and lay on our stomachs. Peering out between two tall cactuses, we saw the herd feeding, partly obscured behind some bushes. As near as I could count there were fifteen, all colors, shapes and sizes. I spotted the old Billy standing on a rock, looking attentively toward where Carmen and Tony must have been.

We crept nearer. Fritz's rifle bolt made a slight snick as he slid a cartridge into the chamber. We were within thirty yards of the goats and could see their rumps. Their heads were down, nibbling the leaves. I noticed Fritz picking out two that looked young, a brown one and a black one. The young ones were the best for eating.

He searched for a small stone and hurled it into the middle of the herd. Immediately the goats lifted their heads, giving him a good target. He fired twice in rapid succession. Two animals dropped. Fritz jumped to his feet and waved his arms and yelled. The other goats panicked and plunged in the direction of Carmen and Tony. We heard two shots. Fritz grinned. "There are our four goats. Carmen never misses."

It was the work of a few moments for Fritz to gut the animals and hoist them on our shoulders. When we came up to the others, Carmen had her animals already cleaned.

"That Carmen," Tony said to me. "You should see her shoot and use a knife. And with the looks besides. If she wasn't married I'd be in love with her this moment."

"That's a tough break, her being married," I said sarcastically, "but maybe you will find somebody else in Polynesia."

It was harder going with the goats on our backs, but Fritz and Carmen still moved swiftly. Panting, we tried to keep up, determined not to be outdone by a woman. At the barranca, we eased the goats down from ledge to ledge and secured them on the foredeck. It was dark when we landed at Angermeyer Point. Fritz hung the goats in the shade tree next to his boat, inserting a stick crosswise in each of their bellies to allow the air to circulate.

That evening, after a supper with Fritz and Carmen, we crowded into Carl's tiny shack. Seascapes hung on the walls among little pictures painted on turtle bones. In the golden light of kerosene lamps, Gus took his accordion, Carl got a harmonica, Marga carefully unwrapped her violin, and Fritz seated himself behind his drum made from a pelican's pouch stretched over a nail keg.

Lively folk tunes of the world filled the room. We sang and kept time with our feet, the little cabin trembling as if buffeted by a storm. Toward midnight the children were sleeping blissfully on their parents' laps. Little Hunky was nestled against Tony. Her golden hair cascaded across his knee. I watched the music of life shining on all those happy faces, and imagined that the wilderness outside was looking in, nodding its approval.

—⟿—

A few days later, the Galapagos moon cast the silhouette of Gus, me, a boat, and a long, hooked pole on the calm surface of the lagoon. On one side the jagged cliff of volcanic rock, spiked by cactus, made a bristly skyline under the stars. On the other, a tiny stretch of beach gleamed ghostly white, and the dense mangroves to its left were a pool of darkness where even the moonbeams couldn't penetrate.

Gus was standing, peering intently into the water ahead, while I slowly sculled. In his hands he held a long pole with a huge hook attached to its end. A stout line ran down from the shank of the hook to a neat coil in the bow. The stillness of the night was intensified by the soft knock, knock of my sculling oar in the chock, and the melancholy sigh of the turtles as they rose to the surface, exhaled, and gulped another lungful.

A dark spot moved under the water ten yards forward of the skiff. Gus crouched, his grasp tightened on the pole. We glided closer. Gus lumped his muscles and plunged the shaft downward and yanked back against the live weight with all the great strength in his arms and shoulders.

The lagoon exploded. The boat lurched forward, bringing Gus to his knees. He dropped the pole and grabbed the line running over the bow. The skiff shot ahead, spun around, and raced forward once more as the turtle fought for its life. Gus worked it in slowly, pitting his strength and cunning against the beast's two hundred pounds. After minutes it rose close to the boat, splashing wildly with its flippers, soaking us. Gus swung two loops deftly over the front flippers and the turtle lay lashed alongside, breathing in mournful cadences.

Gus extracted the hook from the fleshy underpart of the turtle's jaw and motioned for me to head for the beach. Unlashing the turtle, we pulled it up on the sand and left it, upside down, alongside another we had caught an hour before.

We climbed back into the boat and Gus took a flashlight from beneath the seat and snapped it on. Ever so slowly I sculled across the lagoon while he shone the light into the water. Soon the beam disclosed two red eyes and waving antennae. He picked up a pronged grain and thrust it downward, aiming just behind the eyes. The shaft wriggled beneath his grip. He drew it up and pulled the two-pound, clawless lobster from the four barbs. Again and again he plunged his spear to skewer a lobster, until twenty-five crackling, clicking forms scrabbled in the bottom of the boat.

"Let's have a smoke and head home," Gus said, breaking the silence. "We've got enough for everybody." He laid his spear on the bottom of the boat and sat down comfortably on the seat forward. I laid aside the sculling oar and settled back in a half-reclining position. We didn't speak at first, allowing the night to carry us, two men in a small boat on the surface of an isolated lagoon. We lit our pipes, and the tendrils of smoke rose lazily toward the sinking moon. The soothing quiet, the limpid night, made it seem that the stars were falling into our laps. Our pipes whispered, echoed by the sibilant sight of the turtles rising to the surface. It was close to midnight and there were only two of us in all the world.

"My friend," came softly from Gus. Then silence as if even talking was an effort. "This is living."

"Yes, this is living," I reiterated, strengthening the bond between us.

"My friend," came again from the darkness forward, "when I'm out here at night—alone—hunting turtles or spearing lobsters, I talk to the stars up there. They are my friends. I tell them whatever comes into my head. They seem to listen up there—look down at me and understand—even though it's only nonsense."

"What would you tell them tonight?"

"I would tell them that they're true lights—away from dark and wrong. That they make me hum—tune my heart to sing my song. They help me find my melody—of night and day. Stars and moon—the warming sun."

"Did you ever try writing poetry?"

"Every time I come out here and gaze at the sky, and the barranca, and the water, and feel the space around me, I make up a little ditty. But they are for here—for me and my stars. When I try to

Gus

tell them to other people or try to put them on paper, they fly away, turn to dust, disappear."

"Did you ever try to write the story of you brothers? How you escaped from Germany—your clashes with the Nazis—the adventures you had in coming here—and how you clawed a home out of the wilderness—founded your own free community, Robinson Crusoe fashion? It would make a fine tale."

"Once or twice I've started, written half of the first page but that's as far as I've ever gotten. There's too much to do here, and the truth is, I like being out in the open too much to sit down at a typewriter. I always find an excuse to leave the writing and go goat hunting, or look for turtles or lobsters, catch fish, or just walk off exploring. Maybe someday when I'm older and can't get about, then I will have the time. Right now I'm too busy living." Gus knocked the ashes from his pipe so I took up the sculling oar and headed for the beach.

"Too bad Tony didn't come tonight," said Gus, dropping lobsters in the gunny sack.

"He's rare company, Tony is!"

"I tried my damndest to lure him from his book. Told him to come and live adventure and forget about reading it. But he said we couldn't produce such a glorious woman as he was reading about and he had to see her out of trouble."

The skiff grounded on the beach. Gus hoisted the gunnysack to his shoulders and made toward the path for home. "We'll come around in the morning with my fishing boat for the turtles and the skiff. Why don't you sleep at the house tonight? It would save you waking up Tony to row in and get you."

The moon set behind the barranca as we reached the house. Lying down on the proffered bed, I was instantly asleep.

—∾—

We had more wondrous days enjoying the Angermeyers, their life and islands, so much of which I wrote about in my other book about Polynesia, *Man on His Island*. But all good things eventually end. One day we sailed away for the Marquesas, three thousand miles downwind, then on to the Tuamotus and Tahiti. There were tears in my eyes, holding Gus's hands in farewell. We promised to stay in contact in the months to come. He had taken me into the family and now I had two. I knew, and intuition proved me right, though our voyage was young, that the Galapagos was to be the most magical place of our whole passage and Gus was to live for years in my mind as a beloved older brother. We corresponded until years later when his life ended in a cave that he had made to live in that was as magical as himself. Of all the people I met on the voyage, Gus was the one who possessed such a joy of living and imagination that being around him was inspirational.

On those long nights under the stars, rolling down the trades toward the Marquesas, the mind rolled too, along with the groaning of the rigging and creaking of the old wooden hull. I pictured myself in a burning house with time only to grab my most precious possession. It came without hesitation that it would be the memory of Gus, his family, and the wild bulls with frangipani behind their ears. As he said, "We could dance together across the bridge of understanding."

Carl and his two nieces

Titi in Tahiti

CHAPTER TEN

Tahiti

We sailed to Tahiti, into Papeete after dusk. As we entered the pass, the smell of flowers came down off the land with the gentle breeze. It was a heavy, exotic, sensual smell. Right then I knew this would be a place difficult to forget, although the Galapagos lay heavy on my mind. Tahiti is difficult to describe, constantly changing one's emotions, a sorceress wrapping herself in so many spells and little tricks as to make her true identity hazy.

We moored stern to the seawall fronting the town. The shops and bars and other places of business formed a line cheek to jowl the other side of the grass strip and the main road through the village. We boat people had a site in the midst of the town's activities, making it impossible not to soon know the crews on the other boats, and a goodly number among the stream of humanity passing along that vibrant street. One soon became a member of an extended family, made even tighter by the openness and friendly aura. Distrust was an unknown word. A handshake or hug was the norm, both afloat and ashore. We felt at home immediately. The *pareu*, or cloth around the loins, was the fashion, along with flipflops and sneakers, while white shorts signified authority. I don't think we ever saw a necktie. Beards were a rarity, cleanliness was the norm, and long black hair was an attractive addition to the passing feminine scene on their motor scooters.

However, a beard was one of the first stories to be encountered. It belonged to a man with kind eyes whom we came to call "Sam the Egyptian." He was one of many castaways. Tahiti had its gracious plenty, both on the water and ashore. But in a sense we boat people were all castaways, having left home, not for fame or fortune, but rather to wander, seeking what we really didn't know. Which brings to mind the words of J.R.R. Tolkien: "Not all who wander are lost."

Sam was, perhaps, just a little bit lost. Wealthy in his own country, cocooned in luxury, he grew tired of that life and decided to fulfill a boyhood dream of visiting Tahiti. The Egyptian government would only let him leave with fifty pounds plus the passage. Paris was the first stop, where he stayed first in a 1400-franc hotel, then a 900 one, then 700, and finally 350. "I had to slowly accustom myself to a lower standard of living," he said. Selling his solid gold cigarette case and lighter helped. He was robbed by two girls and said goodbye to his gray flannel suits, except the one he was wearing. Eventually, making it to Tahiti, he bought a fourteen-foot sailboat and moved aboard with a Primus, oatmeal, and the last of his flannels. Four inner tubes were placed in the bottom of the little boat to sleep on and so it wouldn't sink if swamped.

Sam's first adventure was a sail to Moorea, ten miles across the bay. He made the passage but arriving after dark, hove-to as he didn't dare sail in the narrow pass at night. The next day found him back in Tahiti, carried by the current. On trying again, he ran into a gale. After bailing for twenty-four hours it was back again to Tahiti. The third time he made it. Encouraged by success, he decided to press on to find a cheap place to live in some little paradise, such as romanticized in his childhood books. So off he went to Bora Bora, seventy miles away, with a few coconuts and native food. Forty miles into the voyage he got food poisoning and, after lying on his back for twenty-four hours, returned to Moorea, because it was the only land in sight. After that he curtailed his sailing to Papeete Harbor, his boat not far from us down by the shipyard.

Sam's purpose in life was to have a good time. His religion laughed at physical discomforts, so his economic hardships never took away this laughter. His day went something like this: Rising between six and seven he cooked his oatmeal with the Primus on the cement wall behind his boat. Next, if there wasn't much wind to sail, Sam would don the last gray flannels and button-down shirt to stroll uptown, stopping first, probably, at the Croissant Café on Main Street. Here he would have another cup of coffee or a lemonade, watch the people go by, meet his friends, then continue along the waterfront to the yachts where there was always someone to spend a pleasant hour talking to or helping with some little job. Then on to the Cercle Polynesian, a veranda-like bar overlooking the harbor. Swallowing another lemonade, as he didn't drink alcohol, he encountered more friends, who would now have increased to at least four or five. Another hour or two could go by with Sam talking about Tahiti, the pros and cons of this or that wahine, a Polynesian girl, and the dastardly Egyptian government that wouldn't send him his own money so he could live in the style to which he was accustomed. By now the sun would have risen close to the meridian and Sam would have to decide whether the big meal was to be at noon or in the evening. His franc problem was always acute, so it was one meal a day, with just a little something in between.

Today he might decide on a noon meal, so must plan how to extricate himself from his friends. They, knowing his money problems, always tried to take him to lunch, which incensed Sam, being very proud. Breaking away on some pretext, he had his meal, and feeling sleepy from the morning's activities, usually retreated to the small boatyard shed behind his boat for a siesta. Later in the afternoon came perhaps a sail down to the Tropique or Royal Tahitian for a cup of tea and a swim. Usually there was time for a stroll uptown in the evening, a chat with friends and yachtsmen, then to bed before nine. His halcyon days were only disturbed by fits of anger when he sent a cable demanding money and received a reply from the head of the Ministry of Foreign Affairs saying, "No money, come home, signed Father."

The island housed many originals. Mr. Miller, the Dutch concert pianist, was a standout. He had come with his wife from Holland seventeen years earlier, planning to stay two months. She returned to Holland after a year and he remained, living by himself in a little house back in the mountains. People said he talked to spiders and it was certainly believable. A talented musician, Miller had done more for music in Tahiti than anyone else. Aside from music, his passion was animals. Every morning he went to the market to collect leftovers, then on to the hotels where he also had an arrangement to have their scraps. With these our man wandered about the island feeding the animals. They knew the sound of his car and wherever he stopped a pack of dogs and cats surrounded him. One day I remember he had a little bird and I asked where it came from. He had passed a group of small boys who had caught the tiny thing and were whirling it around their heads. He stopped, made them ashamed, and took the wounded bird home. He tried to feed it scraps but it was an insect eater and grew slowly weaker. He would have to kill bugs and spiders or the bird would die. But he couldn't bear to kill a roach, a spider, or even a fly so that was the end of the poor thing. The boys felt so ashamed they brought Miller a little nest for the dead bird to lie in.

A few days after arriving, Tony moved ashore, feeling more comfortable surrounded by things of a land nature going on. Frequenting the bars and being an amateur actor, he found his friends quintupled in a fortnight. It wasn't long before he became known as Jesus Christ, from the night, under the influence of a good vintage, he walked into Quinn's Bar and somebody said he looked like JC. Tony immediately snatched a lily from a wahine he knew. Tearing off the flowers to give a crown of thorns effect, he reenacted the crucifixion as only he could do, with head down and eyeballs rolling. Another man came in, took one look, and shouted, "That is no way to do it," and attempted to surpass Tony. Then several others wanted to get in on the scene. Soon it included Matthew, Mark, Luke, and John. A little Tahitian girl, who happened to be standing nearby, became Mary Magdalene with giggles. Mr. Woof Woof assumed the role of Pontius Pilate (more about Woof Woof in a minute). Two priests entered for a nightcap. Tony yelled, "Here are the employees." When the priests left they called for their donkeys, first in French and when nothing happened, in Latin. Someone in the back of the room gave a bray and soon the place was quivering with the sound of a herd of donkeys.

Mr. Woof Woof was the British consul or ambassador. He could be quite pompous when sober, but the cloak could be thrown aside with the proper good wine. He had a stunning wife whose roving eyes had nothing to do with the resurrection. It was inevitable that they soon crossed with Tony's. So it was that one evening when Woof Woof was out woofing, Tony found himself in bed with the one of the roving eye. Then to their consternation, they heard old Woof coming home early. No place to hide but under the big Victorian bed, so the ambassador took Tony's place with Tony underneath. Under some pretense Woof was lured away temporarily to the other side of the house and Tony bailed out a window and ran at full speed, scantily clad. He was still shaking the next morning. Woof had considerable power, dressed in the proper uniform, and could have had him extricated from the island.

Tony aside, I met a real saint-like person in Tahiti, Commander Francois Faye, a retired French naval officer. He didn't know the word "selfish," dedicating his days doing nice things for others. He had bought a little thirty-foot sloop and for the past two years had been rebuilding it seven days a week. All his money went into the boat. He hoped to sail it somewhere, somehow, some day, existing on a small pension. More worldly than most anyone I met, he looked at things from myriad angles and perspectives. An intestinal ailment had gripped him the last two years, violent enough to wear him down. He couldn't shake it. He also had a hernia rupture so bad one could see the bulge under his shorts. He desperately needed an operation but was afraid. A few years earlier an operation had almost killed him. To die in Tahiti, which he called an inhabited desert, would be too sorrowful an ending to a story with too many twists and turns to recount here.

His boat was almost ready, but his money had dwindled. He needed to find work, but where? His sails weren't good, but he couldn't afford better. His plan was to set off singlehanded, being afraid of taking a shipmate who might prove incompatible. The poor man resembled a scarecrow, all skin and bones. For breakfast he had oatmeal, and for lunch again oatmeal with a bit of cheese. Supper was more oatmeal and another slice of cheese. He knew he had to leave;

otherwise he would die in this place he detested. It was an impossible situation with him having no money and not even being sure of enough strength to sail singlehanded.

Now the amazing part. Although in constant pain, which one saw in his face and twitching body, he always had a smile for everyone. Their problems were his own and there was nothing too small to cause him to stop all work and attend to his friends' needs. Try and do something for him and he came back with a present that made one feel ashamed. I give him a few odds and ends of marine hardware. The next day he arrived with two chickens and a ham, which he most certainly couldn't afford. When *Mandalay* was on the ways for bottom work he would stop by with bottles of beer for us weary toilers, dropping them quickly and disappearing before we could even say "thank you."

Whenever I was disgusted, puzzled, or depressed, I went to him and we talked, about anything. The sense of peace surrounding him made every muscle in my body relax. Problems that seemed so important melted away. Through him I came to understand Tahiti better than I ever would have on my own. One had to cry about Francois because here was a great man, living out the end of his life alone, forgotten by the world. Yet one had to laugh when in his presence, listening to his humor roll on and on about himself and his surroundings. As it turned out, I spent more time with him while in Tahiti than with anyone else but one. As I look back at our friendship now at the age of ninety-two, I see that he has been a reference point in my thinking all these many decades. I have lain awake many nights comparing him to Gus. They both had something in their characters far above the ordinary, but different. Gus was the teller and teacher, Francois the listener. I often conjured a meeting between the two and the ensuing conversation, with me as a fly on the wall, and, of course,

Margaret, always my anchor to windward. In my mind's eye, I saw Francois standing, surrounded by a great ocean, arms upraised, a solitary apostle to something beyond my understanding. And Gus, too. His arms were not upright but dancing in the air, accompanied by words that formed a song that danced on the surface of the great sea like a fairy ballet on a magical stage.

Months later I met Francois' former mistress in Paris. We spent several weeks together, and she showed me parts of France I would never have seen without her. We talked of him every day. I remember her saying, "Pebble, he is the most unusual, yes, the most remarkable man I have ever met. The tragedy is that he felt he failed his country in the war but it was the country that failed him, threw him in the dustbin. He could have gone on to have led a wonderful, productive life. But his pride wouldn't let him. He fled."

Gus, on the other hand, fled a war that wasn't his and created a life that had few comparisons. I was the truly privileged one, having known them both.

Back to Tahiti. Tony decided he'd had enough sailing for a while, so I looked around for another shipmate. The vacuum was soon filled by Bob Grant, a man of many stories, including one involving love. He had arrived on the schooner *Ventura* out of Gloucester with co-owner Jack. They decided to split, a not unlikely scenario among the crews tied along the waterfront. He came from South Boston, had no formal education, and worked on the railroad as a brakeman. His intellect and outlook on life outshone nine-tenths of the people I had met at school. Bob was an artist, in that he noticed little things, human things, like the way a person moves. He saw things a person wouldn't notice unless he or she were a painter, writer, philosopher, or lover. His language was poetry, the poetry of American slang with original expressions. He made Damon Runyon seem a second-rater.

His love story started at Atuona in the Marquesas. Bob was in the tiny house behind the doctor's and had an infected foot the size of three balloons. The doctor had a schoolteacher, his wife, and their maid staying with him. Through his pain, Bob watched the maid, a young girl, move around the house doing her work. Bob gave her the eye and the eyebrows, as he put it. Her name was Titi, a big strapping girl with the brown skin and somber face of a Marquesan tiki. They saw each other for two weeks, aware of each other's presence but never coming into direct contact. She left with the schoolteacher and his wife but first came to say goodbye to Bob. He couldn't get her out of his mind, so on leaving Atuona he took the island boat to Ouapou. There he asked her if she wanted to go to Tahiti with him. She said yes, but as she was not of age she had to get her mother and father's written consent. They readily assented. Off the two went, hand in hand, to Nuka Hiva, the center of government, to make it legal. But the schoolteacher, incensed by an American making off with his maid, told the supercargo of the schooner to say something to the authorities to kibosh the permission. He succeeded, and the gendarme wouldn't let her go.

Bob came to Tahiti and it took two months for the red tape to be cleared up so the girl could follow. In the meantime, Bob ran around with the Tahitians, sometimes a different one every night. At first he thought himself happy after a few drinks but "couldn't get that big friggin' girl up in Ouapou out of my head." She wasn't beautiful like the Tahitian women but had that certain something. He sent her telegrams and one day she arrived on a schooner. Titi had never before been out of the Marquesas, seen a cinema, or ridden in a car, let alone spoken English, or even associated much with whites. Yet she stepped off that boat into all the new stresses and strains with the poise and dignity of a queen. It was beautiful to behold.

Perhaps a word about morality taken from my journal is in order. First of all, one had to throw away the European concept of marriage in Tahiti. Despite the church, which only went skin deep down there, marriage was a flimsy affair at best. A man and a woman lived together by mutual consent. When they grew tired of each other they simply parted and lived with someone else. There was no problem with children. They cost next to nothing to support, and if they didn't go with the mother or father there was always a family to take them in. Having a child out of wedlock was frowned upon not at all in the islands, and only slightly among the upper-class Tahitians, who were almost always half-white themselves. The one thing a Polynesian woman wanted more than anything was a child. Many children there didn't know the names of their mother and father. So in Tahiti, at that time, it was not considered wrong to live with a woman during one's stay. No one expected the man to marry or even come back. What I grew to understand was that—at least during my time there, so many years ago—Tahitians lived a life of today. If they were happy with someone today that was all they wished. The typical remark was, "Maybe you will be back and maybe you won't. I hope you will be, but it has been a good time with you."

With Titi's arrival, I found someone to live on the boat while we three, Bob, Titi, and I, moved out to Punaauia, a small community with some thatched cabanas on the beach for transients like us, a few miles from Tahiti. Tony had already found himself a place there so I moved in with him, and Bob and Titi moved into another. It was

interesting to watch how Titi reacted to the new wonders she encountered every day, along with Bob's efforts to learn French. One of the
first times she rode in a vehicle was when taking a local bus to Papeete. A motorcycle tried to pass the bus with a car coming the other
way. The motorcycle dumped in a puddle and splashed mud on the
bus, through the open sides and over Titi's new dress. The same day,
Bob bought her first pair of shoes. Walking around town that night he
described how "she was sweating out the cars two blocks away, jumping from one side to the other like a rabbit."

I obtained a one-cylinder Vincent motorcycle for convenient
transportation and it was a delight to see Bob up front at the controls while Titi perched on the rear fender munching on a mango. Her
ability to adapt to new experiences was an inspiration.

We settled into a bucolic lifestyle after the months at sea. I gazed
over the lagoon, thought about not much, somewhat rudderless after
my loss, awaiting I knew not what, but confident that Tahiti held yet
another surprise.

Titi and Bob in Tahiti

Stella

CHAPTER ELEVEN

Stella

Punaauia was a quiet place compared to Papeete. A few small shops sold essentials, but one had to venture into town for anything else. Family enclaves nestled against one another with no fences proclaiming ownership. A narrow sandy beach fronted the lagoon. In some places the water was shoal, studded with coral heads before reaching deep water. Other places it went off deep. Out beyond, at varying distances from the beach, the barrier reef, interspersed with passes, broke the power of the sea beyond. It was a multifaceted playground with its fishing holes, boating possibilities, and places to hang out and picnic along its generous miles of length. Coconut palms were everywhere there wasn't something else. In a goodly breeze considerable thudding could be heard as the nuts rained down, providing food, fire material from the husks, or the meat for making of copra.

Our simple thatched cabana housed a couple of beds, and sparse little else, which was fine by us, who were used to small boat quarters. Several windows were just open spaces with roll down woven shades. I was living with Tony. Three Tahitian families lived next door. We called their enclave "The Idiot Palace." The three families looked identical, which might have had something to do with their behavior.

First thing at dawn a man, *pareu* around his waist, came out and sat on a fallen coconut log for half an hour, not moving, looking down between his legs. He then went back inside, probably for breakfast. Next a small girl brought out a pandanus mat and pillows. Looking up to be sure she was not in the range of falling nuts, she collapsed on the mat with her day's work completed, quickly followed by the other women, all spending the daylight hours flat on their backs, playing the guitar, sleeping, or staring into space. Then one of the girls suddenly rose to her feet, staggered to the water fifteen feet away, and lay half submerged, propped on her elbows for three hours and sixteen minutes. The men squeezed in between the cracks of all this bustle of activity. What they did for a living was a question.

Recalling this from my diary makes me wonder what I was doing during those three hours and sixteen minutes of observation. Diary writing was worth a few minutes of the day. Swimming and spear fishing took another segment, coupled with visiting town and friends. Checking on the boat put still more minutes to rest.

Then there was the picture taking, which opened avenues impossible to have foreseen. Colored thirty-five-millimeter film was mailed to the States to be processed. That left the black and white. In town there was a photographic store run by two Californians, Phil and Hazel Mackenzie. They had adopted a lovely Tahitian girl, whose New Zealander father had returned to his home island and whose mother had died. Her name was Stella.

Stella spoke perfect English, and did most of the processing in the darkroom, along with everything else. She was petite with a nice figure and an eternal smile. She spoke in a melodious voice that gave the impression of gaiety and concern for all those around her. She was a lovely Tahitian woman with the added sophistication of being brought up by Phil and Hazel.

We didn't pay much attention to each other at first, but as my visits became more frequent and I became friends with Phil and Hazel, the inevitable happened. I was drawn to Stella. Looking back now, I suppose my heart was sore with Margaret's death and Stella was the first person who helped it heal. Soon, I was in the darkroom helping Stella process my film. There in the dim red light words were spoken, subtle contacts took place, with one thing leading to another in a most logical manner, as it does when young people are together often.

It didn't help that the Mackenzies also lived in Punaauia about a quarter of a mile from our enclave. Pretty soon we were invited down there for dinners and picnics. Phil was a frustrated movie director with no film or equipment. I had a movie camera and film. Again, one thing led to another and we cooked up the idea of making a film based on a wedding, showing lovely people, festivities, Tahitian life, and other good pot boiling stuff. This increased our time together, as of course Stella was part of the movie crew, helping with the casting. Her birth family lived beyond Hazel and Phil, providing a wonderful pool of good-looking actors while also adding to our circle of friends. Because people loved her, some of it brushed off on us and we became a part of the family. More and more sweet words were bandied back and forth between Stella and me until one night I found myself walking down the beach toward the Mackenzie compound. Their main house was at the rear of the property with Stella's cabin closer to the beach.

I vividly remember the night I found my way into Stella's bedroom. The new moon drew the eye to the dome of stars, while the gentle lap of water against the sand was periodically interrupted by the splash of a big fish. Bare feet on the sand, the gentle breeze against my face made the walk a treasure before even arriving at my destination. When her cabin appeared, my footsteps became stealthy. This was crossing a line of serious significance. Right or wrong was banished from my mind with the burden of celibacy weighing heavily on my youth. A tap on the window, hidden from the main house, and I was inside with a person, who, for a spell, made me forget Margaret's death.

On the walk home before dawn, right and wrong raised their questioning heads—I was unsure what should come next—but were quickly shoved aside by the swirl of events that filled the ensuing days. Preparations for filming went forward. Stella's sister Madelaine was the bride, marrying Tamu, a handsome tall Tahitian, who made the perfect groom. Other family members filled in where needed, along with friends and friends of friends. Of course, Titi was perfect for climbing coconut trees, showing off her superb frontal display. The plot was so corny as to be highly amusing. Our group became one large family, with only Phil, the director, taking the project seriously. For the rest of us it was pure fun. My Bell and Howell devoured film, assuming various nicknames like Wicked One Eye, Myth Maker, Pareu Lifter, and other bawdier monikers.

Ostensibly in search of filming sites, we toured the island one weekend, renting a local bus. Bottled goods came aboard, as did a large quantity of food, musical instruments, and other essential ingredients for merriment. At each waterfall and little river, the bus emptied.

It was into the river, instruments and clothes together. I remember one musician with just his head above water, hands strumming on the floating guitar, inducing swaying hips and vocal noises from surrounding comrades.

Back on the bus, a few kilometers farther on, someone would call from the rear, where bottled goods were in serious demand. Another outpouring would take place. The men lined both sides of the road ahead, while the women lifted their skirts to the rear of our chariot. Needless to say, the day was considered a huge success with increased dedication to the filming in hopes that the good times would continue to roll.

Intrigued by the diversity of the island, inspired by our party excursion, I took the motorcycle for a tour of the other side of Tahiti. It was scarcely populated, with few settlements, making for an interesting moment when a tire blew at kilometer sixty. From my past military service experience, the flat didn't worry me, but a patch kit and pump would be critical. I walked along the road, where traffic was nonexistent, until behind a mango and an avocado tree a small repair shop emerged. In the backyard was a Model T Ford, while under the shed an old Seth Thomas was merrily ticking away. The Tahitian shopkeeper could have stepped out of a New England landscape. It turned out his father was a Yankee, with antecedents going back to the whaling era. Again, Priestess Tahiti had pulled aside another of her shrouds to reveal a treasure.

Bob, Titi, and I parted another shroud a few days later by climbing 6,300-foot Mt. Aorai. Near it was Mt. Orohena, at 7,352 feet. Stella didn't go because of her weakened rheumatic heart. As it was, we huffed and puffed and lay on our backs for rest, seriously out of shape from all the easy living. Interior Tahiti was a different animal from the flat land down by the sea. Huge trees towered above us with unknown names, and plants with enormous leaves brushed our knees. We glimpsed a boar with large tusks, exotic birds, and waterfalls that tumbled down stunning cliffs and were in a class by themselves. Their crystal pools cooled our sweat-drenched bodies. We spent the night in a lean-to halfway to the peak. It grew colder as we climbed and that first night I had on a T-shirt and red flannel underwear. The next night at the top was worse. We huddled together, shivering the night away. The view from the peak was worth it. Clouds chased each other from peak to peak. With our binoculars, we could see *Mandalay* tied to the quay in the harbor, in a world so removed from where we stood that it brought on thoughts about the future. We fled down the steep path at dawn, back to the other reality.

Those mountaintop thoughts persisted on our return to lagoon life. The filming was winding down. The hurricane season would soon come to an end. Princess Tahiti had again become inscrutable. It was time to move on. *Mandalay* was very tired. I had to accept that her days were numbered. We had been lucky to make it this far. There were no customers for her here. The most reasonable plan was to sail with the trades, visiting Moorea, Bora Bora, Huahine, Fiji, Samoa, and finally the New Hebrides, where from all reports selling the boat would be easy. Tony was leaving soon for Australia. Sam the Egyptian had finally received some money from home and was leaving for points unknown. The commander was making noises about changes that had to come to his life if he weren't to die here. For all of us, Tahiti had lost her allure. We were replete with her pleasures.

Titi was returning to Ouapou on the next schooner, her gravest concern being that she wouldn't be pregnant. Her Polynesian thinking reasoned that Bob might or might not return some day. In the meantime, her family would be disappointed if she returned with nothing, as she put it. Thus she told Bob in no uncertain terms to work harder. This meant not working hard during the day so he could work harder at night.

I also had one big hurdle to work out: Stella. By now she had moved in with me. Her adopted parents had accepted the inevitable, grudgingly. I had not told my parents about her. Things were a bit tense. Then she told me one black, unforgettable night that despite all precautions, she was in a "family way." Now, as a father and grandfather, I'm not entirely proud of my reaction, but then I was a young man in my twenties and having a family was far from my plan. Selfishly, I just wanted to sail away, but I also knew that I couldn't emotionally abandon her, or the baby, despite my plans. I was in a deep conundrum.

—◊◊◊—

Stella made it clear that she wanted to come with us on the rest of the journey. I told her she wouldn't be happy living in the States with me. She understood, but still wanted to go on the boat for our trip west. Each day, not the future, was the Polynesian creed. She kept pleading, saying she would return to Phil and Hazel before we hit the New Hebrides. Bob was no help. He was very fond of Stella, calling her "sister," like everyone else, as she was such a pleasure to be around. He said it would be a plus to have her along, and besides, she could speak the language. I said no, reluctantly, being also concerned about her health. She said yes. Stella won.

The Mackenzies had by now taken a long-range view. They didn't want her to go. She was their beloved daughter. On the other hand, Phil's health was deteriorating. Before long they would have to return to California for good hospital care, living out their days there. But, on a modest budget, what was to become of Stella? With my name, I could be the answer to their dilemma, providing her and the coming child a sound financial future. We parted friends, remaining so to the end of their lives. As for my own parents, it was easy to avoid the subject a world away in a day before computers and cell phones. I did not tell them for a while.

I was fast coming to see that one's life was a necklace of human relations, each segment special in its own way, if not always harmonious. The Tahiti segment with the commander, Bob, Tony, the Mackenzies, and Stella and our future son was a part of that necklace I would wear until the end of my life. Stella and I never were officially married, but I took care of her and our son, James Stillman Bennett, also known as Wa, for all their lives.

(As Stella aged, her heart problems meant she needed expert care, which continued for the balance of her life and required periodic California visits for medical attention not available in Tahiti. During those times I sent her to the West Coast, and she stayed with Hazel and Phil, who eventually retired there. They were forever grateful as they missed her terribly. Phil died in 1961, making her visits even more precious for Hazel.)

Wa was born in 1956 in Tahiti. When he grew to the age when his education became an issue, he came to me in Camden, Maine, and attended high school. After graduation he decided to return to Tahiti. The pace was slower there, better suited to his easygoing, gentle ways. For years he lived in the house I built for Stella on the Mackenzie family compound, with a nice woman as a Tahitian wife. Stella eventually died from complications with her heart. Then one night, a short time after supper, while sitting in a chair, Wa died suddenly of an embolism. He was in his late thirties. Wa was a lovely human being, beloved by all, including my other children, Liv and Ola.

But that was the future, with many more miles and stories yet to come. At the time of our departure, before his birth, I had no idea what was coming. There were three of us heading out on *Mandalay*, Stella, Bob, and me. In the official paperwork under "occupation," Bob was listed as bullfighter. This was partly in defiance of French authority, and partly because when under the influence he was known to whip off his pareu and employ it as a cape.

It was an emotional parting. All of Stella's family was there, and our many friends, bringing flower leis and shell necklaces. Tony overslept and didn't show, probably on purpose. I was glad for it would have been hard saying goodbye. He had been a wonderful shipmate, utterly useless for anything but taking his time at the wheel but made up for it in so many other ways. The many months we were together I never heard him say a bad word about anyone. His heart was as big as the whole world. Everyone, no matter who they were, loved Tony. Every house was his and all he had to do was walk in and one could see the sincere smiles on all the faces there. Tony was one of those people who gave themselves freely, and in ten minutes with a stranger he knew their life history, joys, and sorrows.

The crowd continued to grow. We had a few farewell drinks together, then the bar across the street played Auld Lang Syne and the Tahitian equivalent, Maruru. Eyes were moist as we shoved off replete with six months of mixed emotions. Sailing out the pass I thought that each place I had been stood out not so much for itself but for some individual and for others met.

One of those was standing apart from the main crowd in a pair of old faded blue shorts and a shirt that had seen better days, along with a battered straw hat that had weathered countless hours under the sun and rain. Francois stood absolutely still not raising an arm in farewell. I lifted my arm and thought I saw a hand twitch. There was in that brief moment an exchange of feeling that was to haunt me for years. I felt I was leaving a part of myself, the better part, and would never see him again. With blurred eyes I turned at last and looked across the bay to Moorea, leaving two exceptional people, Tony and Francois, behind and taking two others with me.

CHAPTER TWELVE

Suvorov

Tahiti was behind, the New Hebrides lay ahead, and Moorea on our bow was slumbering under a white cloud, typical of a South Pacific island, where heat from the moisture-laden greenery rises until condensing in the cooler air, creating a cover to be seen before the island itself. We put Stella at the helm, where she was a natural. It was a pleasure to have her with us. In through the pass we glided that afternoon under a gentle breeze to find Pao Pao Bay well guarded by volcanic peaks. We put up the sun tarp, and contemplated the idyllic setting, wondering what new adventure was in store for us three wanderers.

Naturally, it turned out to be a person. His name was William Alister MacDonald. He lived in one of the few thatched cabins scattered around the bay, fronted by a white beach. He was thin with blue, watery, piercing eyes, spry for his ninety-three years. He climbed out of his dinghy over our gunwale like a man thirty years younger. Before long we learned he was an English watercolorist who had been living here for many years. Known for his London scenes, Alister was now devoted to drawing Polynesian landscapes, with an added fascination for boats. The unusualness of our vessel had drawn him from his work. After a few minutes an affinity developed that resulted in many hours of conversation during our stay. He talked to Stella in fluent Tahitian.

There were few countries he hadn't visited, and he was as cognizant of world events as an ardent reader of *The New York Times*. He had gone back to England for a spell but with no family or friends there anymore, "I returned to this beautiful bay where the heat is good for my age and I can live to be a hundred and much longer perhaps."

On his next visit he brought avocados, papayas, and lobsters. We talked far into the night. On asking about his long life I received this reply: "Two things. I eat very little and most important, I am too interested to die." Then when I asked if he wasn't cynical with all the evils in the world, he replied with great humility, "No! People and the world are far too interesting for me ever to be cynical."

He did a brown watercolor of *Mandalay* floating in the placid bay with the three volcanic peaks rising beyond her bow and his little house nestled on the shore to our port. It hangs behind the computer as I write these words, drawing me back to that necklace of people that made our voyage such a treasure. He was second to Gus in being a contented, happy man, living very simply in small quarters with an elderly housekeeper to help when needed. Working five hours a day with brush and paint, he looked forward to each new sunrise. Alister died at ninety-six, three years after we said goodbye. This year one of his early small paintings of London, for which he was so famous, appeared on eBay for a goodly sum. He will also be remembered for his beautiful cover for *Men Against the Sea*, about the mutiny on the *Bounty*, by Charles Nordhoff and James Norman Hall.

Then it was on to Bora Bora, which I immediately came to regard as a perfect vacation spot after the turmoil of Tahiti. During World War II, the United States used it as a supply base with six thousand men and built a long airstrip. The landing field was the only international one in Polynesia until Tahiti built its own in 1960. I thought the island would have been ruined by the occupation but very little had changed, we were told. Apparently, soon after the Americans left the natives went back to their old way of life with only good memories of the past happy times during the war. There were only two Frenchmen on the island, one a schoolteacher and the other a gendarme. Folks loved the Americans and detested the French. Living was easy under the Americans compared to life before. We built houses on their property with the understanding that on leaving the houses would revert to the landowners. The French, however, went from house to house confiscating what the Americans had left, taking the houses for themselves.

The government at the time of the occupation in Tahiti hated the Americans. Officials weren't informed about the occupation until the troops arrived with ships, guns, and supplies, on orders from the Allied Command. The officials in Papeete were incensed. A trading schooner was outfitted with a machine gun on the bow and the Polynesian skipper was ordered to go over and repulse the takeover. The skipper reported it was an excellent mission. He had gone ashore and gotten thoroughly drunk with the top brass. So ended the repulse.

The best-loved man on the island was a Polynesian schoolteacher called Francis Sanford. During the war he worked with the Americans. Three times the French tried to remove him from the job but failed. It was his duty to keep the army, the navy, the French, and the Polynesians all happy. After the war he was given the Medal of Freedom by Secretary of the Navy for his outstanding work. The French had the gall to try to take the medal away from him, saying he was just a subordinate. When it was presented to him by the American Consulate in Papeete, not a single Frenchman showed up.

I was sad to leave Pago Pago, but more adventures beckoned. So one morning, three weeks after we left Papeete, a lone coconut tree rose from the horizon's rim. As the yacht rolled onward under the push of the southeast trade, another tree rose and then another until there stood a small company against the vastness of the Pacific around them. A low gray outline emerged, and clumps of palms stood on it. Then came the barrier reef with the rollers crashing on the coral. We had come to Suvorov Island. Tahiti was eleven hundred miles astern, Samoa another five hundred miles ahead. Manihiki, the nearest land, lay two hundred miles to the north.

Bob and Stella took turns with the binoculars while I read the pilot directions. Laconic as always, there was one magic phrase: "Suvorov is uninhabited." We were to have an island to ourselves for two weeks before sailing on to Fiji, Samoa, and the New Hebrides. This was just another atoll in the Pacific, perhaps, but all ours and with a history. Treasure had been buried here and $10,000 in Mexican money unearthed. Reputedly a cache of opium lay beneath the sand, and here Dean Frisbie and his four children had weathered the terrible hurricane of 1942, the worst in more than a hundred years. In his book *The Island of Desire*, we had read how he and his children lashed themselves to the branches of the tamanu trees, then watched their island gradually blow away. The hurricane swept sixteen of the twenty-two islets into the sea and leveled the other six. So now there was nothing to bring people to Suvorov. The new stand of palms didn't produce enough coconuts to warrant making copra.

Pearl shell in the lagoon was scarce and difficult to obtain. The island lay slumbering, waiting for time and nature to restore what the sea and wind had taken away. During the war a ship-watching post had been set up, but the men had left at the end of hostilities, so we swept into the pass and around into the lee of the first motu, Anchorage Island, confident of possession.

The motu was small, as such atolls always are, scarcely a half-mile long and a few dozen yards across, with the highest point only twelve feet above the water. The lagoon in its greens and blues extended like a vast lake, six miles across, enclosed by the barrier reef, while here and there at great distance along its length, an islet struggled to survive. The effect of the hurricane, now twelve years past, was immediately evident. A few tall palms, the survivors of the terrible storm, towered high above the new generation beneath them. Great boulders of coral weighing many tons lay strewn about the windward beach, and all but a few of the islets along the reef lay bare, with only an occasional bush as a pitiful reminder of their past fertility.

But the young palms were green on Anchorage Island and the beach was white and inviting under the June sun. Bosun birds, terns, and frigates wheeled overhead, showing that life once again was returning to Suvorov. We swept the shore with binoculars, taking in the reef shelving out from the beach, the rows of young palms halting within a few feet of the water, and a rude dock that jutted out from the beach. Then there it was.

"Rass!" said Bob. "I'm seeing things!"

A crude boat lay pulled up on the sand, tied to a coconut tree. Its sail hung limp and unfurled. Next to it rested a box-crate chair, its back supported by a coconut.

After anchoring we rowed ashore, gaping at the red letters, "Ruptured Duckling," painted with a shaky hand, on the stern of the little boat. Pulling the dinghy up on the sand we spied a path leading back from the beach toward a white shack with a red tin roof. We walked quietly toward the house. Nobody came to greet us.

We called. No answer. Examining the shack, we saw it had two rooms and a front porch. A third room led off the far end of the porch, separate from the others. The first chamber was a study with a desk piled high with papers and magazines. To one side a journal lay open, while beside it a pen and inkwell sat on an old Pacific Islands Monthly. Books were on the shelves behind the desk. A barometer hung on the wall. A little room leading off the porch was a pantry with papayas and bananas hanging. A few tins were on the shelf.

But it was the other room that held us. All we could see from our vantage point was the lower end of a wooden bed. A white sheet covered the mattress. On the sheet were two feet, tanned, but unmistakably white.

We retreated to a respectable distance and Bob coughed loudly. I called, "Anybody home?"

"Who is it?" answered a weak voice from somewhere above the feet.

"We're in off a yacht," we replied.

"Fair dinkum," came the feeble voice. "Come in. You'll have to help me up."

The man was lying on his back, his loins covered with a lava-lava. A glass full of urine, a machete, and two opened drinking nuts were on the floor beside the bed. He looked at us with kindly, washed-out eyes sunk in an emaciated face. It was a matter-of-fact face despite the three-day stubble and the havoc lines around his eyes. The man was tall, and his height was exaggerated by his leanness. Every muscle, rib, and tendon showed under his bronzed skin.

He smiled and weakly held out his hand in greeting.

"Name's Tom Neale. Dislocated my back. Been lying here thirty-six hours trying to get up."

"Christ!" said Bob. "You must be hungry enough to eat a bull. What can I cook you?"

"Thanks," Tom said with a sigh. "I sure could use a cup of tea. But it'll mean building a fire in the stove back there in the cook shed."

Bob rushed out with Stella behind, and I helped Tom into a sitting position. It hurt him badly and he gritted his teeth. "It's much better," he croaked, with the sweat running down his face. "I'll be all right in a minute."

I hurried to the boat to get supplies. Bob and Stella had the crude iron stove going when I returned. We made Tom a hot meal, gave him a stiff drink of rum, and rubbed liniment on his back. He felt considerably revived after tucking away the food. The rum didn't hurt, by the expression on his face.

He told us then, fumbling for words, how he had come to hurt his back and was reduced to this state in which we had found him. On Monday (it was now Wednesday) he had sailed to the Brushwood islets a mile along the reef to gather firewood and plant coconuts. Landing on the motu, he had lifted the iron weight that served as his anchor. When he did, something gave in his back, making him double up in pain. Somehow, he had managed to crawl back into the boat, cut the anchor line, and let the wind blow him home. If the wind hadn't been behind him he would never have made it. As it was it took him three hours to cover the mile to Anchorage Island. On landing, he tied the boat, took two drinking nuts and the machete, staggered home, and fell on his bed. The next morning he could only roll his head, use his arms, and double up his legs. Luckily there was a glass on a shelf over his head. With his machete he tipped it over, catching it when it fell. He urinated in it to save wetting his bed. He thought he had a dislocated disc. It had happened to him once before.

During our three weeks on Suvorov, Tom's story unfolded bit by bit as the days went on. He had been born in New Zealand, fifty-one years before, and had spent his life on boats trading among the islands or tending store. For five years, before coming to Suvorov, he had run a trading post on one of the more isolated islands of the Cook Island group. Five years was a long time to be on an atoll among natives, with only an occasional visit from another white face. Tom had grown tired of it. He had gone to Rarotonga, the seat of the Cook Island government, "for a change of scenery." There he had met his old friend Dean Frisbie. The writer told him about the charms of Suvorov—how it was uninhabited, how during the war the coast watchers had built a small shack there with water tanks to hold eleven hundred gallons. When they abandoned the post, they left everything. It sounded like a perfect setup to Tom.

Although he was sick to death of being continually surrounded only by Polynesians, he was soon just as discontent in the relative hustle and bustle of the white colony in Rarotonga. "I had a hankering to go it alone for a spell."

It so happened that the commissioner wanted to send an expedition of divers to Suvorov to dive for pearl shell, so Tom offered to supervise the operation. They would stay for two months. If in that time he found he liked the place he could stay on for a couple of years, after the divers had left. He bought himself fifty pounds of flour, seventy pounds of sugar, forty pounds of biscuits, two dozen tins of bully beef, six pounds of salt, baking powder, jam, some tinned butter, ten pounds of lard, tea and coffee, kerosene, two axes, a few tools, a fish spear, hooks and lines, a lantern, bedding, a few odd clothes, iodine, and aspirin.

Taking his two cats, Mr. Tom Tom and Mrs. Thievery, and a few chickens, off he went with his supplies and the divers.

"All my friends said I was crazy and that I couldn't possibly stay alive on an atoll for two years all alone. They said I'd be back damn soon."

He found the island more or less as Frisbie had described it. The little shack was in fair repair, the tanks were still good, there was a crude shed in which to store firewood and gear. A cook shed behind the house was easily repaired. The new coconut palms were as yet low, so it was simple to get the nuts without climbing the trees. Immediately he liked the place and when the divers departed after a month, discouraged by the scarcity of shell, Tom stayed on.

"When the schooner left at 5 p.m. eighteen months ago with the divers, I went to the outer beach and watched her sweep out the pass, returning the captain's wave by taking off my pants and using them as a flag. They stayed off until another ship came. That was many months."

Suvorov was off the schooner route. A boat never stopped except in an emergency or on orders from the commissioner in Rarotonga. Either circumstance was rare. An occasional yacht stopped by on the way to Samoa from Tahiti. We asked Tom if he hadn't felt lonely standing on the beach watching the schooner disappear eighteen months ago.

"Never felt so good," was his reply. "Never felt so free or more unlonely. It was one of the nicest moments in my life. I was sick to death of the divers!"

There was plenty to keep him busy. He repaired the cookhouse and made a stove of sorts from an old oil drum. Next he re-thatched the front porch with coconut fronds, cleaned up the yard, and turned to the question of food. The supplies he had brought would soon run out, so he had to depend on the island for nourishment. He made a garden, hauling topsoil from the most fertile spots on the atoll and lumping it on a small plot close to the house. He planted sweet potatoes, bananas, and papayas. On the island, already, were papayas, a breadfruit tree, wild chickens, and five wild pigs. The pigs, left by goodness knows who, proved to be his biggest problem.

"They ran wild, eating every green thing that dared show its head. I had to do something, and I didn't have a gun."

He told us one evening how he had killed them. His back was better by then and we were sitting on the beach cooking supper over a small fire. The lagoon was quiet with only the faintest sounds coming from the trade wind rustling in the palms. We had a bottle of rum and Tom sipped his drink with the pleasure that comes from long, forced abstinence. His conversation grew eloquent.

"I took a broken machete blade, sharpened it like a razor, and lashed it securely to a stout pole. I built a platform in a palm fifteen feet off the ground and made a clearing around it. On a moonlit night I would open a dozen coconuts and lay them at the base of the tree, climb to my platform, and wait, holding the spear between my legs. I counted on the fact that a pig never looks up. It was beautiful up there with the moonbeams drifting through the fronds, making lighted places on the coral beneath me. Turning my head, I could see the pass into the lagoon, the ocean, and the breakers on the reef. In front, the lagoon would be as peaceful as could be. The palms trapped the wind. The noise of the mullet jumping and the jack chasing small fish sounded deafening. An old heron would croak at the edge of the water and terns twittered.

"Looking at the ground again, there would be three great coconut crabs doing a kind of dance with their huge claws waving in the air, pulling at the meat of the opened nuts. They looked ghoulish as they ripped the white strips away.

"A little atoll rat—not the big, ugly, brown ones of the waterfront—would come scampering out, sniff a bit, and nibble at the nuts with his two long front teeth."

Tom leaned forward, excitement creeping into his voice.

"A dark shadow would appear at the edge of the clearing under the tangle of creepers. It would be him. He would sniff and grunt and advance, all black except for the white shine of his tusks. The moonlight made a villain of him and I gripped the spear more tightly. I was all goose bumps. He approached the first nut, ate it, moved on to the next and the next, coming ever closer to my tree. Then he was directly below my spear. He paused and sniffed the air. He smelled me. I saw those wicked red eyes, and aiming just behind his neck, I plunged the spear downward. It sank in to the hilt and he screamed. Spurting blood, he tore the pole from my hands and staggered toward the thicket. I scrambled from my platform and ran after him with my machete raised. I caught him before he made cover and slashed down across his spine. He screamed again and fell, and I cut his throat and saw his blood on the coral."

Tom slumped back and sighed. "With his last convulsion I felt suddenly melancholy. The savage in me was gone and I was only an

169

old man of fifty-one on an atoll, alone. I would walk slowly home, feeling very tired. Five times I did that."

We put some more wood on the fire and watched the grease from the mullet dripping slowly into the flames. The light flickered off the drooping palm fronds and all was quiet but the lap of wavelets on the reef.

"It's fair dinkum this time of day," Tom said quietly. "Often I come here at dusk with my bowl of tea to watch the night fall on the lagoon and think back over the months—the killing of the pigs and what came after. You know, when they were gone the papaya trees sprang up everywhere, seeded from those that were too large for the pigs to kill. I planted spring onions then, and thirty tomato plants. A rooster and six hens were on the island when I arrived. Now there are a dozen roosters and thirty hens. At first they were terribly wild—couldn't get near them. Every evening I would open the soft, pulpy, white heart of the sprouting coconut and scatter it about the yard, first striking a crowbar made from a Model-T rear axle that I brought with me. Soon they knew the noise and would come running. I built a fence of split coconut logs around the garden. What a job—and caught the land crabs that would still get through and eat the green shoots. All the growing things did well except the tomatoes. They shot up strong and husky to a height of six feet with many blossoms, but never gave any fruit. Maybe the absence of bees had something to do with it.

"Mr. Tom Tom and Mrs. Thievery had a son and I called him Suvorov, but it soon corrupted to Sparrow. I neutralized him to keep incest from the family. I wrote in my journal every day and was too busy to consider being lonely."

Stella asked him how he fished. "Easy," he replied. "I go on the reef with my spear and look for the fish that lie in the holes in the coral, or at night I walk along the shallows on the lagoon side and catch mullet by waiting until they approach the lantern's light and then hit them across the back with a machete. Or I take my lantern and walk along the reef on the ocean side and pick up lobsters that come up at night to feed."

I enjoyed the look on Stella's face. She loved to fish so begged him for more details.

"I made a lure of white feathers from a bosun bird I found dead on the beach and lashed it on a hook and line attached to a bamboo pole. Moved slowly over the water at night at the edge of the reef, it was murder on the red fish called 'ku.'"

He went on. "One moonlit night I was using it, dragging it slowly over the deep water with little twitches. I was standing at the edge of the reef, up to my thighs in water. A big fish took the lure in a swirl of spray. I worked him in slowly to the edge of the reef, bent down, and strained forward to take him by the gills. My hand was within six inches of his head when I paused, I don't know why. It was unconscious. A great gray thing rushed in. I saw the rows and rows of teeth. A smashing blow struck me across the legs, throwing me on my back on the reef. I jumped up. The fish was gone, the lure was gone, and my little finger was bleeding. The shark had taken the fish, just nicking my finger, and had hit me with his tail on turning. I walked home wondering where my hand would have been if I hadn't paused that brief instant."

Tom stopped talking and looked embarrassed, as if he wanted to say something but didn't know how to begin. We poured him another drink and waited.

"You see," he began hesitantly, "by then I had come to love Suvorov. It was giving me happiness and contentment. I wanted to do something to sort of repay her. So next I fixed Ruptured Duckling, and using it to get around in, planted coconuts on the islets swept clear by the hurricane. I would set out early in the morning with thirty or forty sprouting nuts, plant them, and return toward evening, thinking that I had speeded up evolution a hundred years.

"The only complaint I had against the island was the diet. My supply of flour, sugar, and rice soon ran out. The lard dwindled so low I only used a trace now and then to fry eggs. My staples came to be eggs, a rare rooster on special occasions, a few sweet potatoes, fish, coconuts, and papayas. Then a cup of tea in the morning and one in the evening. But no sugar sorely hurt, and I didn't feel satisfied without flour and lard. My body seemed to demand them. I missed the flour and lard the most. Only eggs helped to fill the hole. I spent hours searching for nests in the bush. Very few hens laid in the nests I had made for them about the yard."

Tom's journal, which I avidly perused, recounted a chicken incident.

August 5

"Wasted time following the hen that lays away. She went in a wide semicircle and finally eluded me. I waited for half an hour to see if she would return. Not a sign nor did she cackle again. She was in the yard when I returned. Am determined to find her nest; besides now I've got to show something for the time wasted.

August 6

Tried to follow the hen but a young rooster upset her. I chased him and scared the hen. She wouldn't go straight to the nest but hung around in the bush. Couldn't waste any more time so vowed would put that young rooster in the pot. Don't like his crow

Tom Neale

anyhow. Caught him when his back was to me. He being too busy on the job he was on to notice me....

August 7

Found the nest with ten eggs. This morning she started making a noise so I followed her a bit, but she hung around in the bush so I went and hung around in the bush too, in the usual place for ten minutes. When she didn't show up I backtracked and happened to spot her, so hid and waited. Soon she came in my direction, then suddenly disappeared. I couldn't believe my eyes, so waited a bit longer and investigated a coconut stump about ten feet high, which she had disappeared behind. Damn me, if I didn't see her head sticking out of a hole four feet from the ground. I can't write what I said when I found her. Talk about pigs not thinking to look up, I'm as bad. Had been around that stump half a dozen times and reckoned the nest was in that area until the first day when she decoyed me a hundred yards beyond. A lot of writing about nothing but I feel I've achieved a major victory."

We listened as he told how he had turned his attention to the pier of coral blocks on the lagoon side that had been washed out in the hurricane. The blocks were strewn every which way, making an eyesore on his otherwise beautiful atoll. It turned out to be a greater undertaking than he had imagined. He worked three or four hours a day until his back ached and the ends of his fingers were raw. One day he felt something give in his back and the next morning he could barely move. The work went on and on and never seemed to come any closer to completion. It got his dander up. He was determined to see it finished. Not that it made any great difference if it wasn't. There really was no need of a wharf as copra wasn't being produced. However, everything he had started here had been successfully completed. He could use it as a fishing dock.

Then talk went back to food. "I wasn't used to my diet of fish and coconuts. Couldn't eat enough. Got tired very easily and had to take a long rest in the middle of the day. I would have a cup of tea with a papaya or eggs in the morning and when the morning wore on I would nibble uto [sprouting coconut]. I had only two meals a day, with uto in between. For supper there would be tea again, fish, eggs, and once in a while kumeras [sweet potatoes]. I had one tin of bully beef left, which was to be for Christmas. More than anything, I craved bread with lots of butter on it. About this time my tobacco ran out. For the first time, I felt depressed and lonely. I'm not a heavy smoker, perhaps two ounces a week, but I have smoked that amount regularly all my life and it was startling to see the effect when it was suddenly stopped. The first symptom was loneliness with a heavy dose of depression. Then my appetite suffered, and my stomach was upset for days. In the evening after supper the craving for a smoke would be terrible. A month later a yacht came in and one of the crew gave me a package of Players cigarettes. I broke each open and rolled two from one, planning on making them last a month. They were gone in five days and the craving was worse than ever. It took a month before I was cured.

"Next the hurricane season came along. The weather took on great importance. I would look at the barometer three or four times a day, noticing the direction of the wind and its force. I examined the tamanu trees Frisbie and his kids used in '42 and planned how I would use them. They are a terribly strong hardwood with their roots deep in the sand and coral.

"I guess you know how Frisbie lashed himself and his children fifteen feet above the ground to the stoutest limbs. One of his little girls slept through the great wind, until he woke her to make her drink a little rum, for apparently it was terribly cold with the wind and the rain. Afterward she said she was perfectly content until drinking the rum as she was unable to return to sleep after that. Incidentally, while grubbing around those trees I unearthed an old bottle of Worcestershire sauce, a relic of Frisbie. It was still good but every time I used it I had an urge to look at the barometer, and in the end, I wished that it had remained where it was. A few days after my inspection it began to blow strongly from the north, whipped into a full gale, and the barometer started dropping. I could understand Frisbie's description of the wind 'shrieking,' for it actually did, although it was not nearly as strong as he saw it. Coconut palms were falling, the nuts flying through the air, and the tin roof vibrated like a buzz saw. I gathered my ropes, collected a bit of food, and awaited the worst. It was a long day and oh, how I longed for a bottle of rum and some company. The wind backed to the northwest toward evening and at 9 p.m. the barometer went up, accompanied by sheets of rain and by thunder and lightning. I heaved a sigh of relief and went to bed, first yelling into the night, 'Go on Huey, bang those bloody drums.' The cats curled up on my feet and it was one of the best night sleeps I'd had in a long time. That was the only scare I had in eighteen months."

We asked Tom if he had ever wanted to give up his Suvorov life and return to Rarotonga during his eighteen-month exile.

He grinned. "Naturally, now and again. I would get depressed and wish I was back in civilization. But then I would think of all my friends saying, 'I told you so,' and just the thought of that *made me kind of mad. Besides, there was no way to leave even if I had wanted to, and those bad spells never lasted long. But the diet continued to irk me, and at times I would have loved a piece of chocolate. Strangely enough, I never longed for greens. I guess coconuts must supply all the vitamins. Yet there was always something to take my mind off food. I brought back a young bosun bird from Whale Cay where it was nesting. I called him Charlie and he would answer with a noise like 'whoouu.' He gradually grew his wing feathers. One day I took him down to the beach and set him on the sand. He flew a hundred yards out into the lagoon, settled on the water, took off again, and disappeared. He never came back. I felt sad—partly the tobacco, I think—so that evening I tried a new dish to cheer my spirits. I cut several papayas in half and placed them in the native oven to bake. When done, and covered with coconut cream, they tasted just like peaches."*

Tom gave us a list of what he considered to be the bare essentials for living on an atoll:

- KEROSENE (LIGHT)
- SOAP
- MATCHES
- KNIFE AND MACHETE
- FISH SPEAR
- BLANKET
- SNEAKERS FOR WALKING ON THE REEF AND A FEW CLOTHES

To make things easier, he would add the following:

- TEA AND COFFEE
- SUGAR

- FLOUR
- BAKING POWDER
- LARD
- BEEF
- RICE
- TOBACCO
- BUTTER OR OLEO
- SALT AND CONDIMENTS
- FILE
- HOOK AND LINES FOR FISH
- READING MATTER

"With all these," Tom said, "and with what an island has to offer, one can live like a king."

"Tom," Bob asked, "how come you didn't bring a nice squaw up here for company?"

"I wanted a little peace and quiet for a change." He winked. "And you know it would be kind of hard to get a woman to come to this place. Women are kind of gregarious, if you know what I mean."

"I know what you mean," said Bob. "They break out in a rash if they can't pad down to the store or lean over the back fence to chat it up. They're kind of handy gadgets though, other things being equal."

Stella smiled.

We asked him one night, how much longer he planned to stay on Suvorov.

"I'm rather scared of my back now," he answered. "I think you'd better send a cable to the commissioner in Rarotonga when you hit Samoa. Tell him to have the next schooner going to Manihiki pick me up on the way back. I hate to leave Suvorov but I'd hate to have my back go again when I'm here alone. Too much risk. I want to live a little longer. Also, the hurricane season is coming around and Suvo-rov is due. It's been over eleven years since the last one and they seem to strike between every ten or fifteen years."

"Do you think you'll ever come back?"

"I don't know. I just don't know. Some days I think, yes. Some days, no."

That night, back on *Mandalay*, Bob said, "Don't you meet the damndest people in the screwiest places. That friggin' Tom is so damn normal it hurts. He's just an ordinary, stubborn little shopkeeper and here he is living for eighteen months all by his lonesome—starving himself to death. What for? I don't get it. Talk about peace and quiet. I guess people are just naturally screwy."

"Nicely screwy," I countered.

"Yeah, you're right. Hell! I wonder where that friggin' Tony is tonight. I sure miss the old bastard."

I saw Stella looking at me. I knew what she was thinking. How long the two of us could be happy here, alone.

The next day we left Suvorov for Fiji.

Months later when I was in another hemisphere, I received a let-ter from Tom that rounded out his story:

Rarotonga, Cook Islands
Dear Peb,

Two weeks after you left Suvorov a schooner picked me up, thanks to the cable you sent from Pago.

Here in Raro I find myself discontent with civilization. Just too many people, so I am planning to go back to Suvorov, this time with a twelve-foot sailing dinghy and a thirty-year-old Palmerston woman. In the meantime, I'm working for a local firm slowly building up a grub stake to last for the rest of my time on Suvorov.

I had an x-ray of my back and the doctor said an acute case of arthritis, no evidence of a displaced disk, so that's good news. I have had no recurrence of it.

Next time I reckon I'll stay on in Suvorov until the end of me or the island or both. Next time there will be a hell of a lot of work to get the place back in shape again and that's where the woman will come in handy. And being an atoll woman she can like it there. As a young girl she spent six months on Suvorov and liked the place. What that woman can do with coconuts in their various stages of development is nobody's business. She's clever with fish too. I don't want to go back alone. Not that I'm lonely alone, but I know what a difference it would make to live on a place like that with a woman of her capabilities.

I often think of our times on Suvorov together.

Best wishes,

Tom

Note: Tom married the Palmerston woman. They had two children, Arthur and Stella. The daughter was named after my Stella, about whom he had become crazy for during our stay with him. We had a hard time keeping his hands off her during those three weeks. He returned to Suvorov in 1960 for three and a half years, returning to Rarotonga when he could no longer stand the periodic pearl divers. Then he came back for the last time in 1967, staying until 1977, when he developed stomach cancer and was taken off. Tom died eight months later.

Tom Neale and his hut

Bob on a motorcycle in Tahiti

CHAPTER THIRTEEN

Bob

Motoring out the pass, returning Tom's farewell wave, I could see the eyes of Stella and Bob were both looking back, but also far away. As for me, it was the thought that our three futures were presently entwined but soon would scatter to the winds, somewhere beyond the beckoning seas ahead. "Let's up sails," I said to break the spell. "Fiji, here we come."

Fiji did come after the usual parade of rough weather and calm, pumping, and the blessings of shipmate camaraderie. The islands were a pleasant intermingling of British culture and South Pacific palms with the fun-loving inhabitants comfortable in their black skin and hair. One immediately felt at home in the welcoming aura of smiling faces.

But it was a sad time for us, as it was here we had agreed Stella would return to Tahiti. We did our best to keep a "stiff upper," outfitting her with things she desired and presents for friends and family. I had made financial arrangements for her and the baby, and she was contented to go back home for the birth. However, the moment of departure was much harder than either of us had anticipated. We (Bob and I) fled the harbor after the last hug and kiss with eyes hardly fit for seeing. We were silent hoisting sail and setting course for Port Vila, New Hebrides.

In Melanesia we found yet another land with a different culture; part Polynesian laid-back living, part dark forests with native people playing drums, beating on tom-toms, bowing low to fearsome idols, all cemented by strong individuals beyond the ordinary. It was a land of strong men, skilled at survival, sometimes helped by stronger women.

We found a buyer for *Mandalay* at Port Vila in the New Hebrides: Emile was a French planter who needed a boat to recruit labor and haul supplies to his plantation. We hauled down the Stars and Stripes and hoisted the French Tricolor before boarding Emile's launch. The old girl looked at home in that tropical setting. We knew she was in good hands, floating in the crescent harbor with palms coming down to meet the sand.

I looked back at her one last time. She was a part of my life and we had used each other well. She had carried me thousands of miles, hung the necklace of people met around my neck, and brought me safely to this place of palms and sand, old and tired as she was. *Mandalay*, in a sense, had been a beloved nanny like my dog Nana, from a distant childhood. It was now time to turn the page and leave her for the pages yet to come.

For the hundredth time I asked Bob his plans for the future. "I'm taking the first boat to Tahiti, leaving in a few days," he said. "I'm going to buy that sloop off the commander, the *Korrigan*, and sail her back here. I'll dive for shells and trade around the islands with her. I'll be my own boss—won't have to take nothin' from nobody."

"Is a plantation in your future?"

"That's my idea, Peb. If I can get some coconut trees, plant some cocoa, find myself a good squaw who can put up with me and the plantation, I'll have it made. I don't want to make a million dollars; I just want to live."

Before I knew it, Bob was gone. We had a last good night together, and in the morning when I awoke his gear had disappeared. His bed was empty. He had left a note.

"Peb, didn't want to wake you. I hate goodbyes. Will write you General Delivery, Sydney, how I make out. Damn good cruise we had. Bob."

It was strange being ashore after being afloat so long. I felt lonely and disconnected. On a small boat with a good friend it is never "I," but rather "we." It took time to think in terms of "I" again. I explored the outer islands, awaiting the coastal freighter to Sydney, and came to admire the planters. They were a resourceful lot, having to cope with a thousand situations, adept at handling people, knowing when force was needed, or a kind word would do as well. For the most part, they possessed a happy-go-lucky philosophy. Being considered a good fellow was more important than making money. I felt Bob had found his proper place.

But there was a downside. I visited several mean little shacks with just a table, chair, and broken-down bed. Former carefree adventurers in much-reduced circumstances were being cared for by a local woman, with little of their old insouciance on display. Sometimes there would be a few tattered volumes left in dusty corners, all that remained of past education and background.

—◦◦◦—

Two months later, in a swirling crowd of people in the bohemian section of Sydney, Australia, I spied a monstrous mustache.

"Tony," I yelled. The figure gave a violent start.

Tony Richardson

After the embraces came the questions when we were tucked in a cozy bar around the corner, to which Tony quickly led us.

"Well Peb, it was sort of like this. I was going straight home, but then I got to New Zealand. Was waiting for a boat and suddenly met this girl. That took a month and a half and now I'm here."

"Been four months since we parted in Tahiti. What kept you in Sydney?"

"Well, you know how it goes. I met a girl the second day here. We got along fine for a while and then quarreled. Now I've found someone else. Takes time."

I told him I had booked passage to Europe and was on my way to Norway to meet up with the documentary film man, Per Host, whom we had met in the Galapagos and taken around the islands for his filming.

A week later Tony had changed his plans. He said goodbye to his new friend and joined me. Off we went to Scandinavia. While waiting for our steamer, I began to receive letters from Bob:

October 1955
Hog Harbor, Santo

Dear Peb,

This plantation I'm managing is one thousand acres. One hundred pounds a month and all the meat I can eat plus chicken, crab, and pig. Belongs to a Frenchman, Graziani. What a setup. Everything is here and all I got to do is put it back together again and that's what I've been doing for the past nineteen days. I tell you Peb, I ain't had time to have a shit and that's the truth, what with workin' on the trucks, pumps, water tanks. Have to kill all the wild bean and wild flower that's takin over. Place is so rundown you can't believe. I've got enough poison to kill all the people in the world. So far I ain't killed a thing except some cows, pigs, chickens, and ducks to eat. I got four hard head boys and if you ain't got your hands full with them there ain't a cow in the state of Texas . . .

November 14

Jacque's boat came in a month ago with fifteen drunken Wallis Islanders, one half-drunk Tahitian, one 900-kilo bull, and thirteen boys. Things were really fouled up. The bull almost tore the ship apart before they got him off. They tried to hoist him with the halyard and the mast broke at the spreaders. The bull circled the deck three times before deciding he'd had enough and jumped over the side and swam for shore. The captain got the brainstorm for a boy to jump in and grab the bull by the tail and swim ashore with him. It's just as well the boy didn't catch up to the bull.

I've been making copra this last month and this afternoon put the last bag on the boat. Can't say I'm sorry. What a headache! I'm the only planter in the Hebrides who never planted a coconut or made a ton of copra until just the other day. But can I tell you all you want to know about black boys and killing wild bean and blue flower. Now I'm all alone here again with just four hard-headed boys. The rest went back on the ship.

Peb, I tell you I'm getting fed up doing my own laundry and cooking and all the rest that goes with living alone. Emile (man we sold Mandalay *to) has got a sixteen-year-old sister who is just all hands and feet to get up here to Hog Harbor. But she's too good looking, I'm afraid. I want somebody to do the laundry, not me* do hers. And what with her speaking French it would be another *Titi* all over again.

I ain't seen the colors in the bay for three weeks. It's been raining all the time. One of the boys hit a tree with the truck and messed it up so bad it will take three weeks to fix it.

Peb, even though there's only four boys and me in Hog Harbor there's more life here than in Tahiti, Panama, Boston, or Gloucester. I never done nothin' spectacular enough in my life to deserve such a beautiful place. Speaking about life. Did you ever see a wild chicken take off and fly straight up and then level off and fly for a good half mile? Then there's something that lives out in the bush that I ain't seen yet that lays an egg as big as a baseball and tastes better than a hen's egg.

Got two rams and twelve sheep. I keep them fenced in what with all the sprayin' I'm doin'. I think the two rams are fed up being fenced in and about six times a day I'll hear two or three crashes like someone beatin' two baseball bats together. Sure enough, there's the two rams squared off buttin' heads like heaven won't have it. They'll square off two or three times standing about five paces from each other, give each other the eye and then go for it until the blood runs then walk off together like nothing happened. They just hang around knockin' each other's brains out. They take more beating than the three stooges in the movies. I don't know. I've felt the same way sometimes myself.

This morning I started the boys off sprayin' and took a walk over in the blue flower to see what they did last Friday. Up ahead of me I see a wild rooster, a hen and three little ones. They are maybe fifty yards ahead of me. Then I spots this little blue bastard. This little bastard just doesn't deserve to live. I watch him as he comes in to *make his pass at the mother hen. He doesn't say a word but swoops in and gives the hen a bang with his four-inch beak on her head and then takes off screaming at the top of his lungs. The rooster and the little ones take off but the mother hen is floundering around on the grounds. I go over and pick her up. She ain't dead yet but it is just minutes before she cashes in. The little bastard missed her eyes but there is a cut in the back of her head a quarter inch deep. I cut off her head and take her home for supper. I saw him take the eyes out of another hen. All I got to shoot him is a 45 and 30-30.*

Another day

I'm still thinking that I'll put the bite on Emile for his sister. What else can I do? I like Hog Harbor and I want to stay. I'm going down to Santo on Monday to see her and Emile. I got my lines all rehearsed. I had the rehearsal last night, just me and a jug of Rhum Negrita.

Another day

Well, I made a flying trip to Santo. I put the bite on Emile for his sister. He said it was fine by him as she wants to marry me and live in Hog Harbor, but they have to write the mother. Well, I'm back in the race again even though I got my money all on one horse and it's a French horse at that. Knowing it's a French horse I'll try not to get too excited.

Went over and had a look at Mandalay *while I was in Santo. They put her on a reef a month ago. She's had it! I feel sorry for the kid who bought her from Emile and put her on the reef. He's so much like Tony. He can't see any bad in anyone, only good, just like Tony.*

Two weeks later

*Heard from Emile and nothing doing on Miss Lovely Lovely.
I'm going to make a reservation on the mail boat to Noumea on
the twenty-eighth. I've been in Hog Harbor three months now and
I like the place just as much as ever. I'll do anything to stay here.
I'll try and latch onto some gal in Noumea that will listen to what
I have to say and bring her back here. I never went on an errand
like this before and I've got no idea how to go about it. I'll prob-
ably end up on the street down there in Noumea with a bag on
one shoulder and a club on the other. I'm only giving myself fifteen
days to look for a* wahine *so I guess I'd better shave this beard off.
The kind of gal I'm looking for wouldn't care if I had a beard but
I don't know if you can find that kind in just fifteen days.*

*I'm not bragging, Peb, but I'm doing a good job up here. There
isn't a friggin' thing on the place I can't do. I've worked harder in
these months up here than I ever have in my life. If I can find a
gal I'll be all set.*

*Will mail this in Noumea and will give you a squeak and let
you know how I make out with the bag and the club.*

*So long for now,
Bob*

Two weeks later

Dear Peb,

This hotel in Noumea is full of good-looking wahines. *Last
night I picked out one that owns up to thirty-seven and being Aus-
tralian. Nothing to look at but I think she's good people. She took*

me to this house that she lives in. She works for the Pacific Com-
mission translating French and Dutch into English. Well any-how,
along about 11:30 I asked her if she would like to come up to Hog
Harbor. We sleep on it and next morning she says yes.

She doesn't seem the kind of girl who would like a place like
HH, but she says she's been looking for just such a spot. Who knows,
she may be just the squaw. She's got a good education and has class.
Not too much class, I hope, for what would she do with it up there.
You don't need it to get along with me and the coconuts.

Three days later

Well, Peb, the gal gave away her job at the Pacific Commis-
sion and we're sweating out the next boat back to Santo. This gal is
OK. One of them kind that looks better in just an old black skirt
and shirt with the sleeves rolled up, and an old black bra you can
see thru, some open-toed shoes, and her hair just lying all over her
head any which way, and a smile that just won't wait. She looks
better that way than if she had on all the soup and nuts a million
other women wear.

Like I told her, we can't make a million dollars in HH but
we can live the way we want to live. She's been around enough in
the last thirty-seven years to know what she wants and I do too,
so we've got a good start. On top of everything she can and will
cook. With luck it looks as if I'll have a reward for the months I
put in at HH by myself. It will pay up for all the times I walked
down to the beach alone and thought how beautiful things would
be if I could just have someone that could share all the beauty of
the place with me.

I'm dreaming already—about 08:30 every morning up there after starting the boys off to work, I'll go back to the house for a cup of coffee and there this old gal will be in her black skirt and white shirt and her hair blown all over her face. I'll just sit down with her and see the easy way she sits in the chair and listen to the easy way she talks.

Well Peb, I've talked enough. Come on down to HH when you can for some good going living.

Yours, Bob

Weeks later: Bob writes from the New Hebrides.

Shipwreck

Dear Peb,

So much has happened since my last letter. Things didn't work out in Hog Harbor. Couldn't take Graziani anymore and the wahine *decided she didn't like coconuts as much as she thought she would so I gave up the job and got a boat to Tahiti and bought* Korrigan *that thirty-seven-foot sloop from the commander, and got an Aussie to sail her with me to Vila. Goddam Tahiti. If you ain't got a suitcase of money the bastards don't want you around. The port captain squeaked me that I had to go directly to Pago and can't stop any place en route or he'll send the gunboat after me. Well, I put into Bora Bora with a broken compass. I took a wrench and smashed it going in the pass. I had to practice my navigation some-where before I took off on the long stretches and no better place than Bora. The compass was too big anyhow. No place to mount it except right in the way. Sent a telegram to Émile in Santo to send me a new one. Worked like a crazy man on the navigation and took off for Suvorov and Pago when I got the compass.*

Hit Suvorov OK. Just ten months after Tom left, and what a change. The house is about down and rats all over. Killed five with one shot of the .410.

Seven days Suvorov to Pago. Stayed long enough to kick the Aussie off. He said I was a hard man because I told him for Chrissake get out of the sack and do something. Wouldn't even cook the coffee when I was at the tiller.

Sweet Christ, I had myself a hell of a singlehanded trip from Pago to the Hebrides. The first thing I did was see if she would heave-to. She wouldn't—cutter rig and sails stretched too much. But I had good weather for three days.

Then up comes a southeast blow that lasts the next three days. I steered with just the jib up. I soon saw Korrigan *had a rubber stick (mast). The top of it would work fore and aft a good four inches. Jesus! For three days what a beating we took. Did everything to make her heave-to but no soap. Just had to stay at the tiller. Then the wind eased off and I put a half-ass reef in the main. Half-ass because it's got a belly in it like a knocked-up cow and the roller reefing gadget is near worthless. Still had nine hundred miles to Vila. I put the boom in the boom gallows and eased off the sail to make a bigger belly in it, if that was possible. With the wind east or southeast she did all right by herself but as soon as it began to blow I had to be at the tiller.*

When the weather got rough the water came through the deck like a sieve. Had to keep the #214 tables and the almanac covered with a raincoat. I was in oilskins so much that I broke out with little bumps everywhere.

After I passed Fiji I put four more days and nights at the tiller. I never thought I could put more than four hours in at the tiller at one time, but when you have to you sure can. Man, you talk to yourself and the things you can think about. I only asked the Big Man up Top for help twice. I remember one Sunday 150 miles from Vila. All that night I had been at the tiller. Only thing she would do in a blow was lay broadside to the seas if you didn't stay at the tiller. Come that Sunday morning the wind was still making that noise in the rigging I had come to hate. To make my course I was running with a beam sea, easing her off before the big breaking ones. By two o'clock I was all in.

I'm sitting in the cockpit with a line around me fighting to keep awake, when all of a sudden I break out singing opera.

"Oh, calm the sea for Korrigan *and me, beat down the white caps for* Korrigan *and me," I sings [sic]. There were squalls all around. I've got her reefed so there's just a rag left. About five o'clock I run out of opera and am fightin' to keep awake again. I stand up to take a piss. My eyes feel like they're full of sand. Then, Jesus, up ahead I see a patch of green water as green as a Tuamotu lagoon. I'm 150 miles from nowhere. By the time I gathered myself I was over it. That patch kept me awake for an hour and I had quite a conversation with myself. "Did I see it or didn't I."*

Night came. The head is rolling around my shoulders like it ain't made fast at all. I'm saying to myself, "Sleep! Sleep! I'd give a year's pay just to sleep for half an hour." I pour a bucket of salt water over my head but man, I'm beyond even that. I've gotta do something. I untie the line around my waist, dash down and light the Primus, dash back to the tiller. While I'm waiting for the water to heat, damn me if I don't go to sleep, no line around me, and when I come to, I'm head and shoulders over the rail and she has jibbed. I sit at the wheel cursing boats, rubbing the knot on my back from hitting the rail. "Frig all boats, big and small."

But the scare of nearly falling overboard wears off quick and I'm right back in the groove again with my head rolling around my shoulders. I try the salt-water treatment again but before the bucket is set down I'm asleep. When I woke up there was the biggest, blackest island in front of me two hundred yards away. I kick the tiller hard over and ease the sheet so I am running parallel with this thing. If that ain't an island then I'm an aviator. "Bob, for Chrissake, slow down! You must be cracking up! We're a hundred miles from any land." But there it is, the white line of the beach and a great big headland to the south. I pour sea water over my head. "If that's a beach in there, where are the breakers? It can't be land! Nearest land is Pentecost, one hundred miles to the west. I'm wide awake now and reason with myself it can't be land. I haul in the sheet and head Korrigan for it. If it is land so much the better. Then I can sleep. Twice I was tempted to haul her off, as it looked more like an island every minute but then all of a sudden it seemed to lift and I could make out what it was. It was just a big black cloud hanging close to the water, and the beach was a light streak in the sky.

I slide the hatch and take a sweat at the clock. Hell! Only 9 p.m. I can't take this anymore. I go below and drop in the bunk. I grab a blanket and put it over my head to block out the eerie sound the wind is making. Then with the blanket over my head I heard this one coming. I braced myself in the bunk. She took it broadside *and from the noise on deck and the way things were happening down below I thought it was coming right through the deck, dinghy, skylight and all. It sounded like a battering ram. "Rass, the Big Man upstairs must be putting telephone poles in them now." When she hit, it threw me out of the bunk. Cursing I go on deck and grab the tiller. "You ornery bastard! You're only a hunk of wood! People say you've got a heart. I say nuts! Anything with a heart would never give me a beating like this. They say you're alive. Yeah, alive because some silly bastard like me keeps you alive. You don't have to sleep so you don't want me to sleep! I've lived with you for twenty days and twenty nights and I've never taken such a beating in my life from a hunk of wood."*

But anyhow, by the twenty-sixth I'm twenty-five miles from Vila, where I'm going to enter, then the wind goes from SE, E, NE, N, NW, to west. Jesus, right out of where I'm headed, and blowing like hell. I tried everything before I decided to run to Erromango. Four days and three nights at the tiller. I had to get somewhere quick before I collapsed. All night I ran with just the jib, my head rolling like a rubber ball again. Come 05:30 I could see Erromango fifteen miles off to the southeast. The wind had dropped to nothing but the seas were as big as ever. I was all in, so I went below and set the alarm for 7 a.m. She did everything but turn over, but I didn't care. I just died for the next six and a half hours. When I came to, the clock said 12:30. Three jumps and I'm on deck. But I'm one jump too late for the reef is just twenty feet away. I'm broadside to the reef and seas as well. One more swell and I hit like a ton of bricks. Two more swells and I'm in on the reef twenty feet. I quickly gather some gear while I'm sweating out what's going to happen next, she flops from her portside to starboard and I'm in the water with the ship's papers, a pair of shoes, four cans of beans, the .410 pistol, $160, and the watch in a glass jar—everything in a sea bag. I still got on the rain gear and the big green sweater. The seas pounded in and pushed me farther up the reef but when they sucked out I was sucked back too. About the second wave that broke over me, I let go the bag. Between mouthfuls of salt water I said to myself, "Well, Bob, I guess this is it. You're on your way out!" I was eighty or ninety yards from the beach.

But somehow I finally made it. I crawled as far up the beach as I could and put my arms around a big rock and rested my head on it. My ass was still in the water but I couldn't crawl another inch.

I stayed that way for over an hour before I got strength to roll over and over, away from the water. I sat against a rock and heaved up a quart of salt water. My feet were all cut up with the coral, and with the salt water in them they felt on fire. I cut the sleeves out of the sweater and bandaged them up. I caught myself saying, "Man alive! Now I can sleep!" I looked over at the Korrigan where she was beating herself to death on the reef. "Go ahead, you bastard," I yelled. "Now you're getting some of your own medicine. I guess you thought it was fun these last four days. Well, how do you like it now?" I just had to say it.

When I get rid of the spots in front of my eyes I look around. I am in a bay and on the farther side I notice three big caves like great overgrown quonset huts, maybe five or six hundred feet high. Their sides are covered with green but the faces are a dark gray and the entrances are jet black. Spookier places I never see. Any minute I'm expecting to see ten war canoes put out from the beach over there filled with natives with spears and shields.

Korrigan *was well up on the reef by now but still rolling around in five feet of water. I tried standing up but the pain kept me on my knees. The cuts had dried and were full of salt. Eventually I made my slow way, walking on the sides of my feet, over to where the boat was. I got aboard and gathered a few supplies. That night I slept under an overhanging rock up from the water. I lit a fire, wrapped up in two wet blankets among land crabs, mosquitoes and spiders, and I came to next morning hungry as a bitch wolf. All I wanted was oatmeal with heaps of sugar. I just couldn't get enough sugar. For the next five days I ate oatmeal and sugar four times a day.*

Sundown the third day I began to think I was going to have to walk out of there, but I didn't know how. My feet were two pieces of beefsteak. But I was getting my share of sleep. Next morning a native came along with a dog. In pidgin English he told me that he and his buddies were cutting sandalwood and those caves were their headquarters. They came down there every night but my fire was too far under a rock for them to see it. They were going to Dillon Bay the next day in a boat, so I asked for a ride.

The boat came over next morning to pick me up. It was a real native lash-up. It's ten miles to Dillon Bay but that thing didn't look capable of running ten minutes. Two boys were bailing to beat hell, one boy held the rudder in place while another wrestled with the tiller. The clutch was shot, so there was a boy with two sticks pressing in on either side of the clutch band. Still another had two hands on the carburetor, as the bolts were shot. Another joker had found the American flag off Korrigan. *He tied this to a fish spear and held the spear between his knees, looking up at the flag every minute to be sure the wind held it out straight. The exhaust pipe had rusted off where it went through the hull so only some of the cooling water hit the hole and went out. The rest fell into the bilge. The gas tank was a five-pound bully-beef tin with a hose coming out the bottom. No lid on the thing, and still another boy held it on his lap. Sure took a lot of boys to run that boat.*

The engine stopped three times on the way over to the caves and we ran out of gas so had to row the rest of the way. I ended up spending three nights in the caves before we got away for Dillon. We made three starts. The first try they busted the rudder. The next day they hit a rock and folded up two blades on the propeller. The next time with everybody at their stations—two on the tiller, two bailing, one on the carburetor, one holding the bully-beef tin, and one on the flag—we made it to Dillon.

From Dillon I came up here to Émile's place on Santo on a sandalwood schooner, and Peb, right now I'm fed up with all boats. After my feet healed up I went back down to Erromango and tried to salvage Korrigan. *Six times I propped her up to patch her, and six times the sea knocked her down. So I finally sold all the gear off her and got a little something for the hull. So that's the end of* Korrigan.

Right now I'm working on Émile's machinery, but I'm looking around for a plantation somewhere out in the bush I can run myself. I'm still determined to get myself my own plantation, no matter what. Rass, I don't want to make a million dollars, all I want to do is live.

Peb, since we sold Mandalay *I feel a little lost and that's putting it mildly. I have been alone a lot since then. I like people but the people I've met in the last year, I would rather be alone than be with them. I don't know what you and I had in common but I ain't found it in anybody here in Santo. None of these people down here know what I'm talking about. I can't seem to take civilization. I'm fed up with Santo. Down there in Erromango, trying to salvage* Korrigan, *I was living on the beach under my favorite rock in the wilderness and so friggin' happy to get away from civilization I could hardly stand it.*

Well, enough of this.
As ever, Bob

Bob's adventures continued after he put *Korrigan* on the reef. With the insurance from *Korrigan* he bought a rugged fifty-foot sailboat in Noumea for a trading vessel. It had no mast but with his usual ingenuity he bought a telephone pole for $6 and whittled it to shape by hand. With it he carried copra and supplies around the New Hebrides until 1957, when lying in Vila Harbor the boat blew up. Somehow, though no one could believe it, he managed to swim to shore, and was found on the beach, passed out. He had lost several toes, lost an ear, and was covered with third-degree burns. He was in the hospital five months undergoing skin grafts. He went from 170 pounds down to 130. The tycoon, R.J. Reynolds, who had interests there, befriended him and paid all his hospital bills.

Eventually he was transferred to a hospital in Auckland for further treatment. During his Auckland hospitalization he was attended by a nineteen-year-old nurse, Marie, and when released he married her. This was 1958.

But his boating days weren't over. With insurance from the cargo vessel Bob bought *Typee*, a rugged double-ended cutter that slept six. After extensive work Bob and Marie moved aboard to their new home. She continued nursing and he did odd jobs around the waterfront. The following year, with Marie pregnant, they set sail for Tahiti. They landed ten weeks later, stopping at Nuku'alofa, Tonga, Pago Pago, and Huahine. Their son Guy was born in May 1959, and when Bob recovered from a bout of malaria they sailed on to Honolulu. There, for ten months, Bob drove a tug for a construction company before they sailed on to Mexico, as that was the route to catch the best equatorial current. Then it was up to Panama where Bob drove a canal mule, then decided the job was not for him, so tried to sell the boat in the States, and when that failed they ended up in Jamaica hoping to run a charter business in the Caribbean. This failed to materialize so they sailed back to New Zealand via Honolulu. Home again, they lived aboard the boat for many years until moving ashore to the Whangarei district at the northern end of New Zealand, where they spent the rest of their lives.

Bob was a dear friend, great companion, and shipmate. I will always remember his words, "I don't want to make a million dollars; I just want to live."

The *Mandalay*, Tahiti

Lapland reindeer with his sleigh

CHAPTER FOURTEEN

Norway

Meanwhile, Tony and I transversed an ocean, wandered up through Europe, and eventually reached Norway. Miles are one way to measure distance, but from here to there is more than just a linear movement connecting one space to another. It also changes one's mindset by closing a door to the past and opening another, to who knows where.

As it turned out, behind the door to Norway would lie a future more significant than anyone could have expected. The country of the midnight sun proved a mansion of many doors, opening to wondrous chambers that eventually led to a room holding a person who was to remain in my life for years to come.

Per Host, our documentary film friend from the Galapagos, was the first to welcome us. A large man with a booming smile, he had traveled among many cultures, written a book, and enjoyed his travels with mirth and schnapps. He had two suits; one for when he was home and his waist grew rounder and another for his expeditions when he traditionally lost twenty pounds. He was married to a former Swedish model. Underneath her blond hair and striking features lurked a mind that fluttered like a butterfly. Aniti was entertainment, an endearing person we came to enjoy immensely.

Per had a documentary to make in Lapland, starting in a month. In the interim, he suggested Tony and I take the mail packet up the west coast to the Lofoten Islands, site of the cod fishery. He would meet me there for a little filming before traveling farther along the coast to Alta, where we would go inland to Kautokeino, a little town in the heart of Lapland. I would help with the filming, take stills, and be a general handyman.

The packet carried half cargo and half passengers, stopping at every little town, many only accessible by water. We docked at small wharfs, where people and cargo swarmed off and on, and then we steamed away to the next. A family aura permeated the ship and we spent many hours in the pilothouse talking with the officers and crew.

One morning after several weeks of incredible scenery and coastal life, the jagged bastion of the Lofoton Islands rose from the sea two miles off the bow. All around us boats were fishing for cod. There were large purse netters, the smaller gillnetters and long liners, and then the babies of the fleet—the hand liners. These little craft were built on the old Viking lines with their bows and sterns swept up in a graceful arc. They were proud little ships whose heritage went back to the beginning of sea travel. Their ancestors had braved unknown oceans and sighted lands never seen by Europeans before.

Tony was transfixed, watching as they danced lightly on the white caps, tossing first their bows and then their sterns like little hobby-horses on a lark. Suddenly he turned to me. "I've got to have one. I've fallen in love."

I smiled condescendingly, accustomed to his whims. But to be polite inquired, "What would you do with it? Aren't you headed for the States?"

"I'll sail it, of course. I can take it through the canals of France then back across the Atlantic to America."

"Tony Leif Ericson Richardson," I added sarcastically. But he didn't hear me, pacing up and down the deck, pulling viciously at this mustache. Within an hour he had plans for the interior drawn out, the route he would take, and a sketch of his private ensign. Without giving me a glance, he mounted to the bridge, disappearing into the pilothouse. Much later he emerged, all smiles. "The captain told me where I can have one built. I'll be getting off at the next stop and taking a boat back to Bindal." He smiled, almost sticking out his tongue. "When I fall in love it is always sudden. Stop in on your way back from Lapland. I'll show you a ship to make you envious."

Half a day later I said adieu to Tony, and explored the Lofoten fisheries with Per, who had brought along his dear friend Gunnar Rollefsen, head of all the Norwegian fisheries and marine research. Gunnar was a fascinating, charming man, a combination of scientist, humanist, and storyteller. He talked about the fish as if they were human, saying his studies of them had increased his knowledge of people.

Hearing him talk about the mating of the cod was like listening to a love story. The male gently bumps the female on her side. There is no visible reaction but in cod language she says either yes or no. If no, the male swims away. If yes, he rests his head on hers and they swim together, male on top of the female. Then the male sinks under the female and turns belly up so their orifices are together. Eggs are fertilized and float to the surface. If the Lofoten cod eggs, in those golden days of fishing, were laid in a line they would reach the sun as one fish roe contained three million eggs.

He went on to tell how intelligent the cod were. They quickly learned how to avoid purse-net capture, sounding before the net closed, necessitating closing the purse quicker. Cods in a tank for study at his research institute in Bergen had a shield all around except for peepholes. The cod used the peepholes more than their observers. They could tell when a stranger entered the room. How they did was a mystery. With known people they would take food from the hand. When they were nervous their oxygen consumption went up and they changed colors, with dark and bright appearing spots. Oxygen control served them well when being transported live to market. Other fish in the same environment had a high mortality, but the cod could decrease oxygen intake when stressed.

He told of a little cod he had in his tank that became pregnant after only two years, a rarity. In the tank was also a large sculpin with a huge ugly mouth. When it came up behind the little cod, and opened its mouth, three other cod would quickly swim between the two. It was some kind of sexual play between cod and sculpin and the others got jealous.

One night at dinner in Svolver, the major town, Gunnar told us about his long-standing friend of twenty-five years, known as the Lofoten Blacksmith. He had been on a British destroyer during the war. One day the destroyer had its bow blown off by a torpedo. The blacksmith went down to the powder room, which was bulk headed off from the bow, and somehow, with his acetylene torch, cut off the rest of the dangling bow, then built a reinforcing structure so the warship could limp back into port.

Gunnar said he had a poet's understanding of steel with no formal structural training. His only wish now at sixty-six was to die without debt, but with failing health he was unable to keep up his blacksmith shop. Gunnar had told him, "Your emotions are your strength and your kindness your weakness."

One day a fisherman brought him his boat engine that a skilled marine mechanic said was unfixable. The result turned out to be a masterpiece of reconstruction that became known throughout the islands, "a work of art and love," as Gunnar said. "I felt it a sacrilege to be paid for a job I loved doing so much," he told Gunnar.

The people, the fishery, the place itself, comprised a wonderful story, starting with the three currents converging off the west coast of Norway that resulted in a greater concentration of herring and cod than anywhere in the world. The year before we were there, the catch was three billion pounds! Today, the fishery is no more. The cod have been fished out with the advent of large ocean trawlers and climate change.

It was a scene to remember, being surrounded by six thousand boats and thirty thousand fishermen in that tightknit little group of islands. A good catch for the day with a purse netter was 35,000 kilos, with gill netters 10 to 15,000, with long liners 15 to 20,000, and with hand liners with one man, 100 fish or 400 kilos. Each method was given its own area and time people could fish. When one fisherman was asked why he didn't change his boat over to catch more fish he replied, "I love my boat too much to damage it for more codfish."

It was stirring seeing the fishermen return to port after a day of work, standing in the bow, their rugged, solemn faces filled with the serenity of the out-of-doors.

Once the boats were in port, the fish cleaning was close to a ballet. One man made an incision like a surgeon, touching none of the organs. Another stripped livers into a barrel, another did the same with roe, and guts went into another barrel and stomachs into yet another. The stomachs were frozen and sent to France to clear the sediment in wine, while others were salted and put on racks to dry in the spring.

One evening I watched a boy of about seven and his sister with their yellow oilskins cleaning out fish guts in what seemed a charnel house of blood. Those cherubic faces radiating smiles, happiness, and pride in what they were doing were as uplifting as the islands rising from the sea.

Finishing, the fishermen would clean themselves and their surroundings with a hose. The last were the mittens. They, too, were hosed, then put on the ground and pounded with their owners' rubber boots. This was known as "the cleaning dance of the dirty mittens."

Those precious days in Lofoten were another wonder in the Land of the Midnight Sun.

⎯⎯∿⎯⎯

After "the dance," it was on to Hammerfest where we took another boat up the Alta Fjord to the little town of Alta. Here we disembarked and boarded a Canadian snowmobile to Kautokeino, an outpost in the heart of Lapland. This took eight hours. We were at capacity with seventeen people, thirteen adults, and four children. The terrain was a vast plateau of frozen tundra with only a few scraggly trees and an occasional ridge to break the monotony of the vast snow fields. Twenty miles from town we came to a stop to pick up bread baked by a Lapp family (also called Sami) who supplied the hotel. Afterward, we came to our first reindeer with a Lapp urging it and a sleigh off the road to let us pass.

The government lodge sat on a hill overlooking the village. From my window I watched the Laplanders come and go bundled in reindeer furs and their bright-colored dress. They hurtled down the slope on sleighs pulled by their panting deer, swerving wildly back and forth across the icy track.

Lapland 1955

They were small people with gnomish faces, looking like Santa Clauses without beards. Most of them were bowlegged and had a rolling walk that came from a lifetime spent on skis shuffling across those barren, treeless plains.

They were a happy, fun-loving people. I delighted in watching the children skiing down the incline by the inn. There was a small jump and out into space they would fling themselves, frequently losing a ski in midair, landing in a snowy tangle of arms and legs and merriment. Frequently they would lie down in the snow and drop off to sleep by merely pulling their heads and arms into their reindeer parkas like self-sufficient turtles. They wore boots that curled up in front and hooked into the simple single-strap ski binding. Going up an incline they let one ski slouch off to the side for traction. For socks they gathered different varieties of grasses. Stuffed into the boots, the grass and moss kept feet toasty warm. Often one would see them skiing down the slopes in just their boots, holding out arms to the sides for balance.

When not helping Per I would take ski trips through the surrounding country, stopping to chat in sign language with the Lapps tending their herds and watching the deer paw away the snow to eat the tundra reindeer moss. As I went by their tents they would ask me in to share a sugar cube with a few drops of ether poured on it. It was definitely an acquired taste, but it did give one a mellow feeling.

On reindeer grazing trips Lapps measure distance by "coffee boils." That place could be two boils or three boils, depending on whether they had to journey up the terrain or ski down.

Sami families living away from town came to Kautokeino once a year to settle all reindeer disputes. One was going on when we were there. There were boundaries and fences and often distances to separate the herds. Sometimes deer got mixed with another herd in their roaming. Meetings were held to sort out the intermixing. A family could possess several thousand animals. There was also stealing. A man would steal and when his neighbor found out would steal back. A couple's daughter got married and the husband asked his wife how she liked her new son-in-law. The response was, "He's not very rich but he steals well."

We heard about the case of a Lapp who was a notorious thief, taking far more than the accepted amount. One day the neighbors came to his tent with a rope and strung him up from a tree, hoisting him five times off the ground until he confessed to his crimes. He remained alive by grabbing the rope to keep from choking. His wife came out and said, "Please don't hang my husband, but if you do please take him down into the woods where I can't see."

I enjoyed learning about the Lapp culture. They were a superstitious folk, placing scissors in bed so as not to dream. The previous year a man had drowned. The fellow who found his skeleton thought it was his ghost and shot it with his shotgun.

A reindeer untrained for pulling was worth 250 kroner—a trained one 500 (kroner were worth about $.14). A normal herd increased 25 percent a year.

The children had their special play. They would take frozen red foxes and stick them in different positions to play games when the pelt price was low—only ten kroner when we were there.

They would make snares in the low bushes to catch ptarmigan, the arctic partridge, and two children would play at lassoing, one holding a set of horns over his head and running around the other. It was a necessary skill in everyday life.

Taken with their reindeer robes called pesks, I bought one from Johan A. Sara, one of the Lapp chiefs who had two to three thousand deer. I wanted to wear it to a party at the inn that night. Sara said, "No! If you wear it only a moment it will be secondhand and you can never sell it." I asked if the chief's wife would be happy with the 300 kroner I paid for it. "No, now she will have to start all over again."

Pesk or no pesk, the party that night was comical. There was some kind of bingo with a popgun and a target. A big orange cake was the prize. Lapps were going from room to room playing bingo, eating cake, or fornicating with the girls. Their laughter made one's heart sing.

There was the famous story of Nansen taking two Lapps with him on his historic crossing of the Greenland ice cap. A huge welcoming crowd awaited them in Oslo on their return. "Isn't that a beautiful sight all these people coming to welcome us!" Nansen said.

One Lapp replied, "Ah yes, if only they were reindeer."

Per and I had a conversation one night with one of the biggest reindeer owners in the area. He spoke excellent Norwegian and had a very gentle face and demeanor. Per asked how he spoke so well. "I learned it in jail in Oslo. I killed a man with a bottle. Of course, it was an accident."

I loved going skiing in the afternoons by myself in the absolute stillness of the Arctic. Nothing moved. A sense of vast space came with the sinking sun. At utter peace, I felt reluctant to return to the hotel. One windy day, skiing alone through that wilderness, out of sight of any man, animal or house, I imagined being back on *Mandalay* again. The blowing snow became the twin spinnakers billowing, obstructing the sea ahead, while the moaning wind of the frozen Arctic was the sighing of the rigging. When I came to a hill with a few stunted trees, it was as if I had arrived at Suvorov Island—Tom must be on the other side, I thought. I climbed the grade, powered through the pass, and on the summit saw a Lapp tent huddled behind a clump of bushes. Its owner waved to me, beckoning eagerly. Kicking off my skis I entered the tent and shook his hand, calling him Harry. The sooty skins of the tepee, the smell of rancid reindeer fat, and the blackened pots and pans were a reminder of the cabin of our friend's yacht *Molly* in distant Taa Huka in the Marquesas. The Sami handed me a lump of sugar dipped in ether. It was the Galapagos puro mixed with Karo syrup that we used to drink with the Angermeyers.

As I waited for the coffee to boil, I looked around the Sami's austere surroundings, wondering how anybody could live where the sun never shone for three months, where the mercury dropped to forty-five below zero, and the only music was the howling of the wolves or the crackle of a feeble faggot fire. I felt a restlessness descend. For the first time came the thought that the world was round and eventually one returned home again.

—⁓—

The month passed. It came time for the spring migration to the coast where the deer would swim the Alta Fjord, a mile and a quarter wide, to the islands on the other side and their summer pasture to get away from the bot flies that arrived in the warm months. We met them there to witness a scene never to be forgotten. The herd was driven down around the small mountain to a corral by the water's edge. Babies, born during the trek, were rowed along with their mothers and other sick ones, across the fjord.

For the rest, a crowd gathered waving sticks and shouting, driving the deer into the water. There was a lead reindeer on a halter tied behind a boat to entice the herd to follow. On several crossings we saw the herd spook and turn back to shore. It was quite a sight to see close to a thousand reindeer swimming across with the rowboats containing the sick and young alongside. We waited all one day for the big event, but no deer came down. We learned that the boy and girl shepherding them had stopped for sex and then fallen asleep. One couldn't help but like people who took their hard life so casually.

Eventually we bade goodbye to our Sami friends. Per returned to Oslo while I took the mail packet down the coast on the chance of finding Tony. I didn't have much time as the boat only stopped an hour in Bindal, but I asked the first pedestrian I met if he knew of a mustached American building a boat. "You mean Tony," the man said. "You'll find him in that second house to the right. His hotel burned down. Now he's staying with the dentist."

I hurried to the indicated door and knocked. Footsteps sounded and there stood Tony, one ankle bandaged.

"Tony! Wonderful to see you. What's this about your hotel?"

"Burned to the ground. I had to jump."

"Were you hurt?"

"Not seriously," he replied, hobbling into the living room. "Just sprained my ankle. But I broke five bottles of scotch and this is a dry town. I had them sent all the way from Trondheim to celebrate the laying of the keel."

"Did you lose all your gear?"

"Yes. But I've got some real news, Peb."

"Giving up alcohol?"

He gave me a withering look. "I'm getting married."

"Don't joke about things like that," I said. "Haven't much time. Boat leaves in an hour."

"Don't believe it myself. But it's true. We're getting married in three weeks."

I sat down heavily in a chair. "What's she like?" I asked weakly.

"Her name is Anne-lo. She is so sweet she drives me nuts. Got all the good living stuff. None of those impossible qualities you find in most women. Not pretty but wholesome in every way."

"What does she do?" I asked.

"Radio operator in the Norwegian Merchant Marine. She's practical. Can sail a boat, cooks superbly, loves to travel. And she's strong as anything, a good sport, and just full of culture. I'd be an absolute dope to pass her up."

"What does she think about your Viking boat and cruise?"

"To be honest, Peb, I think she fell in love with the idea of the boat before she did me. She thinks we can make a living traveling around writing about it—almost without working. I'll take the pictures and she will do the writing. She's an excellent journalist."

The mail packet's horn blew for departure. I shook Tony's hand, gave him a hug, and ran to the wharf.

—◦—

Tony married Anne-lo, built the Viking boat, calling her *Julie* after his mother, and cruised the canals of France. They had two children and bought a place outside of Oslo where they lived for ten years. Then he grew tired of being a parent in Norway. Ten years was a long time for Tony to remain in one situation. They divorced, and he moved to Maine, buying a house near where I eventually settled. My wife, whom I met in Norway (more on that in a moment), and I were extremely fond of Anne-lo and remained dear friends until her death many years later. Tony married a woman not the equal of Anne-lo and we saw him less and less as age eroded his earlier carefree years. He died young, and that closed another story. Bjorn, one of his offspring, remained in Oslo. The other, Lars, moved to the States, and to this day runs a restaurant on the West Coast, visiting me occasionally. Tony, like Bob and Gus, was a wonderful part of my life. A conflicted character who bore his brain injury well, he rose above the crowd, creating his own space, allowing us a visit from time to time. Often, I can imagine him cavorting with the angels and leprechauns when I look up at the sky at night with clouds moving across the moon.

Liv at her loom

CHAPTER FIFTEEN

Liv

In Oslo my thoughts were turned from Tony by a call from Per. "Pebble, Aniti and I want to give you a little party before you return to the States. Just a few people and we have invited a girl who lived in the Marquesas you might enjoy swapping anecdotes with. How about seven on Friday?"

Idly I wondered who the woman was. Some kind of scientist probably, interested in facts and figures. We would talk about Polynesian taboos and sex customs. Well, it was only for an evening. I had a plane ticket the following day for New York.

Come Friday evening Per pointed out his guest across the room, giving me time for a quick appraisal as we threaded our way through the crowd. She was a surprise—certainly no dried-up cerebral type. There was something wild and untamed about her. She didn't have the languid grace, the dark mysterious eyes of the South Pacific *wahine*, or the golden skin that had attracted me so much. She was blue-eyed and white-skinned. Her brown hair was unruly as a tropical jungle. And there was something far from ordinary in the face. Suddenly I felt shy. My mind was already in the States, settling into Cobble Court, back in that precious past with Margaret and her dog that didn't like me.

In fact, I had been thinking a lot about her in Lapland while skiing alone in that great stillness where her presence was as elemental as the subtle sense of movement of the continental platelets beneath my feet.

As I made my way toward the woman she stamped her foot, apparently in response to a remark made by a man standing next to her. I liked that. She was her own free agent, not a follower, and her faced radiated kindness and humor.

She took my hand with a mischievous grin. "So you are the man who lost his heart to the South Pacific."

"I guess that's me," I said inanely.

"I'm Liv," she said. "I left a piece of my heart there also. Were you in the Marquesas?"

"Yes"

"Oh good. Let's sit down. Tell me all about it. Which did you like best, the islands or the people?"

"It's hard to think of them separately," I stammered, adding quickly, "What were you doing down there?" I wanted her to do the talking.

"I used to be married to a scientist," she said. "We lived on Fatu Hiva for a year, next to a cozy old cannibal called Terai. My husband looked for artifacts while I enjoyed Terai."

"Enjoyed?"

"Every day he would feel my forearm and tease me that I was too skinny to make a good roast. The forearm of a woman is the sweetest, he told me. My friend preferred his nine days old—when it was just like porridge. You could see his teeth had fallen out."

I was beginning to feel very comfortable. This was my kind of talk. "Were they still really eating each other while you were there?"

"No, not really," Liv replied. "The old man said a good corpse was hard to find. He complained bitterly about the changing times. Relatives were guarding their deceased kin too carefully and everyone was getting a taste for bully beef in tins. Long pig was rather out of fashion."

"You never worried then," I said, enjoying this woman.

"No," she said impishly. "Even Terai thought I wouldn't be worthwhile to cook. Just too skinny."

"You look good to me," I said, then mentally kicked myself for being an ass. Her eyes sparkled dangerously. They had warmth that made me slightly dizzy. I almost said it would be nice to be in the same pot with her but caught myself in time. I wanted to say something brilliant but nothing came. All I could do was look at her stupidly, thinking how nice it would have been if we could have met before my last night in Norway.

"Pebble," she said, interrupting my thoughts, "is it only the west coast and Finnmark you've seen of my wonderful little country?"

"Yes, but it seems a long way from here to Kautokeino and two very different worlds. I did enjoy the Sami and their culture. A charming people. Their outlook on life is rather Polynesian."

"You haven't been to Lillehammer then! That's the heart of Norway. I have a cabin there, high on a hill—on top of the world. If you came for a visit you might see the Nisse, the little gnome with the red cap, who lives in my neighbor's barn. Every Christmas Eve the farmer puts out porridge for him so the little chap won't knock over milk cans, tease the cows, or do other mischief.

"And there is the Balberg troll who lives in the shaggy mountain hill. You could get acquainted with him. And there are moose right outside the door of my cabin, eating the tops of the little pine trees."

She had my attention right by the throat. "Go on," I urged. This woman was right out of my storybook.

"I could take you up Nevelfjell Mountain on a clear day and you could see all the most beautiful mountains of Norway—Rondane, and Jotunheimen where Per Gynt was lured into the bowels of the earth by a hulder. You know Per Gynt?"

"Yes." I was on solid ground here. "He's an old friend."

"And now it is spring," Liv rushed on. "You could see the black cock doing their mating dance, going cock-a-loo-loo-loo, fluffing out their feathers, proud as anything."

"I'd give a lot to come but I'm leaving for the States in the morning," I said, and I meant it.

Suddenly I wanted to tell about my country—share with her all the things I loved. On impulse I said, "In America I could show you how to call an alligator out of a Georgia swamp, and I could teach you to bleat like a fawn so the mother would come running. I could show you raccoons washing their food in a little stream at twilight, or mullet jumping in the moonlight."

Abruptly I became aware of other people in the room intruding on our precious privacy. I wanted to be with this woman—alone.

"Let's go to the kitchen and hunt up something to eat," I suggested.

Once out there amid the clutter of dirty plates, glasses, and empty bottles, I got down on my hands and knees to show her how a sea turtle comes up on the beach at night, digs a hole with her flipper, lays her eggs, covers the nest again, and slowly returns to the ocean, from whence she came. I made alligator grunts, hawk cries, and fawn bleats. Then she flapped her arms and cockalooed like a capercaillie.

No longer were we in a city house. We walked the mountains at dawn, sat by an inland lake at dusk, or padded softly along a lonely beach at night watching the leviathans from the sea perpetuate the mystery of further generations.

Later I took her home. We stood on the steps. I could hear her two teenage boys inside. It was an awkward moment, neither of us knowing how to say goodbye. Then she put her hand on my shoulder. "Thank you for a wonderful evening," she said.

"Better than anything in the South Pacific," I replied, taking her by the hand. At the bottom of the steps I turned. She was looking at me. I imagined her eyes were misting and I did a little Tahitian dance. She flapped her arms and waved.

I walked through the night happy. Very, very happy. There was a moon shining down. I imagined it was smiling, too. I felt the tectonic platelets stirring under my feet again.

Next morning the gray Atlantic scrolled by five miles beneath the wings. Was I going home or just changing continents once again? Across what bridge of understanding lay home, making me think back to that night with Gus Angermeyer in the Galapagos surrounded with the sighing of the great turtles under a starry heaven?

Johnnie the bear

CHAPTER SIXTEEN

The Vinalhaven Bear

The coming of the bear to a Penobscot Bay island was circuitous, man induced as it was, spurred by this new love for my Norwegian beauty. It began with my return to Maine, several weeks after that momentous night in Oslo, when I was back in the house, big as a ship's cabin, overlooking Hurricane Sound. Margaret had bequeathed her special corner of Vinalhaven to me in her will, and it had been two long years and many sea miles since I had seen The Only House. Yet with that first glimpse of Liv, my mind placed her there, with me, irrefutable as the tide. During our first momentous conversation I told her of The Only House and Margaret Wise Brown. Later in our letters I also told her of Peter the deer, who lived with me that summer: How he had a cowlick behind his head where the fur came together from all directions. How he could rotate his ears almost 180 degrees. How he would stand like a ballerina on his rear legs to nibble my earlobe without touching another part of my body. How I loved that deer. Together we put new sills under The Only House. Peter was enchanted with the hammer. He would bang it on the ground or chew on the wooden handle when not butting me from behind to gain my attention. I had to saw off his spiked horns from sheer distress. His favorite food was

Quaker Oats and he once went to jail for being a bad boy on main street in Carvers Harbor trying to hump a maiden. In turn, Liv told me of her own wild animal. "We had a wonderful bear in Canada at Little Norway during the war."

Liv's bear was named Peck. He also liked Quaker Oats but never went to jail. We parted that first evening, not knowing then that a bear would soon come to Vinalhaven, but certain that other things no less momentous had been unleashed. I had returned to the United States the following morning, but the broad Atlantic was no barrier to my thoughts of a blue-eyed girl, who loved bears, living in a distant Norwegian valley. From then on time alternately stood still or raced ahead as several reunions and separations and letters made us realize that together we were one, and alone, deer and bears did not have the same allure.

In the beginning we wrote back and forth over a string of months. My greetings went from "Dear Liv" to "Darling" to "Darling future wife." Alas, there were obstacles to overcome, starting with the reality that we had met for only one brief evening. Liv was divorced from Thor Heyerdahl, but they had two sons, Thor and Bamse, now teenagers who couldn't be left without at least one parent in charge. Thor the father was often abroad, so the boys needed their mother in Norway. As for me, I was wary of another entanglement with Stella and Margaret still heavy on my mind. Yet I knew the time had come to think about having a family with a person to be happy with in the years ahead. My father had an expression for it: "getting broody." So it went—the corresponding back and forth, up and down and sideways. "I don't want to hurt you if it doesn't work," became her theme. Mine retorted with, "I will take the chance." That brief meeting in

Oslo when the tectonic plates shifted beneath my feet had left a seemingly deep impression on us both.

Anxious months prevailed until she crossed the Atlantic to see firsthand what there was between us. We spent idyllic months together on Cumberland Island, alone. After she left, the letters turned more urgent in "the darling future wife" period, with sentences like, "For a Christmas present I offer you my love. That is the most precious thing I can give." Thus it came to pass that, soon enough, in the spring of 1955, a plea telegram went out from The Only House.

"Liv! You are sorely needed. Marriage set for June. Stop. The Only House waiting."

The reply came back and it was positive. My stars were now aligned, irrevocably pointing to a certain garbage dump in Canada where bears were known to bat around tin cans at dusk, as I needed a wedding present. A gift suitable for a Viking queen. I knew that a bear was necessary.

Swift as the hour, I bid goodbye to the red squirrel scolding from the spruce, untied the punt from the pulley line, and rowed toward the distant point. I was bear-bound.

It is true. Confronted by love, barriers topple. Three days later a young man presented himself at the U.S. Customs on the Canadian border with a cage on the backseat, and was queried, "What have you to declare?"

"One small black bear."

"Value?"

"Five dollars."

The grizzled eyebrows arched and the uniform retreated into its bunker to open a bible of sorts. I waited, wondering where bears came in the international order of things. Somewhere between baskets, brandy, and brassieres, perhaps.

Customs returned. "Where are you taking the bear?"

"Vinalhaven. An island off the Maine coast."

His face was as inscrutable as a lobsterman eyeing a summer person's yacht. "Is the bear for resale? Zoo? Animal farm?"

"No! He's a wedding present. I'm to be married in a month."

His mustache twitched. "Son, if that's the case, bears are duty free. Good thing you didn't choose diamonds."

There was a snarl from the backseat, accompanied by the sound of claws against wire. I called the bear Johnnie. He was not a cuddly teddy. His baby fur was matted and scraggly. His eyes were right out of the deep woods. Considering his market price of a dollar a pound, his value lay only in the eyes of his beholder. He clawed, snarled, and growled all the way to The Only House. During the crossing on the Vinalhaven ferry, matrons clutched their children and the natives dropped into a hunting crouch. But I was young, in my own special world, and rowing up Hurricane Sound with Johnnie in the cage was truly a blissful moment. Even Johnnie momentarily forgot his bearish tantrums at the introduction to a world of water, floating objects, and screaming gulls. The wedding gift was in hand. Now all that was wanting was the bride.

Johnnie and I were cast together like two people on a raft. Once a week I'd row after supplies; otherwise we saw just the lobster boats, once in a while the herring fishermen, and always the gulls. Something had to give and it was Johnnie. Like Peter the deer, he discovered Quaker Oats. I became Father Oats. He graduated from a cage to a leash, then to no restraints. Handled at first with gloves, he soon came to tolerate my touch and then having his belly scratched. His hair turned black and shiny. His muzzle went from being pointed like a

coon's to more like that of a black Lab turned up at the end. He would
stand on his hind legs to look around, and in very little time I considered him an endearing personality worthy of my bride. He would lie
on his back amid the Indian paintbrushes, clasp an errant daisy in his
paws, and delicately dismember it petal by petal, humming the while.
He liked to hide in a tree and pounce when I walked near. Swimming
was also an adventure, but I never did get him to retrieve. What was
his was Johnnie's and he would brook no interference. However, he
did like people as long as "people" meant me. He was basically a shy
soul, but there lurked a jealous streak as we shall see.

The bear was now in place, somewhat domesticated. Only the
bridegroom was pacing back and forth along the water's edge awaiting an arrival message from across the sea. It came one day via peapod with old Maynard standing up rowing not more than four strokes
to the minute, smoke erupting from his pipe like exhaust from a
one-lunger. He handed over the telegram and waited. Telegrams
didn't grow on Vinalhaven trees back then. "Finally comin' ain't she.
'Bought' time before you wear a groove in that rock. What you going
to do with the 'bar' while you go for her up New York?"

What was I going to do with the "bar"? I couldn't park Johnnie at a kennel, even if there was one, and he was not a house pet
welcomed by the everyday, animal-loving neighbor. There was only
one option—Keith. Keith had the same shape as a bear, walked like
a bear. The only difference was that his honey came in a bottle. He
was a plumber, part-time lobsterman, bon vivant, philosopher, and
wit. Keith was inventive. He had the first answering machine on the
island. Its message was succinct: "Keith Carver. State your business!"

Because he had the answering machine he could lie up in his
camp between jobs on a little island in sight of where I stood, do a

little lobstering, drink a few red ones (S.S. Pierce Red Label), and think about things. The timing was perfect. Keith needed a reprieve. The week before he had fallen out of his boat. No enemy of comfort, Keith had mounted a swiveling office chair in his outboard skiff so everything was to hand. He could lobster, take refreshment, and think about things with a simple rotating motion. He must have been rotating too fast, or perhaps the weight of his thoughts toppled him, for over he went. His ample proportions didn't allow for an easy reentry so there he lay spouting water, grasping the gunwale, hollering for help. It so happened Sheila Perkins, my nearest neighbor, was out for a row. A wee slip of a woman, she was, however, a mariner to the bone and resourceful in emergencies.

Unable to reunite Keith with his office chair despite their combined efforts, she took some pot warp, lashed him alongside, started the outboard, and beached him out on Strawson's Point. He surely needed to caretake a bear to restore his image. Plan in hand, I gave some Quaker Oats to Johnnie to keep him from following, grabbed a red one, and rowed down the bay to Cranberry Island. Three hours later the deal was struck. It would require six red ones, twelve cans of sardines in mustard sauce, and half a case of beans. Keith loftily said he would supply the Quaker Oats and perhaps throw in a herring or two.

I rushed down to meet Liv in New York, and almost before the lines were secured to the quay, hurried her out to Greenwich, Connecticut, where my parents lived. There was no time to shilly-shally about getting married, what with the bear on Cranberry with Keith. The evident distrust they had for each other from first sight had been palpable. We sprinted to the town office for the appropriate paperwork. Here the clerk delivered a bomb. "It requires five days, sir, from the time you apply until a license can be issued."

Five-day waiting period! My wedding present might be in serious trouble, compromised, even lost. "There must be a way around this," I pleaded. "No way can we wait five days."

The wretch placidly sucked her pencil. "Legally, you can apply for a waiver. But a word of warning: Judge Hershberg doesn't make exceptions."

Warning or not, an appointment was granted, and we rushed home so I could put on my $15 suit bought in Fiji, then stop by a shoe store on the way to the courthouse. My mother had told me the judge was "old school." The shoes might counterbalance the beard. The desk behind which he sat was large, the platform high. The judge himself was small, elderly, with eyes infinitely wise in the ways of mankind. I remember my new shoes squeaking as I shifted nervously before the bench.

"I understand you request a waiver of the waiting period."

"Yes, your honor."

"Reason?" The owlish eyes were neither kind nor unkind.

"I have a bear in Maine," came blurting out. "Wedding present for my wife."

The more I said the worse it sounded. Hershberg's eyes never wavered, never gave a sign as I poured out the problems of bear keeping. When I had finished he turned to Liv. "Miss," he said ever so softly, "I understand you come from Norway. In that country are bears an accepted wedding present?"

My bride smiled that smile of hers that made one feel bright and tingly. "Yes, your honor. And the fault is mine. I made the mistake of telling this man that next to him I loved bears best."

The gavel rose to shoulder height and crashed down with astonishing force. "First-of-a-kind deserves a waiver! Plea granted. Next!"

We were married and off to Maine before the ink congealed. The Kittery Bridge never looked better. However, my fears were confirmed when we hit Hurricane Sound. Johnnie had escaped his Alcatraz of Cranberry Island. A trail of herring led from Keith's bait barrel to the shore. Liv's comment held little comfort. "There is always method in a bear's behavior. He misses you. Perhaps he will not go far."

She was right. Johnnie had swum from Cranberry to the shelving beach on Strauson's Point where Sheila had grounded out Keith. An island being what it is, word had spread quicker than plague and a search party discovered Johnnie in a nearby raspberry patch. For the last twenty-four hours the good citizens had left him tethered to a tree. He was most happy to see me but his elation stopped short of Liv. He allowed himself to be ensconced in the bow of the punt by Father Oats, content to have him pull smartly up the bay toward The Only House, but he pointedly ignored the soothing little bear noises of proffered friendship from the blue-eyed girl sitting in the stern sheets.

Drawing near home I saw the Billings Brothers of Stonington had set their herring twine by the wharf. Their boat was moored nearby. They waved us over.

"Got Johnnie back, I see." They dug each other in the ribs, grinning at a dubious bear who tolerated them more than other folks as they smelled strongly of fish and had been known to toss a few his way.

"And you finally got the Mrs." They welcomed her in such a way I could see she was touched. "Heard you were comin', ma'am. Not much doing the last two days so we cooked you up a little something for your first night."

Winnie disappeared below and reemerged supporting a large round chocolate cake with soft white icing. Liv accepted it with Scandinavian graciousness. Johnnie wrinkled his snout, and we made for shore feeling warm inside. It was wonderful walking up the path to The Only House with my new bride exclaiming how everything was as I said. Johnnie shot up the lone apple tree to survey his old kingdom. I warned Liv not to let him in the house unattended, even if he might deign to go in with her. Last time I had allowed him in he had made a bear scratching post out of the little horsehair couch on the first floor when my back was turned. Liv was right. Bears were lovable but definitely out of the deep woods.

Looking up the path to her new home, Liv sensed the personality of the place. Originally built as a one-story office for the manager of the granite quarry, it had been moved twice before nestling next to the whale-shaped ledge. With yet a different owner it had been jacked up to allow for the keeping of goats and chickens on the first floor. The tiny kitchen, sitting room, and bedroom on the second floor were reached by outside steps leading onto a porch from which in turn one entered the kitchen. There was room for two people. Three was an intrusion. The original front door in the sitting room opened to the sea and a ten-foot drop. On it was a brass nameplate saying "Belle McCann" if one took the trouble to lean a ladder against the house and go up to read it. Kerosene lights handled the utilities. Water was hand carried from the well. Perishables were kept in the spring. Liv wanted the story behind each piece of furniture, the pictures, the bric-a-brac collected from several lives. However, dusk was only an hour away and I wished to show my bride the wonders that lay outside before retiring within for the wedding supper complete with cake.

Ceremoniously, I placed the Billings Brothers gift on the pine drop-leaf kitchen table beside the window opening onto the porch. It was more than just a cake, representing as it did our union, the start of a lifetime together, coupled with a special welcome from the island and the people so dear to me.

Johnnie was out back on the grass pretending to investigate an Indian paintbrush as we descended from the porch. I called for him to follow for it was fun to have a bear for company on a walk. He always noticed things not readily apparent to the human eye, loving a ramble along the water's edge or through the woods. However, behaving unlike himself, this time he continued to investigate the paintbrush even though I knew he preferred daisies. Oh well, I thought, he is just thankful to be home.

Liv and I had a wonderful ramble, Johnnie or no. We sat on the deep moss in the forest, explored the back cove, climbed atop the mountainous ledge, and looked down Hurricane Sound at the setting sun. Finally, the ever-increasing whine of mosquitoes drove us homeward.

Arriving at The Only House I called for Johnnie as we stopped at the well to pull up a bucket of water. But no black butterball came bounding to greet his Father Oats. Concerned, we climbed to the porch and started for the door. Immediately our eyes were drawn to the kitchen window. A great hole was torn in the screen, framing the surface of the table upon which but an hour before the wedding cake had so tenderly been set. A great chunk of the cake had been torn away. What was left no longer had the contour or consistency of its birthright. Rushing in we spotted sticky paw marks crossing into the sitting room and then disappearing into the tiny bedroom.

"Johnnie!" I called but there was no snuffling reply. We tiptoed to the bedroom door. In the dim light the bridal bed appeared untouched. However, on second glance, the desecration came into focus. In the center of the white counterpane loomed a brown and steaming mound worthy of a far larger bear than Johnnie. My face must have shown anger and shock for Liv took my hand and squeezed it. "Don't be angry," she said simply. "Johnnie was just being a bear."

The tide has come and gone for six decades since that wedding night. The bear is gone to some distant forest. Liv is gone. But The Only House still stands, and the voices of our children and our children's children now compete with the gulls, the screech of the osprey, and the sea against the shore. With the passing of time, The Only House has become an elixir of the good and beautiful, the wistful and sad, solitude and partnerships. Each visit is a rediscovery, a looking back and a pondering as to what lies ahead. Not all of us need a bear. Only some of us are lucky enough to have a good mate. But we all need an Only House no matter the shape or place.

Lapland child on skiis

CHAPTER SEVENTEEN

Lillehammer

The fall of 1956, after saying goodbye to our newlywed days and The Only House, we returned to Norway and Liv's Lillehammer cabin to be with her teenage children, Thor and Bamse, as their father was off on another expedition. They required a bit more schooling under parental supervision before sailing off on their own. We broke away from a farewell visit to my parents with Ma's last words to Liv being, "When you come back I expect you to present us with a little 'grand.'"

We arrived at Idlewild (now JFK) to be confronted with the Pan American scales. The bulk of our baggage struck home for the first time. The weighing attendant smirked, coming forth with, "I guess you know you have a little overweight—120 kilos to be exact. It's really 120 and a third, but I'll give you the benefit of the fraction."

"Well," I said to Liv, "there goes our little family trip to Spain after Christmas to see Tony and Anna-lo. No nice wine, azure water, and blessed warmth."

"Oh darling, don't be so gloomy. Think of all the enjoyment we're bringing the folks in my little country. This is going to be the best Christmas—ever."

I dutifully nodded, wondering how a generous man like me could think so many nasty thoughts with Christmas coming up and with 120 kilos overweight in presents for my new family. I thought of the lead cavalry complete with artillery pieces, along with the two pairs of heavy hiking boots for the boys, the electric iron with spray attachment for her mother, Christmas stockings for everybody from my mother. The holiday spirit was not upon me as we boarded the plane. "What price Christmas," I wailed.

"Cheer up darling," Liv said gaily. "Don't be such a stingy bastard. Open up that beautiful new briefcase sister Nancy gave you and let's celebrate with that bottle of rum you were so clever to stick in."

As the miles passed underneath and the briefcase continued to give forth cheer, my mood brightened and was happy by the time we landed in London. The mood remained gay until the luggage was piled on the inspection bench at the London customs. Once again, the enormity of it made me want to give up all material things and live like a monk—a monk with a wife, that is. As we piled into the Lilliputian taxi, Liv anxiously inquired, "Are you sure we have all the pieces? Don't you think you'd better count?"

I, the veteran traveler, airily replied, "Certainly they are all here. I don't need to count. I can tell all is well by one look at the aggregate bulk."

"You know best dearrrrrr!"

We arrived at the hotel. Liv wanted something from her medium suitcase. No medium suitcase! That took the rest of the day as we had to go out to the airfield again to retrieve it from customs.

The next morning the maid came in to clean the room. "Lovely day," she said sprightly, looking out the window. I looked out the window. It was drizzling. We were in London three days and it continually drizzled.

—∿—

From London we went to Birmingham and picked up our Land Rover station wagon, complete with four-wheel drive and tractor tires for serious camping. We were given a tour through the factory. Even though I knew little about mass production methods I saw that the work was excellent. The way they did it, though, was outmoded and time consuming. For instance, the two steel beams that formed the chassis were not made from one piece of steel, but rather each beam was made from four sheets, which they had to weld together. They put the four strips in a jig, tack welded them, and then ran down each seam with a continuous weld. The beams had to be carefully checked and then painted. It seemed an awful waste of time when they could get whatever form they wanted directly from the rolling mills like our car manufacturers did in the United States.

Overall, the car was excellent but certain things I questioned. The Land Rover was made for out of the way places where often maintenance was at a premium. Therefore, the car should have been mechanically simple so it could be serviced easily. This car of ours had as complicated an electrical system as our flossiest "Caddies" in the States. Even the fuel pump was electrical, so if the battery went dead—brother, you'd had it. The Lucas electrical system was known as "The Prince of Darkness" by car aficionados. Then the heater was put in such a position that one had to wriggle the leg under it to get to the accelerator pedal. Next the starter button was in such a position that one had to get around both the heater and the gear shift to get at it. The clutch and brake pedals were over to one side so far that a person's legs had to go down at quite an angle to strike them. The gas tank was located under the seat so every time we wanted to fill up we had to remove the seat. The de-icer was located so that it only de-iced the section of the windshield one didn't look through. I'm not bitching about all this, as I loved the car dearly.

Anyhow, we rolled our "baby" east from Birmingham to the ferry for Holland, which left from Harwich. The country was lovely, with little villages and pastureland, but the thing that struck us was the medieval quality about it. It seemed we were back in another century. In all my travels through Europe, which weren't many, I had never felt I was in the "Old World" as much as I did in England. Everything was so dark. After dusk when we drove through a village there was hardly a light showing. Even the hotels and inns were so dark we had to actually go inside to see if they were open. It was spooky. All the transportation seemed to be on a small scale. The railroad cars were half the size of ours. They were the smallest of any in Europe, by and large, as if the trip were designed for tiny people. The food was awful everywhere we went. Even in London we couldn't find a restaurant that served a first-class continental meal. The Italian restaurants didn't even cook with garlic. The country won the war but seemed behind in most everything and too steeped in tradition to break from the "old way" and try the new. An Englishman described the gas rationing to us. "Well, we British will take anything from our government." That summed it up. They took it and were such good sports and so bloody decent that the revolt, the reaction against hardships, never came. They just grinned and bore it.

In England, they always played fair and would never stab a person in the back, like they did in other countries I had been in. Whenever we looked confused an Englishman would come up to us, unasked, and inquire if he could be of assistance. And their faces were so nice. In big cities one often saw the sharp ferret faces, the cruel faces, the hard faces. This wasn't true of London. We felt people could trust the locals with their best silver if they possessed good silver.

Watching the people strolling around the colossal government buildings in London on a Sunday one could sense them telling themselves, "The days of empire aren't over, they can't be—look at those buildings, how solid, how big, how all enduring." It was hard for them to convince themselves that all they had left were the buildings. So much for England—God bless her.

Everything was humming in Germany. The roads were the size of our roads, the trucks were bigger than our trailer trucks, buildings were modern, people were working full blast. But the scary things in Germany were the uniforms. Everybody wore one—from the farmer in the field, to the boy on his bicycle, to the worker going home from the plant. And two people walking together inevitably were walking in step. It was unbelievable and altogether unsettling. Especially so when one thought back over their atrocities of the last war. One could forgive it a little bit if Russians had done it. But for one of the most civilized countries in Europe, with its cultural background, to do something like that was unforgivable. There was something innately terrifying about the Germans. However, the northern Germans were the scariest. The southern ones in Bavaria were another breed. The Prussians from the north I didn't trust.

Coming into Denmark was like coming home, and it was the same in Norway. It was amazing how the two countries next to Norway differed in personality. Both the Danes and the Norwegians detested the Swedes. The favorite occupation in Copenhagen was rolling a Swede. The amazing thing was that the Swedes didn't realize they were disliked so intensely. But then things weren't that simple for there were the Swedes from Goteborg who were good and helped the Norwegians during the war. Then there were the bad Swedes that came from Eastern Sweden. Then of course nobody liked the Belgians, and the Dutch hated everybody. And until a few years ago it was worth a Norwegian's neck to go to Spain because of some unfavorable trade agreement. Oh yes, the Danes couldn't stand the English for they were closely tied to England economically and England screwed them apparently. So it was the same the whole world over. People were just no damn good.

Finally, we came to Norway. The first person I met was the famous man with the raft who sailed to Easter Island, Liv's remarkable former husband, Thor Heyerdahl. When we went to pick up Liv's boys at his house, I expected the meeting to be very tense, but it wasn't at all. We got along famously with our mutual love of the Pacific as a common denominator. He had picked up some extraordinary stuff on his last expedition, and even discovered a hidden prehistoric village in the Tubuai group that lies to the South of Tahiti.

Liv's boys were extremely nice and very different in personality. Thor, the oldest, was the proper young man who didn't smoke or stay out late. His only vice was playing Polynesian songs on his guitar, complete with Tahitian words. He was helpful, kind, and considerate, liked the out-of-doors, and was generally the "all Norwegian kid."

Bamse had long hair complete with ducktail. In front it rose swiftly in a large mound, and then like a ski jump, took off and sailed over his eyes, which usually sported dark circles. During the vacation he rarely arose before noon, arriving home at eight one morning after an all-night session somewhere, spitting blood. There was a beautiful story about "no bus home so caught a sleigh and fell off and landed on my back and started spitting blood so taken into a house and saw a nurse and she said must have busted a blood vessel because of my bad cold and . . . " After that Liv lowered the boom and Bamse was restricted to quarters. He was sixteen and loved the girls and rock and roll.

Anyhow, on a visit to Oslo we had a hectic three days meeting all of Liv's ex in-laws. She was considered a part of the family, divorce or not, and her ex mother-in-law firmly believed Liv was her daughter. It was rather a colorful family. I'd never seen a person so universally loved as Liv. In Oslo everybody called, from bank presidents to char women. People came to drink from her goodness and joy of living and go away again feeling refreshed in themselves and with the world.

We escaped after three days, with Bamse, Thor, and a chow called Fan Kee, which means frivolous woman, belonging to Liv's ex mother-in-law, Mama Heyerdahl.

I still hadn't met my mother-in-law. That treat was coming. She was waiting at the cabin. We pulled into Lillehammer and chugged up the monstrous hill or semi-mountain behind town. We powered up and up. The snow was five feet deep and the air was not warm. We pulled into a stor *skog*, big woods, and the trees looked like trolls and *hulders*. I thought to myself that it was damn lucky I liked nature and the simple life, for by the looks of it, they had a gracious plenty of it. About the only person I was going to find to talk with might be a lonely moose.

By now we were at ten thousand feet it seemed. Thick woods everywhere. I didn't see anything that looked like a house. "Don't worry," my wife said. "We're almost there." We pulled into a tiny road off the other narrow road and I dropped into four-wheel drive, low range. "Not far now." Thor strummed his guitar and sang, Liv bubbled happily, the chow dog yowled, Bamse hiccupped. I glued my eye to the wilderness outside and anxiously listened to the clicking of the tappets and the snarl of the exhaust. I thought to myself I should have an American flag I could plant when we reached the top.

But come out on the top we did, and the view was something to behold, even though it was night. Lillehammer lay far below at the edge of the great lake, glittering at the corner of that white ermine robe of snow, like a gem-encrusted brooch.

"We're here!" everybody yelled (the boys spoke perfect English). I looked around. There was forest on three sides and a view on the fourth. "Isn't it rather hard to keep warm with just a view?" I asked Liv. She looked at me scornfully, told me to get the car off the road somehow, and so saying, put on her knapsack, grabbed a forty-pound crate of groceries, and took off into the woods. The boys and the chow dog followed with skis and a case of beer. I was left with the two bottles of rum and the Land Rover. Make the most of every moment was my motto, so I up ended one of the bottles and felt the courage flowing into me. I had started searching for a shovel to dig a niche in the road for the car when I heard a hell of a noise.

I froze, knowing I was about to see my first moose. The "thrump, thrump" of heavy feet approached, with a crackling of bushes and the swish of snow. I crouched behind the car and tried to pierce the darkness. The rum was doing good work. I wondered how one greeted a strange moose. I gripped the shovel tightly. The noise was headed straight for the car. It stopped.

I held my breath. "Where are you?" it said.

"I'm here," I replied. "But you're not a moose. I can tell. You sound like my wife."

"Darling, what are you doing?"

"I was about to see my first moose," I said, sighing and feeling chagrined. "But it was only you."

"Darling, you've been drinking. I can smell it on you. What is Mother going to say? And the boys! Here, help me get this load on my back."

"Can I climb up too?"

"Stop being ridiculous and get that car parked! Isn't it lovely— the woods, the snow, the view, the brisk air, the falling snowflakes?"

"I'm cold."

"What? Cold? I'm sweating. And all this beauty. Men folks! You just don't understands. Get to work with that shovel. Tra-la-la, it's so nice to be home. Oh, I forgot to tell you. It seems Mother has moved in with us."

Eventually I discovered the cabin, quite by accident. It was hiding under a snowdrift with just its chimney showing. It would have made a delightful Christmas card. Mother met me at the door. We embraced. We fell apart and Mother regarded me with eyes like an adder. "Nice to meet you," I said lamely. "I've heard so much about you."

Mother nodded, said something between a whine and a snuffle, and backed behind a large pot of sausages simmering on the stove. We continued to peruse each other from the corners of our eyes. About some elderly people one could say, they must have been beauties or very good looking when they were younger. In all fairness one couldn't say this about Mother. She was of medium height and build with a face half between Old Stone Face and a Galapagos tortoise. Her smoldering, inky eyes lay in the shadow of her Neanderthal eyebrows. I saw quickly that we were going to have an interesting relationship.

The cabin was real *koselig*, which means cozy in Norwegian. One entered through the kitchen, and off the kitchen on the left was the combined living room and dining room. To the right of the kitchen through an open portal was a small room with double-decker bunks. Not even a curtain separated it from the kitchen. A bedroom opened off the double-decker room, complete with a door and blissful privacy. That was the only place in the house where one could close the door and be alone, and the only place with a double bed. Mother informed us she was sleeping in there. Now Mother had an apartment in a farmhouse only a mile away, yet uninvited she moved right in here taking the only private room in the house. I sidled up to her and put the bite on her where she expected us to sleep while she snored in the double bed. She gleefully informed me that she had made the double-decker bunks ready for us and we would be very comfortable there right outside her door. Daughter's chastity would be preserved while Mother was in the house.

I retired into conference with myself, and after essaying the coldness of the climate, the width of the bunk, and the warm coziness of my mate at night, I decided the double bunks were not for us. Liv was of the same mind, and in turn, not a little irritated at Mother. She led me out to the woodshed with a conspiratorial air and showed me a little room at one end that had been fixed up like an office. It was tiny, poorly insulated, with only a miniature stove in the corner, but at first glance I knew this was going to be "home."

I poked in dark cupboards and corners of the cabin and located a rusty saw, hammer, and nails. With inspiration born of passion, I wrought a double bed in the room out there in the woodshed. When it came time to retire, I triumphantly led my spouse to the bridal suite, while Mother twitched and wrung her hands as her daughter was led away by a stranger. For the first ten days she twitched every time we went to the woodshed. Poor Mother, she had had an unhappy married life and couldn't understand that husband and wife could be happy together, enjoy being in the same bed together, and like being alone, occasionally. Poor Mother was a mattress thickness from the analyst's couch.

Two days after we arrived she was invited out by one of the neighbors for supper without Liv. However, Mother saw to it that her daughter was asked and couldn't understand why Liv refused to go and leave me by myself for the evening. Mother was a sly one. Coming home she petulantly asked Liv why she hadn't come to the neighbor's and walked her home, knowing her mother was afraid of the woods. Mother had been going back and forth in those same woods for years.

It became rather a game after a while, the battle of Liv and me against Mother. Liv was on my side, but being a daughter, was prone to fits of guilt. I kindled the fires in the house and organized breakfast while Liv tidied the house. Mother had to have her hot water and morning coffee carried to her room before she could get up. Liv did this, as nobody else was allowed in the room of the double bed or would have gone in if they had been. By bringing Mother her warm water and coffee just as we sat down to breakfast, we had a delightful meal with the boys, sans Mother. A small triumph, but in this struggle for survival, it seemed a major victory.

Then finally Mother moved back to her apartment. The air became quieter, but the struggle continued. One week she told all the neighbors she was so destitute that she was eating mink fish, the lowest grade of fish the farmers used to feed their mink. It came to Liv's ears that her poor mother was slowly starving while the daughter lived in luxury up on the hill with her Rockefeller husband, who signed his name with zeroes. Liv was upset. She rushed down to the lawyer who handled her mother's affairs to find out if her mother was in need. It was impossible to get anything out of Mother herself. The lawyer showed Liv Mother's bankbook containing a very tidy sum. Liv saw Mother and gave her hell. "Oh dear, I'd forgotten all about that account," was the only comment.

We asked Mother up for supper once a week. When she went home, we walked with her as she was still afraid of the woods. Slowly the battle was being won. Mother was coming to realize that I intended to stay married to her daughter and with marriage came certain unalienable rights in which she had no part. I guess I was too harsh on her. Time and distance should cure everything.

Other than Mother, life was pleasant here. In zero weather the outhouse junket was like sitting on a cold enema. Hell of a country to have piles. Dawn came at ten o'clock and sunset at three. For the first thirteen days we didn't see the sun once. I began to feel like a miner. However, the days did start getting longer and the sun was beginning to shine. We figured we might get through the winter yet.

Before we arrived, Liv painted in glowing terms how healthy the place was. No sooner were we there than she contracted a terrible cold and had it for a month. On closer questioning it appeared that this happened every time she was home. I contracted the flu. And the flies! It was hard to imagine that flies could live in this cold, bleak country in the dead of winter. Not only live but prosper. The house was full of them. Working at the typewriter I watched them drop down into the machine. One day it was so bad I thought I was running an IBM, what with all the buzzing and crunching.

The chow dog came into heat and the house was surrounded. It was like the Kentucky Mountains in feudin' times except there was a dog behind every tree. I half expected a moose to appear.

The neighbors were real personalities. One chap, by the name of Ola, was a true mountain boy. He lived off the land for years, way back in the hills, evading game wardens and shooting moose. A big figure in the resistance, he caught moose with his bare hands and once chased a fox for three days. He finally got it.

A saving grace was my venture into the distilling business. Liquor in Norway is terribly expensive, and the Norwegians enjoy a drink or two or three. However, every hardware store sported the salvation; a brewing kit, consisting of a large glass demijohn and a glass gadget that plugged into the top to let out the bubbles from the fermentation. Every food store offered essences to mellow the result. One could buy a scotch essence, rum, bourbon, gin, and all the rest. Experience showed that after a week to ten days the raw alcohol mellowed to where the adding of an essence made it palatable. My fondest memory of that winter was the subtle bubbling noise coming from the corner. God bless my wife's country in winter.

Good Old Boat, Vinalhaven

CHAPTER EIGHTEEN

Good Old Boat

Our little family grew. We parented Liv's two children part time. Our daughter, Liv, was born in 1957 in Lillehammer. Son Ola followed soon thereafter in 1959 when we were living in Oslo. Our American family settled four years later in Maine after trying a stint in South Carolina. We laid claim to an old 1850s farmhouse on a high hill with a line of sugar maples leading downward toward Penobscot Bay, that inland sea of myriad islands and lobster boats. For dwellers of coastal Maine, lobster boats are as synonymous with living here as woodpiles in the fall or black flies in spring. Their jaunty shapes adorn postcards at our neighborhood stores and the oil-skinned drivers of these symbols of independence, toil, and grit are part and parcel of the local lore.

Once we were settled on our hill overlooking the bay, some months passed while tired sills were put to right and loose boards nailed secure again. But inevitably, thoughts wafted to the bay with increasing intensity. Thus, the following spring when the freshets from the fast disappearing snow rushed to meet the sea, I followed in their wake. There at water's edge where boats gathered, I poked, prodded, and stabbed a treasure trove of keels, frames, and planks from

Friendship to Bar Harbor. Few things in life hold so much promise, so stir the male emotions, as keel thumping at black fly time. It is a romance wild and compelling.

This romancing of the keel truly blossomed one breezy morn in Matinicus Harbor. A brisk southwest wind was artfully nudging winter to take early retirement, causing the white flaring bow of my instantaneous affection to rise and fall with the moderate chop in a motion that bespoke sea kindliness and strength. Her sheer line joined deck and house and transom into such singleness of purpose that this young lover pulled ever more lustily at the oars as we rowed toward her. Here was a boat Ulysses would have chosen for a quest.

I stood in her pilothouse caressing the well-worn wheel. Those drafty rooms on our distant hill, the bad plumbing, the leaking window sills, the enduring loved ones, all vanished as I gripped the bronze spokes, rolling them from side to side as if cradling a child.

The present owner of this paragon was Clyde Young, six-foot-six and lean, whose family tree lay firmly rooted in this island on Penobscot bay. "Where's the compass?" I inquired.

He pointed to a box nailed to the bulkhead. I opened up the lid. The compass was one of those old-fashioned box types, ten inches across. Pushing down on one side of the bowl to see if the gimbals were free, I saw three small cylinders under the bowl. I well knew the shape. Gingerly plucking out one I proffered it to Clyde. He carefully rolled the dynamite cap in his fingers as if making a cigarette, then stuck it in his shirt pocket, reached down, and retrieved the other two.

"Been having a little trouble down here lately," he said laconically.

I made small conversation, not wanting to seem overly eager. "Don't dump on the first call" is the standard expression for a shrewd Maine trader, a trait absent from my repertoire. Buy high and sell low seemed to be my fate. In retrospect, I must have resembled an innocent codfish eager to take the jig. He followed my gaze to the windshield where the glass was slightly glazed with streaks. I raised my eyebrows, conveying I missed nothing. "Dogfish," he said with a slight movement of the lips. "Dogfish thick down here. When it's rough the bow flings them out of the water and they slap the windshield. Skin is like sandpaper."

I asked why he wanted to sell. A softening came to his face. "Time to move ashore," he said. "Do you want her or not?"

Decades have passed since the deal that day, struck over three dynamite caps, and Clyde telling what a good boat she had been to him and the previous owner, Harold Bunker, who had her built. Now it was my turn and I lived with her more than twenty-five years until all the children grew up and left home. She proved a thread of continuity through thick and thin that became more precious with each passing year. She was my window to an inland sea called Penobscot Bay, since my deep-water voyaging days had been traded for a wife and children and a windy hill. Often when I met an old friend, he or she would ask, "Do you still have that old lobster boat? I still remember the day. . . . "

Clyde's boatbuilding brother, Merrill, carved the model for her hull from a block of pine. She was built at Camden Shipbuilding, in 1948, by that master shipwright, Malcolm Brewer, who put together those exquisite coasting schooners designed by Murray Peterson. She was planked with fir left over from the mine sweepers built there during the war and her power was a Chrysler Crown of one hundred horsepower, the standard engine of the day. Harold Bunker, her first owner, said she cost $6,200 new, the most expensive lobster boat ever built in the state, and people had lobster sandwiches and lots to drink at the launching. "She was a good boat," he repeated several times.

"No, never put her aground, but did have one amusing experience. We called her Albert and Vance after my boys."

He went on to tell how one day he had been hauling down back of the Wooden Ball. His son Albert was coming up from Malcom's Ledge in his own boat, throttle in the corner. Father Harold watched him closing fast astern, but thought nothing of it, conjecturing he intended to come alongside for a gam. Next thing he knew Albert drove the bow of his boat right through Harold's transom and up into the cockpit.

"Damn fool of a boy was sitting on the washboard eating his lunch. Never even saw me. Kind of comical, it was," Harold said, chuckling. "Albert put his boat hard astern. Scared of what he'd done, I guess. Backed off and headed for home full throttle. I had to go full tilt myself to keep from sinking, headed after him. Funny thing was he broke down half way home and I had to tow him in. Cost me $80 for a new stern."

Harold's wife added, "Poor Albert, he took an awful ribbing going off like that, scared as he was, leaving his father to sink. You know, when he got married, he and his wife came out to the island in that boat with everything they owned in the world. Yes, she was a good old boat to all of us."

I drove the good old boat home to Camden, painted her transom red, and called her *Mandalay* after my earlier love and our journey to the South Seas. Boats serve as flypaper for the mind. People, incidents, pieces of our lives stick to them.

We took the new *Mandalay* out on so many trips to The Only House on Vinalhaven; past the Fiddler, past the ledges to Dogfish, through the beautiful passage of Leadbetter's Narrows into Hurricane Sound. In calms and gales and fogs and on crystal days. They are one big blur, along with the cargos of children, cats, dogs, wives, and the innumerable supplies, from fertilizer and boards to the spare burnoose. In seasickness and in health—a marriage of voyages in eighty-minute sequences.

Gunning the outer ledges each fall into early January was another series of voyages that would require a sea chest of paper to document. Someone asked me once what made one get up before the dawn with ice on the puddles outside and a keening wind, just to encase one-self in clothes of many layers, haul all that sundry gear aboard the "Old Ducker," steam out to the offshore ledges for two hours, set out tollers (decoys) in that frigid water, row one's ass off for four or five hours chasing crippled birds, slip on slippery rocks and weeds, risk one's neck on a tidal ledge, and then repeat the process in reverse, all for a few fishy tasting ducks.

"It extends the yachting season," I would say facetiously, to shunt away the conversation, for there are few souls with whom one feels comfortable sharing one's personal religion. To me those days from dark to dusk, the quiet harbor before the dawn, the sea and the wind and the frozen weeds on the barnacled rocks, the unspeakable beauty of the eider duck, and the boat were the essence of living on coastal Maine. The Old Ducker, linking them all together, was a church of my own choosing. The physical exertion, the sights and sounds and smells, the moments of terror, the reverence to the god of weather, the multifaceted path from safe harbor out and home again, were a spir-itual experience akin to the aborigine walking his dream line in the Outback, or the bushman trekking his beloved Kalahari.

My comrades on these adventures were many and varied. On one particular day they included Edward, proprietor of the Tug and Grunt Yard Boatyard, and Merv, a blacksmith from a town out back of the Camden Hills. Edward was a land surveyor of some repute. When asked by a North Haven lady of impeccable pedigree how she would recognize him when he stepped off the ferry to document her bounds, he replied without a falter, "Dear woman, naturally I shall wear my leotard and hold a lily in my mouth."

I picked up Merv before sparrow fart, as the expression goes. Merv had a face chipped from stone and his hands resembled monkey wrenches mated to a ball-peen hammer. Approaching Edward's, where the boat was moored, I remarked, "Last time here there were three geese feeding on the front lawn. Seemed a silly place to be what with Edward inside with his double barrel."

Merv fondled his ten-gage blunderbuss and growled, "No understanding the reasoning of a goose."

We set off from Edward's mooring that December morn and had progressed only five hundred yards down the Mussel Ridge Channel when off to port we noticed this thing swimming. From the distance it looked like a stubby tree with branches at one end. I put over the wheel, and on drawing closer saw it was a ten-point buck swimming for the shore a hundred yards away.

"Jesus Christ!" said Merv. "Going to be a corkin' day." He snatched at his waist and came up with a knife that would have frightened a Turk run amok. "Come up alongside," he barked. "I'll reach over and slit his throat. You grab the horns!"

"Merv!" said Edward. "I live here. Deer season's long past. You'll have every eye on this coast out on stalks, ringing up the warden."

An expletive cannonballed from Merv and he waved the knife about with a ferocity that would have slit a dozen throats, including ours. "Season be damned! Anything fool enough to swim out here this time of year is better off having its throat cut."

We progressed on down the channel toward Two Bush Light in silence, mooring in that bight on the southern end of Monroe Island,

and rowed around the point to set out the tollers. Merv shot the first bird with that monstrous ten-gauge that required blacksmith arms to lift. Only then did his equanimity return. Those were the halcyon days for a sea-duck hunter. There were rafts of birds by the thousands. When the boat roused the eiders at one end, the other end of the black and white carpet was as yet undisturbed.

We shot the tide down, hardly noticing the breeze had gone from north to southwest as the day progressed. An hour and a half before dusk we picked up gear and birds and rowed back around the point. To our consternation the Old Ducker had swung around with the change of wind and fetched up on the one rock in that little bight. There was nothing to do but wait for the tide to come again and lift her off.

By now the boat was heeled over at an uncomfortable angle, so we took several birds, the alcohol stove, and a bottle of Jack Daniels and went ashore, determined to make the best of an awkward situation. We offered Merv a drink with his fried duck breast to ward off the cold. He squinted at the label and shook his head. "That whiskey is too expensive for me to drink."

Later, huddling in the dark in the little cabin as the tide slowly righted *Mandalay*, we saw Merv reach for the Jack Daniels. Edward caught him up sharp. "Merv, I thought that whiskey was too expensive for your . . . ?"

"Ed," came the immediate retort. "Too dark to read the label."

Eventually we floated off and steamed for home about eleven that night. Halfway there, we were intercepted by a Coast Guard cutter sent out by the frantic wives. We had no radio aboard. "Women!" Merv snarled. "Just a mite late for supper and they ship out the National Guard. Thank God I'm single."

Like Harold Bunker and Clyde Young, I never really ran *Mandalay* ashore, just grounded her out down there at Munroe Island. But my son did over on Vinalhaven one evening with a friend, running full tilt for town to snare a pizza. When pumped out, the Old Ducker was towed around to the local boatyard at Carver's Harbor for repairs. I called up a week later to see how things were going.

"Drained the water out of the engine," Kevin said. "Seems to run OK. But had to take the stem out of her. It was cracked right down the middle. Your boy must have hit that ledge full clip. Must be hard on you. She's a good old boat."

"Damn hard," I said. "Save that cracked stem for me. I'm going to hang it over my boy's bed as a reminder of what he did."

There was a pause at the other end of the phone. "Hang it over his bed? If it was my boy I'd shove it up his ass!"

The salt water didn't do the old engine much good. A year later she packed it in off the Fiddler with night coming on in a breeze of wind. Luckily, the North Haven ferry came along and gave us a tow. Then decision time. Should I buy a new engine or rebuild the old one, now almost forty years old? A new, more powerful engine would cut down on the eighty-minute commute. And after all, even iron got tired after forty years of service and a dunking. On the other hand, the years of pleasure coming and going were not to be overlooked. What difference would it make if we got to where we were going ten or fifteen minutes earlier? And just as the good old boat had been a thread of continuity in my life, and had served me well, the old Chrysler Crown had been a matron of good service. Thinking back through the countless voyages with family and friends was what tipped the scales. The boat, the engine, and I were no longer young. We had been through a lot and knew each other with an intimacy that would make any wife jealous. A new engine would speak with a different voice—an alien in our midst.

So it was the Old Crown went to Banks Brothers in Belfast to be given an immortality of sorts. Once again, she barked up through the dry exhaust with that same throaty roar as on the initial launching back in 1948. Little else changed. We put in a radio in deference to the grandchildren, but I never used it. When we switched from six volts to twelve, out went the old fathometer, never to be replaced. The windshield wiper, in turn, lost the battle of the voltage, and was cast from view never to be missed until my in-laws presented me with another, which was installed so we didn't hurt their feelings. A radar reflector, given by a kindly soul who worried about us crossing in pea soup fogs with the increased traffic up and down the bay, added to the improvements. Time and course heading, allowing for wind and tide, had never failed to see us reach Hurricane Sound, or come back to Curtis Island at the entrance to Camden.

Now it is 2018, almost fifty-one years since I first saw her in Matinicus Harbor—almost sixty years since she was built. The Old Ducker is still very much alive, almost as good as new, sitting in a slip at the end of Tillson's Wharf in Rockland. She belongs to the O'Hara Family of Journey's End Marina, who so often shared passage with us when our children were young on those countless trips to Vinalhaven. She has new frames, a diesel engine, and modern navigation gear. But under the modern trappings she is still the same Good Old Boat, carrying yet another generation.

The *Taube*

CHAPTER NINETEEN

Building the *Taube*

Sadly, Liv died in 1969 of melanoma, when she was fifty-two. There was some speculation that perhaps it might have been the result of her extraordinary honeymoon with her first husband in the equatorial sun of Fatu Hiva in the Marquesas. She had contracted a nearly fatal skin disease and infection while engaged in their grand experiment to see if modern man could truly go back to nature. Therein lay the seeds of what would someday become Thor Heyerdahl's masterpiece, *Kon-Tiki*.

Our children, who were only eleven and nine at the time, and I continued on in Maine; a dark time for all. My love of things mechanical kept my mind busy as my heart tried to heal. And while I always had the needs of my children at the forefront, with one eye strayed to the shore, the other could often be found looking to the sky. Once an explorer, always an explorer, I guess.

The building of the Etrich *Taube* has the ingredients of a fairy story. It could begin: "Once upon a time a man called Jim had a little landing strip on the side of a mountain in the town of Camden by the Sea. At the bottom of the grass runway was a pond where children swam along with trout and turtles and other things. From the sandbox with its toys, guarded by schools of minnows, the green grass pitched upward until it crested the hill to disappear down the other side. Between the pond, the hill, and the shortness of the runway, only pilots very comfortable with their strapped-on wings cared to land. Today, the airstrip is still called Bald Mountain International and the control tower is still run by a herd of equine operators, constrained behind a fence defining the eastern perimeter."

Back then, those many years ago, it so happened that on a sunny afternoon with the grass at its greenest, a little yellow plane touched down so softly on that airstrip that the operators never raised their heads. A tall man uncoiled from the small cockpit and introduced himself as I was rolling out from the hangar my own small plane of like configuration. I knew who he was, and he knew who I was. The aviation community is small in Maine. It was an honor to have the CEO of one of the most famous companies on the globe land on my little airstrip and then hold out his hand. Tom Watson of IBM had a summer place on an island just off the coast, with his own airstrip and a passion for aviation. Sentences were exchanged, and the meeting turned out to be the start of a story about a plane, a bird, and other things.

Time passed. The solar calendar turned green to brown to white to green again, bringing a day when I opened an envelope to find a commencement program, which was curious since I had no family commencing. Turning the parchment, I found a note. "Wouldn't it be nice to have some old aeroplanes flying around Owls Head." Apparently, the commencement attendee had other things on his mind than listening to what was going on. The attendee was Tom.

Small incidents do sometimes big things bring. Within a year, the Owls Head Transportation Museum was born. In its first two years the baby institution held transportation rallies of cars, planes, and engines to stir interest in the community. It was a quest for mother's milk, financially speaking, as the baby had to grow beyond its one red aeroplane and a car, given by the tall man with the hawk-like eyes, if it was to become more than a sandbox for hobbyists.

The sun shone and the moon waxed and waned and the green mother's milk began to flow. The baby grew rapidly. One day an old man arrived in a battered camper to take in the scene. The old man was Austrian and had learned to fly in a pioneer plane called a *Taube*—one of the most bird-like flying machines ever built. The name was fitting for taube means pigeon or dove in German. The Austrian told how the designers of this bird-like creation were a father and son team. Ignaz, the father, was an Austrian textile machinery manufacturer and aviation buff. Igo was his son. They had explored the work of those who came before them, starting with George Cayley (1773–1857), considered the father of aeronautics with his study of forces acting on a wing. In 1849 Cayley designed a glider that carried a boy aloft. Next came Alphonse Penaud (1850–1880), father of model airplane building. He proved models were an excellent method of experimentation. Then onto the stage arrived the towering figure in aviation history, Otto Lilienthal (1848–1896). Skilled in engineering, he studied bird flight and built gliders for experimentation. So important were his studies that later on the Wright Brothers closely examined his writings. Lilienthal had gone so far as to construct a small hill to serve as a launching ramp. From its summit he made more than two thousand glider flights before killing himself in the process. On his deathbed he wrote his final scientific notes.

Innovation is the ability to take all the old bits and pieces that have come before and build a new creation. So it was with Ignaz and Igo Etrich. The father and son acquired two Lilienthal gliders after the aviator's death and studied bird flight like their predecessors. They even kept two flying squirrels to observe how they soared from branch to branch. In 1898 the Etrichs designed their first glider. It was very unstable. This set them off on an extensive search for a way to correct the problem.

By some quirk of fate, a winged seedpod from a tropical vine in the Malay archipelago caught their attention. This particular vine produced football size gourds, which hung high up in the tropical forests. The gourds contained hundreds of winged seeds that when released spiraled down in twenty-foot circles and often traveled even farther with any wind. This seed from the *Zanonia macrocarpa* vine had a wingspan of five inches. One scientist had waxed ecstatic watching its descent. In a scientific journal he wrote, "Circling widely, and gradually rocking to and fro, the seed sinks slowly, almost unwillingly to earth. It needs only a breath of wind to make it rival butterflies in flight."

This intrigued the Etrichs. The history books told how Ignaz and Igo, inspired by the stability of the seeds, had used the basic shape in their paper gliders. This in turn resulted in the creation of their Zanonia Glider. Built of bamboo, it had a wingspan of forty feet, weighed forty-four pounds, and was so stable the inventors made hundreds of flights using sandbags to simulate passengers.

More experimental gliders followed with ever greater performance. The final step was to install an engine. Improvements kept coming, and presto, an operational *Taube* burst upon the scene in 1911.

The finished product was easy to fly, unlike other pioneer models of its day. With its extreme stability it promptly became the premier sportsman and military trainer, built under license by many different companies with their own individual modifications. In all, five hundred were born between 1911 and 1914. In 1912 Igo flew his creation from Germany to England and back, a remarkable feat for the times. He painted ETRICH under each wing for advertisement and was enthusiastically received in every country except France. The French didn't like to be outshone in aeronautical matters, or in any others for that matter.

The *Taube* had the dubious distinction of being the first plane used for military purposes, dropping two-kilo bombs in the Libyan War of 1911, and participating later in the Turkish Balkan hostilities, where hand grenades were thrown over the side along with the firing of an occasional pistol shot. The *Taube* was also the first to drop a bomb on the English at Dover and took part in a bombardment of Paris. Six months into World War I it was quickly outdated, being relegated to training, and soon faded from aircraft history. One final note: with its transparent wings, the *Taube* was hard to see from the ground and was declared a "stealth plane" by the French.

The Zanonia vine had truly dropped a seed into the minds of the Etrichs. It did the same for the owner of Bald Mountain International Airport. I had already built several airplanes in my boat shop beside the airstrip. The *Taube* presented an irresistible challenge, given the bird-like structure, the botany connection, stability, and a pioneer heritage that would fit well with the new museum's mission. The search for construction plans began.

So I went to Austria, Germany, and Norway. The best remaining *Taube* was in the Norwegian Technical Museum outside of Oslo. I also consulted with a Colonel Devries, who had written a book on the *Taube* and was probably the best living expert on the subject. I knew I was going to fly the plane and I had a family depending on me, so I went one step further. Dave Thurston, the dean of American aeronautics, was on the board at the museum. I consulted him on stresses, strains, and materials, along with guarding against what the Scottish call "things that go bump in the night." The original fuselage was wood, braced with wires, state-of-the-art in those days. Thurston suggested steel tube for greater strength, and a 1940s Ranger aircraft engine, which had about the same weight, horsepower, and configuration as the original Daimler. Suitable bamboo poles for the flexing wingtips were difficult to find so Thurston suggested fiberglass rods. Otherwise, the replica would remain true to the Etrichs' creation. I believed that truth was a slippery concept that could be stretched in most directions and yet retain the original idea. From fifty feet the difference between the original and the replica would be nonexistent.

I laid the keel, so to speak, around 1981. The next year saw the fuselage sitting on wheels. There the project stalled, pushed aside for seven or eight years by other projects with higher priority. My boat shop could not survive on building airplanes for pleasure. In September of 1988 the work began again in earnest. The crew was now smaller but more diverse. First came Fred, who had worked for me since he was a child. He had learned to mold metal, build boats, and fit wood together so nigh a crack could be seen. When obstacles arose, he walked around or over them. Next was my stepdaughter, Genevieve (I had married her mother, Marilyn Moss, in 1983), who learned new words unknown even to her mother, some of them not to be uttered among the old tea party set. From those days forward she became a do-it-yourselfer with an excellent grasp of tools. Then there was George.

George was a history lesson in humanity. Fisherman, sculptor, aircraft mechanic, inventor, he brought to the workshop one of the most inventive minds I had ever encountered. With increasing age, he had taken on a gnome-like figure, complete with ragged beard, and walked in a manner peculiar to his Curtis clan. George claimed he could recognize his kin by watching their gait. It had a side-to-side rocking motion with a small forward component, with the arms swinging back and forth as if using a scythe to harvest grain. He lived in an old house with his wife, cast-iron stove, and a pet crow. A pack of rats lived under the house. George said one could tell he was eating well because the rats had long shiny coats. His children had fled on becoming of age.

Often of an evening, he and Kosti Ruohomaa, the internationally known photographer, would knock back a bottle of bourbon, discussing artistic matters and others that did not reach the light of day. One troubled night George was arrested for OUI. Car transportation was very dear to George. Having his license snatched, restricting his freedom of mobility for thirty days was hell. He never took another drink the rest of his life.

George drove a car kept alive by ingenuity and duct tape. On arriving at the shop one day he proudly opened the hood and pointed to a copper tube snaking back to the trunk, where it mated with a propane tank. Long before the thrust to alternative car fuel, he had rigged up his engine to purr contentedly on bottled gas.

I had a long and valued relationship with George, trusting him in all matters outside of parental guidance. I learned from respected sources that George had minutely laid out a plan to Wa, my Tahitian son, on how marijuana seedlings could be planted not far from the airstrip, grown, and marketed with no danger of discovery. It never came out what he had also imparted to my stepdaughter, but she always referred to George with the greatest respect, storing the swear words in her arsenal for future use as a nurse practitioner.

Aside from George, the building of the *Taube* had another magical ingredient. This was in the form of a bird that appeared one day out of nowhere and stayed for eight months. The wondrous creature had feathers of many hues, and for reasons unknown, fell in love with me, who had an office above the boat shop with a balcony outside. The bird took up residence there, protected from the weather by the long overhang.

Where I went the bird followed, often landing on my head, emitting cooing noises hard to ignore. That the bird was a pigeon, and taube means dove or pigeon in German, was not lost on the me. When I went for a walk with the dogs the bird followed, flitting ahead from tree to tree. When I went inside the house, the bird would fly from window to window looking for me, flapping against the panes.

This attachment was troubling. The bird obviously belonged elsewhere and probably became lost on its way home. I expected a departure any day and that would be that, a wonderful interlude not to be forgotten. But the bird stayed and stayed some more. There was plenty to eat, what with the barn and all the grain left by the horses on the ground. I would also toss more food when he thought it was needed. I was troubled, remembering the wild bear cub I had raised for Liv. Needless to say, the bear cub had grown bigger, a lot bigger, and lived a short, happy life beloved by husband and new wife, but ultimately met with a sad end. I had learned my lesson from this about the keeping of wild things. The bird was different, but there were also too many similarities. I grew very fond of the bird, occasionally even letting it into my office when the weather was terrible outside. There it would sit on the desk and peck at the manual adding machine. When the handle was pulled down the tape arose from the top accompanied by clicks and clacks of the ancient workings. The bird would cock its head and grab the tape. There was often a puppy playing on the floor with a ball. Bird, and the puppy called Oliver, developed a relationship that was quite touching.

So the bird stayed and the days passed and the building continued apace. The crew installed the engine, fitted the cockpit with instruments and controls, while George kept laying his tools on the floor, saying that was their proper place where they could fall no farther. The plane's tail came next, followed by the wings. The rigging was a maze of hundreds of turnbuckles and fittings. The fabric covering came last. For days the shop smelled of nitrate and butyrate dope, that heady essence associated with cloth-covered planes.

There came a day in spring when the engine had been tested, the controls had caused the wingtips to flex, and checklists had been checked and rechecked. The moment had arrived to journey forth to the museum in Owls Head for testing. Down there the runway was longer and flatter, so the margin for mishaps tilted more in favor of plane and pilot. The *Taube* was loaded onto a flatbed trailer with its wings tied to the side of the fuselage. During the loading process the bird flew around and around with what appeared unusual intensity. It followed the trailer and truck down the hill to the end of the driveway.

When I returned late that afternoon the bird was nowhere to be seen. Day after day passed, but the bird never returned. It was as if with its namesake gone there was no longer a reason to stay. I was both sad and relieved. Even more, the timing of the departure caused me to wake in the middle of the night and wonder about all those unknown things that made up the inner workings of the world.

In the ensuing days at the museum, the builder sat in the cockpit of the reassembled plane, testing the engine and the controls to be certain all things moved in the proper direction when the commands were given. Finally, after six thousand man-hours of construction, the great moment came on a cloudless day with a gentle breeze right down the grass strip that ran alongside the paved four-thousand-foot runway. The plan was to do gentle taxi tests to feel out the controls and see how the plane would react when the throttle was pushed forward. The first run went flawlessly. Directional stability was good. The tail rose nicely when the speed increased. The museum staff turned the plane around and the builder taxied back to the starting point for another run.

Again the throttle was advanced. The plane moved forward, and looking out the side, I saw the ground falling away. The *Taube* climbed as steady as a ship of state. I reached to pull the throttle back then hesitated. The engine was running perfectly. The ground was soon several hundred feet beneath with the end of the runway fast approaching. The decision was easy. I turned the wheel to the left in conjunction with the left rudder. There was no immediate reaction and then the plane slowly banked like an old Packard powering around an inclined turn. I flew the airport circuit, making turns right and left and doing gentle climbs and descents to test the controls. At one point, I took my hands off the controls. The plane flew onward, steady as a draft horse pulling its load.

The feeling of security was so profound that the legend, supposedly told by the Red Baron in World War I, came back to me about the old unpiloted *Taube* taking off from its aerodrome, flying the pattern and landing without a hand on the wheel.

I didn't land with the circuit flown but went around again, reluctant to settle back to earth. Later, when asked how it had felt piloting the old dinosaur, I replied that it was like flying a four-poster bed.

Living things have a lifetime and turn to dust. Machines also turn to dust unless saved by people and places that believe dinosaurs should be preserved for future generations to see from whence we have come. Long after I gave up flying, I would stand in front of the museum buildings on an event day watching the *Taube* float by, with ETRICH painted in black on the underside of its wings, like the designer's original a century ago. And in my mind's eye, I saw a small bird with purple feathers flying alongside, embodying all the people, seeds, and circumstances that had made it possible.

My wife, Marilyn, photo courtesy of Kari Herer/*Maine* Magazine

CHAPTER TWENTY

Marilyn

As the Etrich *Taube* took time coming into being, so did another momentous chapter in my life. It began with an encounter with the woman who would become my wife: Marilyn Moss. In the time between losing Liv and meeting Marilyn, I was married, unhappily, to another woman for twelve years. Her name, strangely enough, was Margaret, but she had little in common with the Margaret of my heart. My second Margaret (number two) came at a low point in my life. With the death of Liv, I thought someone was needed to help me raise two young children. She came with baggage, in the form of a curmudgeon of a mother who refused all entreaties from her daughter to change a certain skirt and blouse, which she wore winter and summer, day in and day out in the furtherance of some personal cause of which only she was aware. Margaret's mother referred to me as "the other idiot." Idiot number one was a humorous friend with whom I was wont to talk nonsense about the vagaries of life. The fact that Margaret turned out not to particularly like children didn't help. She introduced me to sports cars, racing, and argumentation. I longed for a return to enduring love, planes, and boats. Bluntly put, I was miserable—until one chance evening.

I met Marilyn in 1982, at a fireplace where the flames danced on her long raven hair. Her eyes were luminous, imparting the notion she knew things at that fateful dinner party that I would like to know. We had a short conversation. Later, she admitted I talked about things that caused me to appear rather odd. On my side, the image of her sitting there followed me home, setting in motion a quest requiring many moons to consummate.

I came to that dinner party with my own baggage: Margaret number two. By then the bonds of matrimony were so severely frayed that if they had been mooring lines tying ship to shore the slightest breeze would have caused boat and dock to part company. Camden, lying on the Maine Coast, is a small town. Little happens that remains unknown. Before long I looked out my bedroom window at a not too distant ridge, having learned that my newfound jewel, Marilyn, lived there with a husband and their two children. In the other direction toward town, she ran a tent factory beside the river flowing into the harbor. The location in previous times had been the site of a water-powered gunpowder mill.

The fuse to the old romantic powder mill site was lit, causing one event to run into another, until we were on talking terms and I was drawn ever closer to the present mill building. One day she invited me down to have a look. It was a two-story structure on the steep bank of the rushing stream. The top floor was on the level of the parking area. On entering one was serenaded with the gentle chatter of sewing machines, cutters at the patterning table, and the swish of fabric being inspected at the end of the production line. The operators had pleasant faces conveying a sense of well-being. They looked up as we passed, and it took no forensic wizard to understand that they were more than comfortable with their boss, addressing her by the first name, as she did them.

The bottom floor, just above the river, was the design center. Here her husband, Bill Moss, held forth with his design and sales team. And here, I was to learn, dealt intrigue, dubious goings on and other factors sufficient to nurture future events. Maestro Bill, the design genius, had glass fronting on the stream so he might, just possibly, see a jumping trout—he was an ardent fly fisherman. His human passions also lay elsewhere as I was to learn, and his marriage to Marilyn was not a mutually happy one. Outside his office was ensconced a flaming red-haired woman, his sales representative, and beyond her a lithesome woman flowed among the machines and tables. She embodied various dimensions I was yet to learn, coupled with a personality as open as a locked vault. She was the one who brought to life the concepts of the maestro.

I was surprised to learn it wasn't my charm that had elicited the invitation to have a peek. The one of the raven hair had other motives. Finances of the enterprise were as shaky as an aspen leaf, and Marilyn was looking for investors to keep the business afloat. Although the backpacking tents flowing off the production line were considered the best in the world, with acclaims from mountain climbers, campers, and explorers from around the globe, money flowed out about as fast as it flowed in.

I was soon to learn there was a tension between the two floors that needed attention, along with developing more sophisticated production techniques. Marilyn was sitting in the captain's chair only because of the pleading of her stepfather, who had been inveigled to invest and saw his beneficence fast disappearing. Now, she was casting her net over friends, acquaintances, friends of friends, and other potentials, in the hope of luring new pockets to share in her visions of future wealth. Moss Tents was a household name among the sporting set, much as the rubber-bottomed boots of L.L. Bean. Husband Bill was revered in the fabric trade as an innovative fabric designer.

The stage was set. Marilyn baked French bread, adding wine and cheese. A crowd gathered, partook of the offerings while listening to a glowing presentation by Marilyn and Bill on the global allure of Moss Tents and other products to come. The company lawyer warned us this was a high-risk investment but was ignored. The French bread alone sold the day. The $4 a share was a small amount for what could blossom forth. It took years for the blossom to flower but blossom it did through Marilyn's perseverance and grit. When the company sold several decades later, a share was worth $46.80.

Five of the largest investors were invited to comprise a board as we had the most to lose should things go awry. I would not be totally honest if I didn't admit that in my heart I was looking for more than just monetary gain. Being part of the inner circle would place me closer to what I considered to be the true prize: Marilyn.

We five on the board were a mixed bag. There was Bill, whose family owned the local woolen mill that was a pillar of the town. Another Bill owned a Portland company that manufactured aircraft parts. Gordon was a local surgeon, using his love of entrepreneurship to help him forget the horror of service in the Vietnam War. Then, aside from me, there was Bronson, a Quaker, an antiwar activist, and a role model of service to humanity, with business acumen to boot.

We met and we talked but looking back I find it hard to say how much we helped. Marilyn, although relatively new to business, was a fast learner with a tenacious will to see things through to a successful conclusion. This wasn't easy. Husband Bill, a maestro of design, was an artist with all the errant traits of the breed that often collide with running a business. He was also as attracted to women as they were to him, adding to the turmoil of the business and the relationship with his wife. Things went on in the basement not meant for the director's table. As time passed the path became harder, the basement intrigue grew unbearable, and it was not difficult to see the toll it was taking on Marilyn. She had a business to run, two children to tend, and a marriage obviously breaking up, like my own. One day I couldn't stand it any longer and gave her a call.

"Marilyn," I said, "as a director I am very worried about your mental well-being. You have to somehow get your mind off the business now and then."

"What do you suggest?" she asked.

"Well," I said, "you could have an affair or learn to fly."

"This town is too small to have an affair," she answered.

"Then I will lend you my Super Cub. Just take out insurance and get an instructor."

So it came to pass that she found an instructor and took out insurance. My little white-and-red Cub was soon flying out of Bald Mountain International, piloted by the One of the Raven Hair, with instructor Manning sitting in the back seat. Days also flew by, and soon Manning was no longer sitting in the rear seat and Marilyn was alone in the sky, building up the required solo hours toward her private license, going cross country, landing at other airports, and acquiring confidence and skill.

Then came the fateful day. It was nigh for her private pilot test. The afternoon was perfect, no wind, blue sky. Manning told her to fly down to the local airport and practice a few landings on the grass strip alongside the paved runway. She called me to see if the plane was available. I rolled it out and prepped it for her. She took off and I wished her well. She looked wonderful in the cockpit with earphones and focused expression, and that something I couldn't get out of my mind. I stood there, chest pounding, until the plane disappeared.

The weather was mild. The afternoon wore on. Evening approached. Dusk arrived and still no little returning plane. It grew dark. There were no cell phones back then. Something must have gone wrong. I assembled cars, the truck, anything with lights to illuminate the landing strip.

Long minutes passed. Then a car came up the drive and drove out to where I was standing beside the strip. The window rolled down. There were tears in Marilyn's eyes.

"Pebble. I have crashed your plane."

When she got out of the car, Manning was driving. I couldn't help it and gave her a hug with tears in my eyes.

"Machines can be fixed. People can't," I said, overwhelmed with relief. "I'll drive you home."

The story unfolded, bit by bit. It had been a perfect afternoon flying down the coastline to Owls Head. Not a ripple on the water or in the sky. The sailboats on the bay were becalmed. She had entered the airport pattern and announced her intention to land. The touchdown was perfect. Then suddenly she lost her concentration, a bad thing in a tailwheel aircraft. The plane veered right into the bushes and she gave it a hard-left rudder and brake to bring it back on the grass strip. The plane went up on its nose, the propeller hit the ground, and then the plane settled back down to the ground again and she heard a slight ripping of fabric.

She sat there, taking in the situation. The plane didn't seem to be badly hurt but she would immediately have to call the FAA and report the accident. She took out the logbook in the pocket beside her. Then George Curtis, the mechanic of the *Taube* who worked for me from time to time, tore across the airport in his car, and opened the side window and folding door to look in.

"I hope I haven't hurt Pebble's plane too badly," she cried.

George examined Marilyn and the interior. His eyes grew large. "Jesus Christ, Marilyn!" he burst out. "If you had been two inches to the left you would have been a popsicle."

Marilyn looked down at her right leg. It was bleeding. A stout, dead sapling had ripped up through the fabric covering of the plane and grazed her leg. George helped her out and they walked around the plane. The damage to it was considerable. They went across to the administration building and she called the FAA, expecting the worst.

"Marilyn," the inspector said, "you'll be a better pilot because of your accident. Get right back in a plane tomorrow before you get scared. Then get your license."

George drove Marilyn home. It was uneventful until they turned to go up Howe Hill. George's car hiccupped and Julie, a friend of my daughter, came barreling around the corner and slammed into their rear, snapping Marilyn forward. George ran to the other car and then came back and told Marilyn he'd better rush Julie to the hospital as it looked like she had broken her wrist and was badly banged up. Marilyn had walked halfway up the hill approaching our drive when Manning tore around the corner, picked her up, and carried her the rest of the way to where I was waiting at the side of the grass strip.

The next day Marilyn went to the doctor. She had a bad whiplash and the nurse spent half an hour removing splinters from her leg.

Marilyn, being who she was, did get back in another plane and went on to get her license. We rebuilt the Cub in the shop with the help of George. During that time the frayed mooring lines of our respective marriages gave away. We both were divorced from our respective spouses and free to be with one another. We spent a long weekend over in the embrace of The Only House, so it was not surprising one morning soon thereafter to find us in the lawyer's office mentally practicing our vows. It was Saturday and he was dressed in shorts.

I said, "I do."

Marilyn said she did also.

The lawyer shook our hands, saying, "no charge," and we walked away toward a new future.

That was 1983. Now it is 2018. During those three-and-a-half decades the mooring lines of our marriage have thickened thanks to family, friends, animals, projects, sickness and, most of all, each other. Humans are not unlike trees that put down roots that intertwine with those closest, nourishing and helping both grow upward toward their respective sun. Marilyn's sun has been service to organizations, others, and her writing. Mine has been to dance across the Bridge of Understanding with other people who have made my life and those of others a joyous, better place with—always—Marilyn by my side.

CHAPTER TWENTY-ONE

A Nonagenarian Day

As years form an ever-narrowing pyramid, the days assume a new rhythm, collapsing into one another at a faster rate. The present loses some of its immediacy, bleeding into the past and future, while the view from the window becomes ever more furtive as to where it will channel one's thoughts. Such is a day in the life of a nonagenarian.

This one started with the questioning call of a crow from the tree outside the window, followed by a stronger reply from its brethren atop the barn. The brain sleepily synapsed the noise, initiating a sidewise rolling of the legs for blood flow to the lower back where age had taken its toll on the worst design of the human body. Then feet met the floor as the clock turned six.

Next came the urgent whisper of little padding feet, belonging to Oliver, the Norwich terrier. For sixteen years Oliver had blessed us with his winning ways, always ready to please and happy to accompany us wherever we went. Sixteen years is a long time, longer than any of our other animal friends. When he started to decline these last years, with dimming vision, loss of hearing, frailty of limb, and finally bewilderment of where he was, it brought home my own mortality as ninety-two approached. We had seen so much in our lives together, through good times and bad. Indeed, it was like a marriage for he was a part of our every happening during that decade and a half.

Time had been kind to Oliver but had rearranged his plumbing protocol from necessitating the out-of-doors journey to lift a leg or do the squats. Puddles were a morning hazard, and this one no different. One had to be careful where to step or it was like a slide into home plate with the umpire declaring "out!"

The sequence of closely spaced morning events, choreographed by practice, was now up and running. Marilyn stirred from the other side of the bed and sleepily rose. We eventually descended the steep and narrow stairway of the 150-year-old house. T. S. Eliot, one of our other terriers, so-called because to him all food was a poem, also jumped from his reclining position beside my head, transitioning from repose to action with a sprinter's start toward food promised below.

During breakfast, the door shoved inward and a bearded man entered wearing a presence that demanded attention.

"Morning," said the man.

"Morning, Fred. What's up?" Fred has worked for me more than fifty years.

"Starter on tractor shit the bed. Your car free to go to John Deere? Can't use truck, loaded with gravel. Mario [the backhoe] has a flat front tire."

"Free until ten. Anything else?"

"Horse fence needs a new post. Saw a mangy fox in the park. Baby turkeys everywhere."

The door slammed shut and breakfast for man resumed. For the four-legged, breakfast was already digesting.

By eight o'clock a slender man on a bicycle appeared over the steep hill and disappeared into the barn, reappearing almost instantly, heading for the stable, coffee cup in hand. Dave, Fred's assistant, lean, tall and handsome, an artist with the paintbrush, was given to biking and also to the stable. It wasn't so much the horse interest that attracted his attention but rather the lovely creatures that leapt on and off their gorgeous mounts in tight-fitting clothing suitable for their equestrian pursuits. I was not surprised to see him quickly engaged with a tall, slender woman with long black hair. And I could imagine the conversation that probably started with a remark about her new black BMW, followed by a comment on the latest boyfriend. Her rapidly changing paramours often arrived on motorcycles, in sports cars, or in flashy trucks with loud exhausts. This friendly, outgoing girl, loved by us all for her joy of life, had one day told Dave that she was an expensive keeper, suggesting that was the reason for the rapid turnover of lovers.

Dave's curiosity apparently satisfied, he retired back to the workshop for the orders of the day and I retired to my mental workshop to do the same. The little woman, or the wife, as one says jokingly in Maine, decided to go up to her writing studio for the morning so there was nothing left for me but to retire to my place of business. Here the hours pass slowly with bill paying, gazing out the window, working with words, watching the activities revolving around the stable, or engaging in the always amusing pastime of following the antics of crows. Long ago they had decided there was no harm in the figures below and ignored the wandering of man and beast, unless, like the terriers, movement suggested a handout, for which the stable was a happy hunting ground.

With lunch at noon, intelligence came in from various sources, some requiring action, the balance to file away for future reference. Dogs needed to be vaccinated for Lyme. Shopping was needed for supper. Social engagements were to be avoided by clever maneuvers. Also, an offspring's problem surfaced, and a nonprofit suddenly demanded attention. The added burden required a nap, disguised as a moment to think things through; thus more hours became tombstones of the day.

Upon waking, I felt an irresistible enticement waft through the open window, initiating a voyage to the out-of-doors to take visual command of the birdfeeder, the sight of Marilyn's garden, and the fields beyond. The garden with its palette of colors, overhung with bees and butterflies, served as a barrier to detach one's thoughts from the outside world. All around was quietness filled with visual noise: of colors, the reds, the blues, the yellows, and all the shades in between. The towering mantles of the oaks and maples were drums of sound beneath the buzzard hanging in his circling space, talking of wind currents and freedom from the ground. At my back the wise old rocks looked down from the bank where I had placed them, with the wise old woman, the dwarf Alberta spruce, caressing their sides. Together they muttered incantations to the breeze about things only they could know. I mused about my own orb in this little kingdom, created with many other hands along with mine, over half a century now.

There was much to muse about. Take the ancient lilac tree, her trunk thick as my thigh, gnarled and twisted like an old cheroot, with branches radiating out, sparse as hair on a balding head. We had known each other more than fifty years. She probably started life about 1840 when the house was built. Every morning birds sang in her branches outside our window, excited about the new dawn. Many arborists had said her time had come, that lilac heaven awaited, and more beautiful specimens should take her place. On their departure I would put an arm around her trunk and an understanding flowed between us that she would remain until my dying breath. She was my icon of Mother Earth, new each spring if old in years, beautiful with her fragile trunk hollowed out by the years. Placing a hand against her connected me to my universe.

If one is a good listener, trees and rocks, water and sky will talk. Thoughts are beams of energy and listening to them we simply rearrange their force to a form our brain can understand. Because trees and rocks, water and sky, do not have vocal chords, we must communicate by thought—more universal than voice. Just ask a person you love.

Take the pine standing at the end of the lawn where the ground slopes downward, drawing one's eye to the distant bay with its islands forming the horizon. I planted it in memory of Liv, mother of our children, when she died forty-nine years ago. An eight-footer back then, the tree has grown to sixty today.

How well I remembered, in the labyrinth of my mind, our initial meeting, Liv and I, in Norway; not unlike that other meeting at Plum Orchard some years before with Margaret, but without the instant, wild flow of minds intertwining. Rather it was like two animals sniffing one another. I remembered how the sniffing continued across the Atlantic by airmail, a method totally inadequate for communication between someone I had come to feel strongly about. Over the years I had reread our letters many times, which brought back thoughts of her on this summer afternoon. It is a trick of time that the older we grow, the more we live in memories. The pine prompted my thoughts to wander back, tracing my journey with Liv.

After that solitary summer on Vinalhaven, described previously, Liv and I lived those blissful years with our two offspring. It seemed so long ago, sitting out in the garden today, and yet the images were so clear as if preserved on glass photographic plates. It was a marriage that started with letter writing and evolved into enduring love. Rarely was there a harsh word, with each day bringing a new adventure, whether it was voyaging over to The Only House, making apple cider in the fall, or setting up her loom from Norway where she sat for hours making beautiful rugs, covers for pillows, or other works of art.

But like beloved old Oliver, Mother Nature, and her companion, Fate, were kind only so long. The thought made me bow my head and close my eyes while sitting in the chair, thinking back to Liv's slow demise. The melanoma caused a nasty lesion on her thigh, and the cancer spread to her lymph nodes before being diagnosed. When they were removed she had to use a leg pressure pump to keep the fluid from building up. We remained upbeat until the doctor, knowing more than we did, suggested she go back to Norway for a visit to her family and friends. That was the beginning of the downhill slide. On the return she grew weaker and the pain increased until the bed became her home. The time came when a morphine syringe with accompanying vials rested on the dresser top. When I plunged the needle into her arm, with increasing frequency, I felt like plunging it into mine as well to ease the pain in us both.

My mother descended to snatch our two children away so they wouldn't witness the end, a mistake for which I never forgave her or myself. Death is a part of living to be shared, no matter how hard, but I was too weak to stop her. I had called Liv's sons. We sat in the library drinking aquavit, singing the Norwegian songs she loved so dearly.

Eventually Liv went into a coma. Lying beside her at night, I would reach out a hand and squeeze hers, imagining I felt a small squeeze in return, and winced at her labored breathing. The doctor came each morning to renew the vials. She died on his third visit.

The grim memory of her death turned me from the tall pine. I walked the dogs to temporarily forget those awful days. Then, with the approaching drama of evening, I returned indoors, back to my favorite chair. The light turned golden, casting its mystical hue on all things that glory in its light. It was time for the fawn, hidden in the tall grass of the orchard, to expect its mother back so she could guide her child along the fenceposts to the upper pasture where the mowed fields now sprouted new tender grass. I had purposely not cut the orchard early, knowing that late spring into early summer, there would be a fawn lying there, secure.

Then the breeze, as it does most every day in summer, reversed itself, carrying the heat of the day out to the coolness of the bay. The moment had come to fold all the events from dawn to dusk into a single package. Time to gather doe and fawn, rocks and trees, birds and bees, friends, family, and beloveds, past and present, along with Marilyn preparing supper inside. Gather all into a wondrous necklace, woven by the industrious hands of time, and clasp it gently around my neck as darkness fell.

Me (back, right) and my children (from left) Ola, Liv, and Wawa

CHAPTER TWENTY-TWO

Looking Back

Evening descends. The water is a mirror, only distorted by the gentle pull of the tide or a swimming bird to show that time is running. From the end of the granite wharf I look back at the familiar shore. A granite ledge, smoothed by glaciers and colored by lichens, is the division between land and sea, drawing the eye to a small rock shelf above it. Here a piece of driftwood has landed, hurled by some forgotten storm. Around it daisies and hawkweed have made a home. Behind the ledge the tiny meadow slopes gently upward, enveloping the well-head and flows on until it meets the storybook house with its two guardians, the ancient apple and patriarchal pear. Behind them the weathered gray clapboards convey an enduring quality above the temporary riot of wildflowers and tasseled grass, with the steep pitched roof adding a gothic connotation, hinting of past inhabitants weathering tempests and tragedies, coupled with the rigors of living on a Maine island in a different age. Beyond the house the spruce forest is a curtain to hold the intimacy of the scene secure from an outside world, as it has for my six-decade acquaintance.

More than sixty years ago, I rowed down here to The Only House for the first time in a gray punt with a person I loved above all else in that period of my youth. Our few short weeks together in this enchanted land were so idyllic as to form a benchmark for happiness ever after. It was from here I sailed off to the Southern Seas in a tired old Friendship sloop while she crossed the Atlantic to die suddenly in a foreign land, leaving a young and bearded man stripped of heart and soul.

This evening, those precious cupfuls of halcyon days lie cradled in my mind like a warming ember. For sixty plus years The Only House has been more than just a way station in my life. It has long since become a part and parcel of me. The eye roams up the small grassy clearing. There at the side of a mighty spruce stand two gravestones: two anchors against life's shifting winds further moor me to this magical place—a place that has lovingly cradled us temporary visitors with our individual needs and understandings.

One for Margaret, for whom the place excited wondrous creativity to translate thoughts and sights into classic children's books. Sharing in the pastures of her imagination was like walking through an enchanted forest. She framed the window that would forever provide my looking glass to the world outside. Taking my hand, much like an adult leading an adoring child, she led me through a world of innocent wonder that can only happen once.

Next to her is Liv, mother earth in human form. A priestess of goodness, she possessed an inner radiance that lighted faces of even the most chance encounter. Her religion was in giving, and of all the saintly people in my life, she stands the tallest.

Though her grave is not physically there, I think, too, of Stella of the South Pacific, mother of Wa, my eldest son; beautiful and beloved companion who gave me care when I needed it the most. Together we had a youthful love affair that blossomed into a lifetime friendship. I wish I could talk to you again. There is so much left to say.

Now in the house readying supper is Marilyn, my dearest living friend and wife. From her Cherokee father she has derived a love of earth and sky, but her working world, with its demands and ethics, lies far beyond the spruce forests. She has climbed a ladder of her own making and in the process has become a role model for others trying to construct their own. I stand in awe of her hard work, understanding, compassion, and intuition, and the incredible skill she has to extract the best from us, placing it to the most productive end.

I sit here, humbled by these extraordinary women, hoping I have given back in some small way a part of what I have received from them. It is true that from stardust we have come and to stardust we shall return. The individual track for most of us is a process predictable as the voyages of those bits of seaweed drifting past the wharf, to be deflected around obstacles, spun in eddies, temporarily pinned against ledges, or violently disturbed by a propeller's wake. These beloved women, and now Marilyn, have laid the steppingstones to a life not to be traded for any other.

A lifetime is a grab bag of thoughts and things and happenings, a progression of emotions, changes in perception, subtle colorings of time and fate. My office in Camden is a museum to these memories. There, scattered, filed, displayed, often hidden, rests the distillation of a lifetime. The paneled room of native cedar, trimmed with mahogany, is a testament to the boatbuilding crew that toiled below. Surgeons at fitting wood together, their reflection is in the reverse curves, the bevels and the fiddles for the counters with the deck beams overhead. Of them, only Fred remains to keep alive the buzz of the planer, the whine of the jointer, the whooshing roar of the table saw.

Albert, who loved dairy farming, installed the porthole beside my desk so I could command the berry patch and garden. That massive bronze casting with one-fourth-inch glass is an icon of protection from adversity, whether it be crashing seas or shore events that crash with equal force. On the walls are tributes to those builders who toiled below—an eighteen-foot double-ended sloop with tan bark sails, hull finished bright, and a reminder of bygone Viking craft in faraway Norwegian fjords. There is a Friendship sloop heeled over in a goodly breeze, going as fast as a Friendship can, while underneath hangs the double-ended forty-foot power yacht of twenty tons, planked with Alaskan cedar, not sporting a single knot or blemish and giving off a scent like sandalwood.

There is a picture of the 1913 Etrich *Taube* that was the most birdlike of the successful early flying machines. This was the machine that brought the pigeon to perch on my head while the plane was being built here. Flying the *Taube* became an icon of my several thousand hours above the ground.

Mandalay of the South Pacific has her nest in a charming little painting done by Allister MacCloud, that Englishman in his nineties, when he caught the rugged volcanic peaks, the greens and blues of the lagoon, and the smallness of the boat in relationship to its surroundings in a snug harbor on Moorea within sight of Tahiti.

There is an oil of a ghostly square-rigger, sailing under a gibbous moon down churning valleys as it forges ahead to its own particular fate in a watery world so removed from land and man as to be on another planet. It draws me back to those nights under the star-filled sky a thousand miles from nowhere with only the creak of the rigging and the occasional crack of canvas as the tired old Friendship groaned her way down the Southeast Trades. How I treasure the memory of those long nights with my companion asleep below, my mind in delicate balance between the sorrow of Margaret's death and the adventures that lay behind the line where sea and sky were one. On those nights, alone for all intents and purposes, except for the rare passing of an albatross, giant fulmar, or stormy petrel, I felt the life force of youth reborn in me and Margaret became a jewel securely locked in the *nimbus* of a meaningful future.

On the long counter below the bookcases stand two figures. The first is a small New Guinea god that obviously knows things I have never seen or understood. It was given to me by a charming lady, Thelma, whom I befriended, or she me, on a tramp steamer going from the New Hebrides to Australia. She was roaming about the islands to keep the life force pulsing, burdened with advancing years and declining health. In the three weeks it took to reach our destination, stopping as we did at every trading post and stand of coconuts, our conversation explored far more ports than did our vessel. I found myself telling things not told to anyone since those days with the owner of The Only House. Thelma knew the islands and their peoples, possessing a reverence for their customs, their black and somber world in the darkness of the jungles where gods and demigods and other happenings controlled one's destiny beyond the grasp of western minds. Shortly after returning to the States a package arrived. In it was the little New Guinea god with a note from Thelma. She explained how it had been her companion and guardian for half a century and now she wanted me to have it since her days were drawing down.

"He has one curious trait," she wrote. "Whenever he falls, for whatever reason, he will always fall facing in the direction of his home, New Guinea."

I placed him on a shelf. The next week he toppled, disturbed by the cat, perhaps. When I returned home that day, there he was lying on the floor, arm broken, facing homeward, a little south of west.

Respecting the unknown, I have never made a move to glue back the broken arm. It has rested all these years in a little box at his feet. Also, I know it was a part of Thelma showing me that what we talked about was true.

This is much to say about an obscure little pagan god from a person "passing in the night." But looking back, I find that it is these little incidents and meetings that stand the tallest in the landscape of one's life.

Next to the little god is his companion, a folk-art piece from Carolina. She is a nurse in a denim uniform with white apron and straps, holding a baby. She is the same height as the little New Guinea fellow. Although fully clothed, her body has a very strong sense, much as a great oak gives one that feeling of strength and security holding aloft its enormous canopy. Her rubicund face is carved wood with wire spectacles, surrounding the eyes that in turn have little crinkles around the corners, as does the humorous mouth, suggesting she knows far more than she is telling. This is corroborated when one lifts off her head and finds hidden inside a half-pint bottle.

My mother gave me that bit of Smoky Mountain folk art way back when I was a boy for reasons unknown. I call them the odd couple, the god and nurse. They represent the structure of my religion, pagan and prosaic, somber and humorous, mysterious, and slightly ridiculous, knowing that gods, like dolls, are merely role players framing the great unknown.

Books wind three deep around two sides of the room. In their varied costumes, shapes, and sizes, they are a sometimes well dressed, sometimes a tawdry mob, celebrating a cross section of the human condition, varied as their bindings and coming from more points of view than the headings of any compass. They are the soup of civilization of which I have enjoyed the sipping.

The gun cabinet holds treasures of its own, heirlooms passed on by father, grandfather, and great-grandfather. There is one rifle, a lever action Winchester, a weapon credited with "the winning of the West," which indiscriminately plugged animals and humans, unhampered by right or wrong, the color of skin, or rarity of species. The bluing is worn off and the steel has a somber, dead color like a stormy sky at dawn. Yet it has a beauty of its own, a classic design of man to carry out his reasoning or lack thereof, back in those good old bad days when black and white were the primary colors of one's philosophy.

The rest are fowling pieces. They have a deeper dimension than the purpose for which they were designed. The engraving on the metal and the selected burled wood of their stocks make them works of art. They speak of the fields and woods of autumn, duck blinds at dawn, the sudden whir of wings, and long tramps with friends and dogs or in solitude through settings where one feels at rest. I was always a rotten shot, perhaps because just being out there was where the pleasure lay. It has been years since I have fired them, for as one ages the reverence for life increases. The guns are icons of happy, healthy days in the great outdoors, where I learned far more of nature than I ever demised.

Finally, we go to the command post, a chair of ancient yew, once growing, perhaps, in some old churchyard in England. Here I sit behind the pine partner's desk built shortly after our thirteen states adopted a constitution. The years have induced large cracks here and there, so if it were a boat no pump would ever keep it floating. The drawers pull out reluctantly on their worn wood slides and I am forever tightening the crude nuts that bolt the pulls to the drawer fronts. It is a wonderful old friend, a comfortable presence, with a large top for work and other things. Over the last half-century the two of us have spent more time together than with any other person or thing. On it sits an old hand-crank calculator weighing twenty pounds that I was shamed into buying at a charity auction forty years ago for $5. I love pulling the handle down, hearing the clash and clank of the internal mechanism that pulls up the levers to print the selected numbers, giving them an importance they seldom deserve. I am left-handed but my right arm is stronger, which I attribute to that old Sundstrand machine.

And at my feet until very recently was Oliver, the Norwich terrier, a loyal little beloved friend who was never farther away than a touching reach. Where he has laid a long line of dogs, each different, each loved, each sadly missed, have also kept me company. I hold our animals in great reverence. They have made life a joy.

Across the room above the pullout settee bunk are pictures of four women. The eyes of Margaret Wise Brown look at me from the first. After all these years I still stiffen at the sight of her face and get that same old knotting feeling in the stomach. It is a precious sensation to carry through one's life.

Next to Margaret is Liv behind her loom and in Norwegian dress. Those twelve years from the days of the bear and the raising of our children were like a summer idyll. I can't remember a discordant word or serious disagreement. Love and warmth and learning to be a father in an old Maine farmhouse was an uncomplicated segment of my life to be enshrined in this special place.

Beside Liv is Stella, in full South Pacific regalia, standing in front of *Mandalay*'s bowsprit on the Tahiti waterfront. In the same frame is a portrait of her face in later years when she came here to have her heart repaired. The calm, sculptured features are in contrast to the gaiety of the grass skirt picture of the other portrait.

The last frame is of Marilyn as a young girl, pixie-like, looking out as if to say, "What next?" And there have been many things since that day. She has won all the challenges through sheer will and understanding of the needs of others. After our thirty plus years together I still look at the young girl of the picture and wonder how she could have accomplished all she has.

Many an hour do I sit here in my museum, talking to these four special people who have shared in a large portion of my life. I thank them for what they have done for me, with the hope that I have given them some of the happiness they have given me.

So summing up this one man's voyage, making my way across the landscape of years, may it be said that at birth we are presented with a ticket allowing entry onto a stage of unknown dimensions and an audience ever changing. Eternity alone has the final word of when we say goodbye.

Me and Marilyn

About the Author

JAMES S. ROCKEFELLER JR. was born in 1926 and raised in Greenwich, Conn., and served in the Army Air Corps during World War II. A graduate of Yale University, he spent his youth traveling and exploring until settling down in Maine. His book about his travels in the Pacific, *Man on His Island*, was published in 1957 by W.W. Norton. He is a cofounder of the Owls Head Transportation Museum and was its chairman until 2017. Rockefeller built boats for twenty years at the Bald Mountain Boat Works, where he also restored a 1912 Etrich *Taube* replica airplane. He stopped flying at the age of ninety, after clocking more than 2,000 hours in the air. Rockefeller has two children, Liv and Ola, with former wife Liv Heyerdahl, now deceased. He married Marilyn Moss in 1983. The couple resides in Camden, Maine.